Animate Literacies

Thought in the Act

A series edited by Erin Manning and Brian Massumi

Animate Literacies

LITERATURE,

AFFECT, AND

THE POLITICS

OF HUMANISM

Nathan Snaza

DUKE UNIVERSITY PRESS

Durham and London 2019

Printed and bound by CPI Group (UK) Ltd, Croydon, CR0 4YY

Cover design by Drew Sisk

Typeset in Quadraat by Copperline Book Services

Library of Congress Cataloging-in-Publication Data

Names: Snaza, Nathan, [date] author.

Title: Animate literacies : literature, affect, and the politics of humanism /
Nathan Snaza.

Description: Durham : Duke University Press, 2019. | Series:
Thought in the act | Includes bibliographical references and index.

Identifiers: LCCN 2018050153 (print)

LCCN 2019013975 (ebook)

ISBN 9781478005629 (ebook)

ISBN 9781478004158 (hardcover : alk. paper)

ISBN 9781478004790 (pbk. : alk. paper)

Subjects: LCSH: Literacy—Social aspects—United States. | Literacy—
Political aspects—United States. | Humanity in literature.

Classification: LCC LC151 (ebook) | LCC LC151 .S624 2019 (print) |
DDC 302.2/244—dc23

LC record available at https://lccn.loc.gov/2018050153

Cover art: Erin Manning, *The Colour of Time – Anarchive*, 2018.
Photograph by Brian Massumi. Courtesy of the artist.

Contents

ACKNOWLEDGMENTS vii

1 The Human(ities) in Crisis 1

2 *Beloved*'s Dispersed Pedagogy 11

3 Haunting, Love, and Attention 19

4 Humanizing Assemblages I: What Is Man? 28

5 Slavery, the Human, and Dehumanization 38

6 Literacy, Slavery, and the Education of Desire 48

7 What Is Literacy? 55

8 Humanizing Assemblages II: Discipline and Control 66

9 Bewilderment 77

10 Toward a Literary Ethology 86

11 What Happens When I Read? 99

12 The Smell of Literature 115

13 Pleasures of the Text 124

14 Those Changeful Sites 134

15 Literacies against the State 145

16 Futures of Anima-Literature 153

NOTES 165

REFERENCES 193

INDEX 209

Acknowledgments

Books emerge through ways of living, and this one springs from an extraordinary decade spent in collaboration with my life's most abiding friend, Julietta Singh. It came into being through exchanges of books, thoughts, and feelings with her over time. I learn from her daily what it means to live, think, parent, teach, write, eat, and desire new worlds. Our experiments in queer kinship and coparenting have been formative to this project, as has our daughter Isadora, whose wonder is infectious and who is embedded in these pages.

And now, two brief stories. In 2011, weeks before defending my dissertation, I was interviewed via Skype for the Copeland Fellowship at Amherst College. The theme, that year, was the Future of the Humanities. The camera on their end was positioned such that I couldn't see any humans most of the time, so it was like being interviewed by a seminar table and a window that spoke in various voices. Near the end of the interview, Austin Sarat, the chair of the committee, asked me what I would think of a proposal to close the Department of German to open, instead, a Department of Catastrophe Studies. While I later kicked myself for not replying, "Thinking of Walter Benjamin, I suspect a German department already is catastrophe studies," in the moment I rehearsed a standard claim that I would oppose any move that would further diminish a focus on the in-depth study of languages and literatures. Austin replied, "So, you're a humanist just like the rest of us?" Needless to say, I didn't receive the fellowship. I want to begin by thanking Austin Sarat for his obvious disappointment, which I took to be not just in me, but in "the rest of us." The affective charge of that response reoriented my reading, thinking, and writing, and without it I'm quite certain I would have written a very different book. *Animate Literacies* is my attempt to wander way from being a disappointing humanist.

The other event that made this book possible was a leave from teaching in the spring of 2013 to stay home with my infant daughter, Isadora. Writing anything scholarly while caring full time for an infant whose needs and schedule are radically unpredictable (despite exerting whatever control we tried) was out of the question, so I filled the small amounts of downtime I had by emailing people. If there is a benefit to not holding a tenure-track position, it is that I wasn't in a rush to publish a monograph and was able to take time to figure out how to unlearn my humanist habits. So I envisioned an edited book on the politics of humanism and schools, both university and P–12, that would gather scholars working across humanities, social sciences, and educational fields. No publisher I contacted could see a way to market such a volume, but those emails set into motion chains of events that determined my antidisciplinary career and brought me into conversation with people who radically changed how I thought.

The folks housed in education programs I contacted became some of my closest colleagues in the fields of curriculum studies and educational philosophy, in part through my work coediting two books collecting their essays. While *Animate Literacies* isn't pitched as a direct contribution to the field of curriculum studies, all of my thinking about these matters has been shaped by my friends and comrades in that field. First and foremost, I want to thank my closest collaborators and coeditors: Jenny Sandlin, Debbie Sonu, Stephanie Springgay, Aparna Mishra Tarc, Sarah E. Truman, John Weaver, and Zofia Zaliwska. I've also learned more than I can ever comprehend from Peter Appelbaum, Sandro Barros, Donald Blumenfeld-Jones, Dennis Carlson, David Cole, Mary Aswell Doll, Rubén Gaztambide-Fernández, Liz de Freitas, Jen Gilbert, Walter Gershon, Sandy Grande, Rob Helfenbein, Mark Helmsing, M. Francine Huckaby, Gabe Huddleston, jan jagodzinski, Jim Jupp, Crystal Laura, Patti Lather, Tyson Lewis, Bettina Love, Marcia McKenzie, Marla Morris, Helena Pedersen, Barbara Pini, Sam Rocha, Bettie St. Pierre, Eve Tuck, and Jason Wallin.

The late William Spanos responded to one of my emails with enormous enthusiasm, and within two months had sent me a full text for the collection. His generosity, to a young scholar he'd never met, kept me working to find a venue for the essays that didn't fit the curriculum-oriented books. He also introduced me to his former students R. Radhakrishan and Asimina Karavanta, who each contributed to the collection. Mina invited me—and Julietta and Isadora—to Athens for the War on the Human Conference, and ended up coediting the collection with me: a special issue of *Symploke* called "Posthumanisms." Her friendship and thoughtful critique have meant a great deal to me, and I owe her an incalculable debt for leading me to the work of Sylvia Wynter. Jeffrey di Leo, at *Symploke*, also indirectly led me to Christopher Breu, who has become one of my most important interlocutors (about literature, music, politics, and pedagogy), and whose Facebook page hosts a dialogue about philosophy and literature that has inspired many of the ideas in this book. Some of the other participants in that dialogue—Stacy Alaimo, Carlos Amador, Sean Grattan, Annie McClanahan, and Rebekah Sheldon—have, whether they know it or not, helped me figure things out.

Jeffrey later invited me to review two books by Brian Massumi for the journal, which led to Erin Manning sending me a message the night before I began teaching for the spring semester of 2017. My literary powers are woefully inadequate to the task of expressing how much Erin and Brian's presence has meant to my life. Far beyond their support of this book, I have come to love their energy, their enthusiasm, and the way they dream better worlds into existence. Erin and Brian came to Richmond in April 2018, and the only word I've ever found that comes close to describing what happened among us is "magic." It was transformative far beyond what I could have ever anticipated.

I want to thank the participants of an ACLA seminar that Julietta and I organized in 2015 called "Bodies/Texts/Matter": Karyn Ball, Christopher Breu, Hsuan Hsu, and Susan McHugh. I read "*Beloved*'s Dispersed Pedagogy" there, and their responses shaped the book that grew out of it. I also want to thank Stephanie Springgay for bringing me to the University of Toronto/Ontario Institute for the Study of Education as a visiting scholar in early 2017, and for inviting me to have the After the Anthropocene Working Group in Toronto read two chapters of this book in draft form. The spirited discussion helped me to clarify many of the stakes of this book. I also shared a portion of the book with participants of the "Nonhuman Encounters" event at New York University, organized by Ann Pellegrini and Katie Gentile, who also happened to be, along with Carla Freccero, the speakers on the Animals panel with me. This was the single most exhilarating and inspiring academic event I've ever been a part of, and I owe a great deal to Ann for inviting me, and for all the conversations we had around it, conversations that haunt the pages of *Animate Literacies*. Christian Haines, Christopher Breu, and Greg Seigworth read drafts of the manuscript and offered crucial feedback when I needed it most.

In graduate school, I spent time in two different PhD programs—comparative literature, where I finished, and literacy education, where I began. Working in and across two fields that are so institutionally separated—at the University of Minnesota, they were housed in different colleges—has inspired my affective dysphoria with disciplinarity. In the years leading up to beginning this book, I often found myself toggling back and forth between the theoretical humanities and curriculum studies (in terms of journals and conferences), even as I have persistently failed to see any benefit to their separation.

My years at the University of Minnesota were shared with a host of incredible teachers, mentors, and friends who animated my education: Richard Beach, Robin Brown, Tony Brown, Thomas Cannavino, Aaron Carico, Siobhan Craig, Patricia Crain, Cesare Casarino, Nicholas de Villiers, Shirley Garner, Andrea Gyenge, Matt Hadley, Christian Haines, Wade Haynes, George Hoagland, Nate Holdren, Qadri Ismail, Kjel Johnson, Josephine Lee, Richard Leppert, Catherine Liu, Cecily Marcus, David O'Brien, Valentine Pakis, Aly Pennucci, Ricardo Rebolledo, Sara Saljoughi, Harvey Sarles, Simona Sawhney, Hoon Song, Matthew Stoddard, Benedict Stork, Gary Thomas, Joe Tomkins, John Troyer, and Julie Wilson. While in curriculum and instruction, I flourished thanks to Tom Friedrich, Kyle Greenwalt, and Mark Vagle. Above all there, I want to thank the members of my doctoral committee: Timothy Lensmire, John Mowitt, Thomas Pepper, Jochen Schulte-Sasse, and Shaden Tageldin.

Working at the University of Richmond has afforded me the unusual opportunity to teach across disciplines and constantly experiment with my pedagogy. I especially want to thank the students across the years in my Vampires in Literature and Film, Modern Literary Theory, Feminist and Queer Theories, Democracy and Education, and Philosophy of Education classes. In the Department of English, I could not have found more proactive and generous chairs than Suzanne Jones and Louis Schwartz, or better colleagues: Bert Ashe, Laura Browder, Abigail Cheever, Daryl Dance, Terryl Givens, Libby Gruner, Brian Henry, Ray Hilliard, Peter Lurie, Joyce

MacAllister, Thomas Manganaro, Reingard Nethersole, Elizabeth Outka, Kevin Pelletier, Monika Siebert, and David Stevens. Conversations with my colleagues associated with the Women's, Gender, and Sexuality Studies Program—especially my dear friends from the Feminist and Queer Materialisms Faculty Learning Communities—have made it possible for me to think most of what's in this book. I am especially indebted to Holly Blake, Eva Hageman, Dorothy Holland, Crystal Hoyt, Lázaro Lima, Mariela Méndez, Mari Lee Mifsud, Melissa Ooten, Andrea Simpson, Kathleen Skerrett, and Sydney Watts. Being able to think with Del McWhorter, and the friendship that emerges from such thinking, has been one of the most sustaining sources of energy for me at the University of Richmond, and I am forever grateful for it. My other comrades on and beyond campus—Myrl Beam, Kate Eubank, Chris Cynn, Kári Driscoll, Jeremy Drummond, Molly Fair, Jesse Goldstein, Nolan Graveley, Christina Hanhardt, Glyn Hughes, Samantha Merz, Erik Nielson, Julia Righetti, Felipe Schwartzman, Gary Shapiro, Tanja Softic, Clare van Loenen, and Peter, Marcie, and Juno Taffs—have kept me thinking and laughing and eating.

I want to also thank the university for funds that enabled Julietta and me to bring Jack Halberstam, Christopher Breu, Erin Manning, and Eileen Joy to campus. In different ways, each of them has shaped how I think about the politics of the university, humanistic inquiry, and what it means to be a teacher.

The city of Richmond has been a constant source of ghosts as the former capital of the Confederacy struggles to think through its past as it rises to a new status as one of the US's hippest cities. Especially because of my involvement with the local public schools—part of it made possible by the Bonner Center for Civic Engagement at the University of Richmond (and especially the work of Sylvia Gale, Amy Howard, and Cassie Price)—I am keenly aware of how the legacies of slavery and a slave economy are woven entirely through the material fabric of contemporary life, and how settler colonialism is an ongoing violence. At the same time, it is a city hospitable to an ecologically oriented food scene that quite literally keeps me alive. Rebecca Ponder and Alistar Harris (and Georgia) at Origins Farm, Autumn and Brian at Tomten Farm, Hunter Hopcroft and the crew at Harvest, Kate from the St. Stephen's Farmer's Market, Maurice from the Birdhouse Market, and Anna from the Byrdhouse Market before that, plus all the folks working toward the Richmond Food Coop: thank you for reminding this kid who spent tons of time in gardens and on farms growing up why it matters so much what and how we eat, and expanding my sense of what it means today to imagine ethical forms of everyday life. Thank you to Lamplighter Coffee for providing a great deal of the caffeine that made this book possible, and often a table at which to write. Thanks to the folks at Salvation Tattoo (especially Josh Autrey) and Black Rabbit Tattoo (especially Jelena Wolves) for the endorphins, and to the whole crew at High Point Barbershop. Ward Tefft, Julie Glover, and everyone at Chop Suey bookstore are the best.

Bobby Egger at Vinyl Conflict made sure I always had records on my turntable to inspire my thinking and writing (and procrastinating). I want to thank Deathwish, Inc., Run for Cover, Sacred Bones, and Southern Lord for consistently putting out music that moves me. Claudio Arrau's Chopin records—both the Preludes and the Nocturnes—and Keith Jarrett also kept me company during many hours of work on this book.

Dan Black, Dan Johnson, and Bill Woitas have been inspiring me for most of my life. My love for Dan Black in particular is unending and unfathomable, and to see him develop something similar with Isadora is one of the greatest joys I know. While I was raising hell with those three, often in class, I met the person who did more to steer me toward literature than any other: Chris Thiem. Thank you, Thiem, for inspiring me in the classroom and letting me spend my senior year of high school reading books like Naked Lunch that wouldn't be allowed as part of the regular curriculum.

I want to thank my siblings Erin, Kelli, and Shannon, my late brother Gregg, and my father, Julian. My mother, Margaret, died as I was completing final revisions on the book. In writing the eulogy for her services, I began the process of coming to grips with the fact that this incredible woman who never went to college instilled in me a love of reading, and the pleasures of being surrounded by books. For giving me my biological life and helping me to find my life's most abiding passion, I owe you everything, mom. David Common, Lisa Balabuck, Christine Common, and Giovanni Geremia are family too.

Finally, I want to thank Ken Wissoker, Elizabeth Ault, and all the incredible staff at Duke University Press. Receiving an email with positive reviews from Ken is, I suspect, the most exciting email an academic working in the theoretical humanities can receive. Being able to work with Liz as she transitions from assistant to an editor at the press has been a dream, and her commitment to the project matters enormously to me. Last, I want to thank the two anonymous reviewers whose suggestions, critiques, and enthusiasm kept me going and significantly improved the book.

1

THE HUMAN(ITIES) IN CRISIS

As any reader of this book will know, we are living through a long moment now when the humanities in general, and perhaps literary studies in particular, are said to be in crisis. This so-called "crisis of the humanities" seems thoroughly entrenched in a polarized debate between sides offering what seem to me to be boring platitudes. On the one side, some claim that the humanities are inefficient, requiring more energies than are justified in the contemporary moment of neoliberal market capitalism. This position seeks to close, consolidate, and de-emphasize humanities programs at the university, leading to some very high-profile closures (and near closures) of literature and language programs. Those on the other side claim that the humanities are the core of the university, transmitting skills that are indispensable for any worker or even citizen in today's world. Although I don't want to give specific enunciations in this debate any more interpretive energy than they claim in the opinion pages of newspapers and the *Chronicle of Higher Education*, I thought it noteworthy that Michael Bérubé could tell CNN that humanities skills even make for good military and corporate leadership.[1] To put this most schematically, one side sees the humanities as a waste of energy (intellectual, instructional, and especially institutional) while the other side expends enormous amounts of energy legitimating their existence in terms that are almost always entirely friendly to neoliberal capitalism. Reframing this in terms of energy and its circulation allows me to pose two questions that I'll dwell upon in this book. One, what would happen if we redirected energy from this tiresome treading in place (one that could not be more stuck in a rut)? And two, what possibilities might open for us if this re-framing of the humanities in terms of energy allows us to see how the humanities is an assemblage that articulates energies across a wide variety of actants, many (or most) of whom are not human? What I am ultimately interested in here is pursuing a nonhumanist reconceptualization of the practices formerly called "humanist."[2]

As an initial shock to our presentist sense of this crisis, I want to note that almost thirty years ago Terry Eagleton wrote that the crisis of the humanities is permanent, resulting from their structural "margin-alization."[3] He speculates that the role of the humanities is to produce the commonsense understanding of the human that allows for the relatively smooth functioning of social and economic life under capitalism. At times when this concept is in crisis, the humanities have to step in to clarify, critique, and shore up the human, but at moments of relative calm this crisis management role is less necessary. I'm not going to spend too much time on Eagleton, and I want to take his assessment with more than one grain of salt. Still, his speculations prompt an interesting question: Is it possible that in our time, the receding of support for and interest in the humanities stems, counterintuitively, from the taken-for-grantedness of the human today?

In one sense, this is an almost absurd, Pollyannaish question. Given the completely unworked-through grappling with evolution and climate change, the ongoing insufficiency of human rights law as a global political framework, the clusterfuck of genetic technologies and myriad other forms of biopolitics, and the increasingly well-known critique of the very notion of the human issuing from the so-called "posthumanism" in the academy, it seems like nothing today is less certain than the human.[4] And yet—and this is a big "yet"—there is something sublime about how little these erosions at the edges of the human seem to disrupt the daily march of neoliberal capitalist empire articulated around a certain version of the human, one Sylvia Wynter calls "Man."[5] Coursing through the entire complex of global relations in the wake of 1492, Man functions as a diagram: "a non-unifying immanent cause that is coextensive with the whole social field: the abstract machine is like the cause of the concrete assemblages that execute its relations; and these relations between forces take place 'not above' but within the very tissue of the assemblages they produce" (Deleuze 1988, 37).

This version of the human—Man—is the object of critique in the linked but divergent discourses of postcolonial and decolonial studies, critical studies of race, posthumanism, queer inhumanism, new materialisms, critical animal studies, non-anthropocentric ecologies, and biopolitics. And yet as long as they operate in the mode of critique alone, they don't seem to offer anything substantially different in relation to the operative model of Man. That is, they, like the antihumanist discourses they inherit and metabolize, end up being able to flourish in the neoliberal university of excellence.[6] But, and here's where I begin to wildly speculate, I think the most interesting thing about these discourses and the ways that they can potentially coalesce is their capacity not for critique but for spurring experimental forms of thinking and being (or, still better, becoming, moving) together. It is not only possible but necessary—and indeed I put a great deal of energy into this in the first chapters of this book—to offer posthumanist critiques of educational institutions and the ways they produce Man as the only permissible mode of being human. What would be far more exciting, though, is to redirect this critical energy to articulating new, nonhumanist ways of thinking about how we learn, together, remembering that this "we" will not be coincident with humanity as a collective, or—and especially not—with some subset of this humanity (Man) pretending to represent the whole.

I have been disciplined to think about the labor of reading, writing, and teaching as a humanist. Without downplaying this, I will argue that we need a significantly enlarged sense of affective participation in the events of literacy if we are to track how literacy gets articulated in relation to a particular conception of the human (Man), and in relation to imperialist states during the period of modernity. Humanists have long claimed that unlike the natural and social sciences that strive for parsimony, they reveal the importance of complexity and overdetermination. And yet, humanism itself—as the disciplined restriction of attention to properly human concerns—disavows most of the material conditions for the emergence of its objects (human societies, practices, cultures) and its own functioning. To play with Paul de Man's phrase, all the insights of humanism are predicated on an unquestioned blindness to virtually the entirety of what matters. That doesn't mean those insights haven't been important—in a wide variety of ways—but it does mean that the whole affair has been restricted and restrictive (this is what "discipline" means, after all).

Rather than take for granted the boundedness of literature as it is humanistically framed, *Animate Literacies* reinserts literature into a much wider field of literacy practices. I attend to how a whole host of actants and agents animate literacy in scenes of pre- or aconscious collision and affective contact that I call *the literacy situation*. This situation is where intrahuman politics of race, class, gender, sexuality, and geography shape the conditions of emergence for literacy events that animate subjects and the political relations with which they are entangled. Bringing together sustained attention to dehumanizing violence with an attunement to what is often called the "more-than-human," this project is at once backward looking and critical (offering an account of how our present situation has emerged) and speculative—oriented toward dehumanist, nonstatist futures not just for the study of literature and literacy, but for politics more generally.

Back to the erosion of the human. There are a lot of problems today (decolonization, global warming, biotechnologies, factory farming, deforestation, etc.) that simply can't be thought in traditional humanist frames. So, maybe, it's time to stop looking for the human. Rather than trying to justify the existence of the humanities by positioning humanist education as a crucial piece of the narrative formation of Man, we might put our energies elsewhere: into seeking out narratives that, in not automatically restricting themselves to humans, take every thing as potentially actant, potentially imbricated in change and growth, potentially at stake even in literacy events (reading, writing, teaching). Learning from Wynter's claim that we have been sociogenically produced as Man (or in relation to Man as inhuman or less-than-human), I think we have to turn toward narratives that don't presume Man and which enable creative, experimental practices of performing the human differently.

Let me propose now a somewhat polemical, extremely speculative project. Instead of seeing literacy events as the signs of a human rupture from all other beings (which is what the humanities propose: literature is uniquely human, so studying literature is ipso facto studying what the human is), I am going to take literacy as an animate practice.[7] That is, some animals make marks that circulate in various media with affective agency, and that are in turn attended by other animals. At least among human animals, some animals are charged with overseeing how other animals develop their attentions to these marks. The particular ways in which these animals do this always require energies from a variety of nonhuman (and nonanimal) actants: soil, trees, power grids, computers, blackboards, eye glasses, Amazon.com, and so on. This description, which is, perhaps, a much more distant form of distant reading than the ones envisioned by Franco Moretti and Pascale Casanova, calls for an ethological and ecological account of literacy, one that does not necessary destroy the particular actions (reading, writing, teaching) that we associate with the humanities. But it inserts these actions into other networks and other narratives. And in doing so, one hopes, it releases us from spending so much energy arguing about the humanities and their importance, freeing up energies to begin making sense of this bizarre, extensive, and extremely fragile ecology of things, events, and actants making up what I call *anima-literature*.

This will involve a refusal to be disciplined. Rather than taking disciplinary borders—or, as will become clear, any borders—as given, I want to think about them as a form of membrane. As Samantha Frost details in *Biocultural Creatures*, "A permeable cell membrane produces a continuously variable chemical or energetic imbalance between inside and outside the cell, a disequilibrium that in turn creates the conditions for the movement, flow, or dispersion of molecules and their transformation from one kind into another" (2016, 55). Although there is a risk in moving from the molecular level to the molar too quickly, Frost's account gives an extremely rigorous way of thinking about what Nancy Tuana (2008) calls the "viscous porosity" of borders. Borders are not things, per se, but activities, and they are particular activities that exist in order to enable the incomplete but functional separation of other activities. As Frost puts it, "What makes a living body separate from its environment are not the substances of which it is composed . . . but rather the activities and the processes that occur within and by means of that body" (2016, 75). I would like to hazard seeing this relation at all levels of my analysis: borders are not stable, given, or solid. Bordering is an activity, a process, and it enables certain things. All of the things I track in this book—literature, literacy, academic disciplines, the human—are processes, actions, movements of energy. Indeed, to the extent that this book has a method, I believe it is something like trying to cobble together insights from a range of disciplinary standpoints and projects in order to construct a machine that asks questions—What is literacy? What is the human? What is a collectivity? What is politics?—and fails to answer them in definite ways. Or rather, like the stoner alone in her room who says a word so many times it loses its ability to signify, I try to look at these things over and over from different directions and distances so that they lose solidity, become uncertain, start trembling. Answers don't really interest me, but questions can disperse energy.

In *Animate Literacies*, I am trying to love literature by failing to understand what it is within the disciplined parameters of my humanist education. As Jack Halberstam has argued, "Under certain circumstances failing, losing, forgetting, unmaking, undoing, unbecoming, not knowing may in fact offer more creative, more cooperative, more surprising ways of being in the world" (2011, 2–3). This book is a record of my failure to be properly humanist, or perhaps it is an archive born of my loving desire to become untrained, undisciplined. Halberstam again: "In some sense we have to untrain ourselves so that we can read the struggles and debates back into the questions that seem settled and resolved" (11). As a thoroughly situated subject, one whose attentions have been disciplined over decades in schools at various levels, I cannot simply break free from such discipline (although I can begin to imagine alternative modes of education that would not discipline others in the same ways!). Rather, I am actively seeking to lose my way, to fail to stay on that paths I am supposed to take as a humanist. I will try to stay not with the disciplines but with the trouble that is "literature."[8]

Wandering off of the disciplinary track, though, doesn't mean a rejection of axiomatics. Indeed, as I get lost, I am doing so only by following my gut, my feelings, my attraction to the affective magnetism of what I love.[9] I would call this *affective attunement politics*, since it concerns how I am touched and how I touch things (and, indeed, how I am a site of touching that is not reducible to a liberal subject). *Animate Literacies* asks both what animates literacies, and how literacies animate particular forms of personhood and politics. In asking this double question, and in proposing anima-literature as a neologism for understanding this thing that I love (and that perhaps we love), I am drawing on Mel Y. Chen's analysis of animacy as it moves between linguistics and politics. Rather than a binary between the animate and the inanimate, Chen attends to how "stones and other inanimates definitively occupy a *scalar* position (near zero) on the animacy hierarchy [but] they are not excluded from it altogether" (2012, 5). In the chapters that follow, I try to feel my way into the presence of a whole range of agencies—many of them nonhuman—participating in this thing called "literature." Many of the chapters begin with the relation between a reading mind and a signifying text—the relation presupposed in the overwhelming mass of scholarship on literature and education more broadly—but then my attention shifts, either pulling back the frame to see these literacy events within much wider networks of relations among entities and agencies, or zooming in to track the microrelations taking place beneath or alongside conscious attention. Sometimes I pan horizontally, following a particular cluster of ideas as it moves through a range of different sites or scales distributed rhizomatically. My aim is not to provide a systematic account of the forces and entities animating literacies as much as to attempt to pressure the borders around literacy that many assume are much more tidy than I do. In this sense, the book has a speculative and polemical edge to it, as I foreground some aspects of literacy (such as its smell) simply because they tend to be significantly disavowed or ignored in humanist scholarship.[10]

As I track the animating participants in literacies, I am aware that not all participation is the same (I do not propose, as do some speculative realists, a "flat ontology").[11] I draw extensively from feminist and queer new materialist scholarship and theories of affect to consider how these actors (or, as Latour might say, actants) have a share in literature, but I also keep my focus on institutions of education where we have a determinate political responsibility to think through intrahuman politics. Indeed, a fair amount of my attention is given to how these institutions shape our perceptions of animacy and, hence, of politics.

I attend, in what follows, to how the questions I ask about literature, literacy, and the human effect and affect those people excluded from political protection as human during modernity.[12] That is, my approach to literature is not humanist but what Julietta Singh (2017b) calls "dehumanist": my attention to literature is focused as much as possible not on the triumphant stories that disciplined academics tell about it, but on its messy entanglements with dehumanization, ecological devastation, and the material-political generation of impoverishment of all kinds.[13] Accordingly, to the extent that this is possible, I am constructing my account by foregrounding the knowledge produced about literature, literacy, and the human by scholars situated at a remove from Man, primarily in feminist, queer, postcolonial, black, brown, and decolonial studies. I thus always attempt "to recollect and foreground the very histories of dehuman-ization too often overlooked in celebratory posthumanisms" (Luciano and Chen 2015, 196). In doing so, I follow Chela Sandoval's affirmative "meth-odology of the oppressed," which responds to a moment of postmodern crisis: "The citizen-subject's postmodern despair over experiencing this condition can be released when the practitioner looks to the survival skills and decolonizing oppositional practices that were developed in response to such fragmentation under previous cultural eras" (2000, 33). That is, when confronting the crisis of the humanities, instead of responding with angst and a defensive desire to shore up this formation, I want to explore alternative, subjugated, fugitive modes of linking literacy, aesthetics, and modalities of being human. As Judith Butler has noted, "There is a certain departure from the human that takes place in order to start the process of remaking the human" (2004, 3–4). *Animate Literacies* is structured ac-cording to a series of such departures, and it is organized into sixteen chapters, each of them shorter than is common in most academic books today. This book's somewhat unusual structure is motivated by my sense that *Animate Literacies* is less about specific conceptual and political argu-ments (although there are many) than about a pedagogical desire to pro-duce affects in the reader.

Chapter 2, "*Beloved*'s Dispersed Pedagogy," takes up one scene of liter-acy education in Toni Morrison's novel and suggests that decisions about how to frame that event have enormous consequences for how we under-stand the politics and materiality of education. In widening the frame, I find that underlying and surrounding the obvious event of literacy is an entire affective field that I call the *literacy situation*. Chapter 3, "Haunting, Love, and Attention," generalizes from my reading of Morrison's novel toward methodological principles that govern this book's account of the literacy situation. In particular, I elaborate on the need to "scope and scale" (King 2011) around literacy events in order to attune to the vast, swirling scene of collisions among bodies and agencies—many of them nonhuman—that animate literacy.

Chapter 4, "Humanizing Assemblages I: What Is Man?," proposes, by examining how literacy animates particular ideas about human persons and their politics, the concept of humanizing assemblages that produce subjects oriented around Man. Taking as my point of departure Lynn Hunt's (2007) provocative (if overly simple) claim that novel reading generates the neurological conditions for global human rights law, and linking this account to Sylvia Wynter's (2003) claim that in the wake of modernity a highly particular version of the human—which Wynter calls "Man"—is overrepresented as the human, I argue that the sociogenic production of Man through assemblages of humanization is woven into the fabric of institutional capture of literacy. This chapter begins to lay out a conception of power as circulating through statist mechanisms of both discipline and control that link literacy to the politics of humanization and dehumanization. Chapters 5, 6, and 7 elaborate this claim in much more detail through close readings of *The Narrative of the Life of Frederick Douglass.*

In chapter 7, "What Is Literacy?," and 8, "Humanizing Assemblages II: Discipline and Control," I lay out this book's main arguments about what literacy is and how it is captured by statist discipline and control. Arguing that literacy names scenes of affective collision among entities and agencies distributed unevenly across scales of space-time, I detail how that gets caught up in modernist politics of humanization and dehumanization, especially as those play out in institutions of education and their disciplinary apparatuses. That is, I attend to how the disciplinary configurations of the university today (but not only the university) are implicated in (de)humanizing politics precisely in how they condition our attentions to literacy.

Chapter 9 theorizes what I call *bewilderment*: an affective condition of disorientation that happens when disciplined attention fails and we become aware of the more-than-human literacy situation that swirls around us and in us. Beginning with close readings of Bram Stoker's *Dracula* and Kate Chopin's *The Awakening*, I generalize toward a concept of bewilderment that can animate non-Man modes of political action and antidisciplinary attention to literacy.

Chapters 10 and 11 offer the book's most sustained elaboration of these antidisciplinary approaches to literacy. "Toward a Literary Ethology" zooms back from the scene of humanist literacy events to see them as part of a much wider ecology of animal literacy practices, while "What Happens When I Read?" zooms in to give an extended account of how literacy affects the reading subject at the prepersonal level. Agreeing with a range of humanist scholars that reading matters precisely because it changes us, I argue that such change is primarily conditioned in the literacy situation where nonhuman agencies and not-yet-human capacities and systems of the reading subject collide. Chapter 12, "The Smell of Literature," elaborates on this claim by examining the role of smell in James Joyce's *A Portrait of the Artist as a Young Man*. I argue that smell gives us a way of attuning to the range of agencies and affects at play in literacy situations, as well as the politics that shape how those situations crystalize into literacy events. Chapter 13, "Pleasures of the Text," broadens this claim by enumerating a wide range of affective pleasures animating and emerging from literacies. By continuing to read Joyce's novel, and putting it into conversation with Paul Preciado's *Testo Junkie*, I argue that literacy is fundamentally erotic, and that the politics of literacy adhere in the ways erotics and pleasures are distributed among humans and nonhumans.

The final three chapters of the book build from my account of the literacy situation and its politics to offer a way of thinking about both classroom practice and the politics of education in noninstitutional sites of study. Proposing what I call *literacies against the state*, I make the case that literacy situations are not pre- or protopolitical but are in fact the very scene of more-than-human politics. In these chapters I think directly about how the arguments in *Animate Literacies* enable us to wander away from tired debates about the crisis of the humanities and focus instead on a range of encounters—always more-than-human—that hold the potential to reorient us away from Man and toward other ways of becoming and relating.

My primary hope is that this book will make the reader feel differently about literacy and the ways it is institutionalized, and that this affective modulation can enable different ways of acting as readers, writers, teachers, and beings in a world woven from dense, bewildering ecologies. This is in keeping with one of my most basic claims about literacy: that it is affective more than symbolic or conceptual. Put differently, *Animate Literacies* is a material intervention into modulating the attention of the reader in order to allow her to attune differently to the affective situation of this book's being read in the hopes that this can "rearrange our desires" (Spivak 2003) away from wanting to be (like) Man. Rather than orienting ourselves in any particular direction, I have tried to write in such a way that the book doesn't just conceptualize bewilderment, it can also produce it in the reader. Let's get lost.[14]

2

BELOVED'S DISPERSED PEDAGOGY

I want to begin again by attending to a single scene in Toni Morrison's *Beloved*, starting at a point of performative action and then tracking outward, redrawing the frame of the scene at least twice. The scene, at least at a first pass, is a familiar one: a teacher and two pupils are gathered, and the teacher is observing the work done by the students as they write in their books: "Schoolteacher made his pupils sit and learn books for a spell every afternoon. If it was nice enough weather, they'd sit on the side porch. All three of em. He'd talk and they'd write. Or he would read and they would write down what he said" (Morrison 1987, 227).[1] We have, then, a familiar scene of literacy instruction. The pupils are learning from the teacher the skills that will be necessary for them to conduct the business expected of them as they enter adulthood in a society, such as that in the nineteenth century in the United States, where print literacy was crucial for economic and political affairs. The particular lesson, though, is not merely about skills in any narrow sense. Schoolteacher corrects his pupil: "No, no. That's not the way. I told you to put her human characteristics on the left; her animal ones on the right. And don't forget to line them up" (228). The lesson concerns the "characteristics" of a human and thus is an instance of the kind of humanizing education called for by some of the most influential philosophers within the tradition called "Western": Plato, Rousseau, Kant, and even postcolonial thinkers such as Paulo Freire and Edward Said. The pupils are instructed to think about what makes the human human and, in contemplating this, they learn to identify with it, indeed to become human through the educational encounter. Schoolteacher's utterances, and the utterances of the students in response, constitute an assemblage in which the contemplation, in and through language, of what it means to be human produces that human.[2] This is, with very rare exception, the highest good imagined for educational institutions within the Western tradition, and it is the one that authorizes the humanities as an academic formation: at its best, education makes us more fully human.

Let's track back though. In the novel, the lesson is reported speech, relayed by Sethe, the black slave around whom the novel unfurls. Sethe is in the grape arbor at Sweet Home, trying to "do the vegetables" with a young child of her own in a basket attracting flies. Sethe leaves the child for a moment: "I headed for the back door to get the clean muslin we kept in the kitchen press" (227). Her movement across the plantation reveals a particular kind of gendering of labor and space, so that Sethe's body tends to be oriented in and toward the spaces of kitchen labor, making her movement from the arbor to the kitchen both habitual to her and unremarkable to Schoolteacher and the whites.[3] As she leaves the grape arbor for the kitchen, she overhears her name. She "couldn't help listening to what [she] heard him say," which is the lesson described above. The antecedent of the pronoun "her" in Schoolteacher's humanizing lesson is Sethe, who, as a woman and as a black slave, has both human and animal characteristics. Sethe is, quite obviously, not a part of the educational scene as Schoolteacher himself would frame it. He is the teacher, and he has two pupils who are proximate in space, and they share, or asymptotically approach, a single object of contemplation. She is aloof, passing by the scene. She is not required or expected or even welcome in it. Following Paul Gilroy and Tavia Nyong'o, we can specify that she eavesdrops.[4] By virtue of the physicality of sonic waves, Schoolteacher's voice travels outside of the presumed limits of the scene, drawing Sethe in. One part of this sonic matter, her name, exerts a pull on her attention, reorienting her body, its affects, its perceptions. For a moment, the arc of her movement, which was tending from the vegetables toward the muslin, is redirected. Between leaving the grape arbor and seeing Schoolteacher, there is one sentence: "The grass felt good on my feet" (227). I will come back to this, but what I want to mark is a shift in Sethe's attunement to the world from her feet (in the movement of locomotion) to her ears, which stop her in her tracks in order to better listen to the sounds coming to her from elsewhere.

Although Sethe is not supposed to be party to the lesson, she is nevertheless already part of it. The students who are being humanized by contemplating humanity in order to become human are contemplating it through dialectical negation: comparing the fully human (that is, white) person to the less-than-human (black) Sethe. Sethe is not humanized by this lesson. Indeed, its performative force cuts in the opposite direction: she is forced, by the capacities of this lesson to affect her as she travels toward the kitchen to get muslin, to contemplate her own lack of humanity and to identify with that (if not in a gesture of affirmation, in one of recognition). Thus, we see that by shifting the way we frame the lesson, by playing with our proximity to it, we are able to construct a rather different account of its function and political force. While humanization is the conscious, explicit logic of the scene within the first account I gave, the second reveals that this humanization proceeds according to a simultaneous and necessary but disavowed process of dehumanization. It might be helpful to see Sethe's dehumanization as a periperformative force of the humanizing performative force in the first scene. As Eve Kosofsky Sedgwick proposes, there is a particular "spatiality to the periperformative"; it is "the neighborhood of the performative" (2003, 78). In other words, it is the widened field of the performative's emergence and dispersal. When the human is only defined dialectically through negation (which it has always been in the West: against the animal, the machine, the slave, the colonized native, the poor, the disabled, the improperly gendered, and so on), it has to produce what Judith Butler calls its "constitutive outside" (1993, 8). Moreover, in the settler colony of the United States, the fact that the primary scene includes only settlers, and this expanded frame articulates that settler humanity in relation to an arrivant whose presence is enabled by the transatlantic slave trade, renders the theft of indigenous land and the United State's genocidal imperialism all but illegible.[5] Humanizing education cannot proceed without simultaneous dehumanizing.

In the widened scene including Sethe's eavesdropping, the direct lesson is dispersed, both temporally and spatially.[6] The second Schoolteacher was done speaking, Sethe "commenced to walk backward, and didn't even look behind [her] to find out where [she] was headed. [She] just kept lifting [her] feet and pushing back" (228). Her corporeal attentions shift from ears back to feet and she's on the move again, although no longer guided by the aim of seeking the muslin. While her body is back walking, the force of the lesson has made her errant. Referring to the lesson, Sethe declares, "That very day I asked Mrs. Garner a part of it" (228). More specifically, she asks, "What do characteristics mean?" (228). Mrs. Garner, her owner, says, "Oh . . . features. Who taught you that?" Sethe: "I heard Schoolteacher say it" (228). The word is one Mrs. Garner does not expect her to know. After tending to the infirm Mrs. Garner's needs, especially for water, Sethe asks again, "You said features, ma'am?" (228). Mrs. Garner responds, "Umm. Like, a feature of summer is heat. A characteristic is a feature. A thing that's natural to a thing" (230). It is only at this point, then, that Sethe is able to understand the denotative content of the lesson she overheard, despite the fact that its force has already been working upon her for an unspecified part of a day.

Mrs. Garner's exchange with Sethe, then, is also part of the lesson, and a crucial part. As I've already said, it enables Sethe to understand an unfamiliar word that played a key role in Schoolteacher's exercise. But it goes a great deal further in that she provides, although Mrs. Garner presumably has no idea that she is continuing or expounding upon Schoolteacher's lesson, an explanation for how Sethe came to be partly human and partly animal. If these are her "characteristics," they are, on Mrs. Garner's explanation, "natural." Sethe, then, learns that she is, by nature, not fully human.[7] The difference between white humans and black nonhumans, then, is "natural," given. I will come back to this later, but I first want to track backward once again.

In a different context in the novel, another character, Stamp Paid, is about to explain to Paul D, a former slave who lived on Sweet Home with Sethe, the magnitude of a particular party at which were served blackberry pies made with berries Stamp had picked. The text reads, "Stamp started with the party, the one Baby Suggs gave, but stopped and backed up a bit to tell about the berries—where they were and what was in the earth that made them grow like that" (184–85). I'd like to take this this as a methodological suggestion, pausing again to back up and attend to the material conditions of possibility for Schoolteacher's lesson. Thus far, my account, despite a crucial shift in framing to include more humans within its orbit, has not strayed from the anthropocentric enclosure of traditional (educational) philosophy. But when we draw back yet again, we have to stray. And like Sethe's movement caught up in the force of the lesson, our movement will necessarily be errant, for we are trying to go somewhere that is not known in advance. Indeed, with this third framing, I confront the impossibility of knowing where and how far back a frame has to be drawn. I, like Sethe, have a clearer sense of what I am fleeing than whither I will travel.

Let me start with the pedagogical materials. The pupils have notebooks and pens. These objects undoubtedly appear from outside the bounds of Sweet Home, manufactured elsewhere using natural resources extracted in places that may even be quite far afield from the factories in which paper is milled and pens are fabricated. This will require me to pay attention to how trees grow in (at this time one presumes still natural) forests and their complex ecologies, and how those trees are felled by humans and their techno-prosthetics, transported via river runs or train, reduced to pulp, combined with other solutions in processing, and formed into paper that is then dried, packaged, and shipped to other sites where some of it will be further refined into notebooks. These notebooks are then sent to scenes of retail commerce where someone has to sell them to Schoolteacher or one of his slaves before being transported to Sweet Home. All of this would take us outside of the novel in order to attend, as Stamp Paid suggests, to how things got to be the way they are for our lesson to unfold.

Within the novel, we read, much earlier than our scene of humanizing education, that "Schoolteacher [wrote] in the ink [Sethe] herself had made while his nephews played on her" (116). That is, the lesson requires a particular material—ink—that has to be made, and it is Sethe who provides the human labor which makes this "ink" something that is ready to hand for Schoolteacher. Sethe, at the very end of the novel, talking with Paul D, seems to register, in some way, how important this ink was for Schoolteacher's entire way of life (which includes, as most of us know, tracking Sethe down after the Fugitive Slave Act, which is the event that causes her to cut her child Beloved's throat rather than allow Schoolteacher to return her to slavery). She says, "I made the ink, Paul D. He couldn't have done it if I hadn't made the ink" (320). Sethe, then, is part of the lesson not only as a conceptual problem but also as a directly material condition of its occurrence. Without Sethe's labor, there is no ink for the scene to unfold. (And as we see most clearly with Mrs. Garner, her labor materially sustains the plantation and the bodies of the whitepeople in an array of ways.[8]) In an obvious way, the point I'm making is simply a working out of a critique of what Marx famously called "commodity fetishism," highlighting the ways that human labor makes commodities like ink possible even though they can be seen as merely there.[9] It's worth remembering here, though, that human agencies are always entangled with multispecies encounters. Most ink during the nineteenth century was made from galls that develop on trees and other plants as a result of parasitic relations with wasps, bacteria, or fungi. The labor that makes ink, and so many other commodities, is more-than-human.[10]

Let us return to Sethe and her daughter in the grape arbor. It is the agency of the flies that provides the immediate situation for Sethe's movement back toward the house to get muslin to cover the baby. This care requires dealing with the agency of flies, flies who obviously exert their agency far beyond anything that can be called control by humans and who have a very obvious capacity to disrupt human action.[11] As she walks toward the kitchen, as I've noted, "the grass felt good on [her] feet" (227). This feeling good, an experience that stands in contrast to the myriad experiences of horror described in *Beloved*, has to be understood as both an affective relation between human foot and grass (which has its own agency and existence quite apart from whatever humans think grass is for) and as an affective priming for encountering the lesson.[12] Learning, as Megan Watkins (2010) puts it, is about "accumulating affects."[13] Perhaps without this brief feeling good, Sethe's corporeal movement toward the muslin would not have been as sensitive to redirection at the sound of Schoolteacher's voice because her attention would have been absorbed into the muslin-oriented movement. Pleasure, then, disorients in opening toward the unexpected.

After Sethe hears the lesson but before she starts to narrate asking Mrs. Garner what "characteristics" means, we read the following sentences: "I commenced to walk backward, didn't even look behind me to find out where I was headed. I just kept lifting my feet and pushing back. When I bumped up against a tree my scalp was prickly. One of the dogs was licking out a pan in the yard. I got to the grape arbor fast enough, but I didn't have the muslin. Flies settled all over your face" (228). Given our extended framing of the lesson as including the entire duration between overhearing her name and learning the meaning of "characteristics," this cannot be excluded from the scene of instruction. Does the tree's force teach Sethe something here? What about the dog's licking? What about this second encounter with the flies on her baby?[14]

A crucial concept for asking how literacy animates persons and politics, and how myriad actants animate literacy, is what I call the *literacy situation*. Most scholars working in new literacy studies conceptualize literacy in terms of events: moments when literacy practices operate in ways that generate meanings of many kinds. While I think the concept of the event, especially as it is theorized in relation to Alfred North Whitehead's philosophy, could be extended to include everything that is caught up in *Beloved*'s widened framing of literacy, the notion of the literacy situation allows us to see how events of conscious meaning production are inseparable from a much wider field of relations and movements.[15] Lauren Berlant defines a situation as "a state of things in which *something* that will perhaps matter is unfolding amid the usual activity of life. It is a state of animated and animating suspension that forces itself on consciousness, that produces a sense of the emergence of something in the present that may become an event" (2011, 5). If the literacy event in *Beloved* concerns three humans as one teaches the other two how to think about themselves as human as they read and write, the situation includes the periperformative dehumanizing force of the lesson and the direct participation across different scales of a panoply of actants both human and non. Talking about literacy situations will allow me to move from the literacy events commonly taken to be the whole of literacy toward a scene of affective movement that conditions these events' emergence.[16] The shift from events to situations also allows me to conceptualize literacy as crucially animated by affects in the sense of feelings (Ahmed 2015; Sedgwick 2003) and in the post-Spinozist sense of how any entity touches or affects another (Deleuze and Guattari 2002; Massumi 2002). This will allow me to generalize from Sethe's eavesdropping and everything that follows in its wake to argue that literacy is primarily about affects and not conscious events of meaning making or representational constructions.

The pages that follow grapple with how to answer the questions raised by *Beloved*'s dispersed account of pedagogy.[17] It seems to me that the task, today, is to attune to the nonhuman agencies that are so disavowed by Western conceptions of education, literacy, and literature that we cannot even properly pose their participation. The work emerging around new materialism, affect theory, posthumanism, and some varieties of ecological thought offers some concepts and intellective habits that I will borrow and develop. There is a tendency in some of this research to take on nonhuman agencies without attending to the difference in experiences of being human that came into focus in my first shift in frame.[18] My task in *Animate Literacies*, then, is to attune to nonhuman agencies at stake in literacy practices, including literature, while remaining intimate with intrahuman politics and violences.[19]

3

HAUNTING, LOVE, AND ATTENTION

I have already sketched how *Beloved* opens onto questions about education, literacy, and agency that cannot be restricted to customary disciplinary ways of asking them, nor to a frame that would see those three things as simply concerning the human. But *Beloved*'s challenge to us has to be extended still further since it is, in an obvious way, a novel about haunting. There is a trauma at the center of the text, as readers gradually learn, and that trauma refuses to stay in the past. After leaving Sweet Home, Sethe runs away to freedom in Ohio with the help of a whitegirl. After the passage of the Fugitive Slave Act in 1850, Schoolteacher and a posse (apocalyptically described as "the four horsemen" [Morrison 1987, 174]) come looking for her. As Christina Sharpe reminds us, "With the Fugitive Slave Act of 1850 slavery was legally extended into so-called "free spaces," and the already constricted possibilities for black freedom in the north were made more insecure" (2010, 11). Slavery is, then a product of statist literacies—the law as written and periperformatively read—which write over the world a grid that, based on literacies of racialization, restricts the movement of some bodies and authorizes the movement of other bodies, indeed that writes some bodies out of personhood and into the legal categories of property. Rather than allow her child to be stolen away into slavery, Sethe hides in a shed and slits the child's throat. Years later, the ghostly reminder of the Misery returns (201), first in the form of a haunted house, and then in the corporeal form of Beloved.

The name "Beloved," as we learn at the very beginning of the novel, emerges from a scene of circulation, literacy, and bodily encounter: it comes from a partially inscribed tombstone paid for with ten minutes of intercourse between Sethe and the engraver (she could not pay for "Dearly Beloved") (5).[1] This name forces the question of how the infanticide might, paradoxically, signify an unfathomable love, one that weighs the futurity of slavery against the violence of sundering the child from any living future. Sethe never falters in her declarations of love for Beloved: "It was a greedy ghost and needed a lot of love, which was only natural, considering. And I do. Love her. I do" (247). Here, love, trauma, memory, and attention are tied into a knot that could never be disentangled.[2]

Early in the novel, Sethe declares, "Some things go. Pass on. Some things just stay," before positing a profoundly materialist theory of history in form of "rememory": "Places, places are still there. If a house burns down, it's gone, but the place—the picture of it—stays, and not just in my rememory, but out there, in the world" (43). In *Beloved*, memory is intersubjective, material, haunting. It is not a question of individual consciousness: you can even "bump into a rememory that belongs to someone else" (43). Haunting and rememory name ways of attuning to the always already collective materiality of the past and its violences, and the ways that those historical violences are present and ongoing.[3] Although these hauntings can and do press in on the consciousness of the characters, thus becoming events, they are always present in situations. Indeed, taking up Christina Sharpe's reading of the weather in *Beloved*, where she argues that "slavery undeniably became the total environment" (2016, 104), I will say that slavery and settler colonial violence haunt every situation in the United States.

In *Ghostly Matters*, Avery F. Gordon analyzes Morrison's *The Bluest Eye* and argues that the novel's evocation of "the thing" is a figuration of "the sedimented conditions that constitute what is in place in the first place" (1997, 4). Attending to these conditions, Gordon tracks "the way in which life is more complicated than those of us who study it have usually granted" (7). Extending this line of thinking and tracking the persistence of haunting in texts by indigenous and Black Atlantic writers, Hershini Bhana Young proposes that ghosts "impress on [us] the urgency of unburying certain social experiences and objects located at the nexus of the subjective and objective" (2006, 47). Picking up and extending Morrison's concept of rememory, Young explores the ways in which indigenous writers like Anna Lee Walters insist that "objects have memory" (88). In particular, in the literatures of indigenous and Black Atlantic writers, it is the memory that genocide and "slavery [are] . . . not . . . aberration[s] of modernity, as liberal humanists claim, but rather essential to its paradigm" (11). And in the context of settler colonies such as the United States, violent dispossession—what Marxists have called "primitive accumulation"—is the ongoing condition of possibility for everyday life.[4]

Places and objects, then, remember. But our attentions, as Gordon suggests, are often trained in ways that limit our attunement to this. Morrison underscores this too, writing of Sethe that "years of haunting had dulled her in ways you wouldn't believe and sharpened her in ways you wouldn't believe" (1987, 117). Young argues that becoming haunted, paying attention to ghosts, leads us toward a responsibility to "recover those marginalized, submerged, transformed corpi who haunt and destabilize the Enlightenment with its narrow rationalism and troubling spatial and temporal sequestration of the spirit world/dead" (2006, 4). In other words, a particular social order—we can call this Enlightenment, or imperial Western modernity—dulls us to particular aspects of our world, and to considering how that world has come into existence, even as it sharpens us in other ways. But dwelling with haunting can unsettle this, sending our attention in other directions, and back toward questions of how that particular social order was able to emerge and at what costs.[5]

In what follows, I experiment with sharpening myself to some things toward which my liberal humanist education in literary studies has dulled my attention. This necessitates taking haunting seriously as an affective phenomenon: "Thinking historicity through haunting thus combines both the seeming objectivity of events and the subjectivity of their affective afterlife" (Freccero 2006, 76). This "afterlife" to which we attend in becoming haunted is materially present in the situations that underlie and enable events, and this is why Carla Freccero can rightly claim that "being haunted is . . . a profoundly erotic experience" (91). I shall have much more to say later about the erotics of literacy, but at this juncture what is important to insist upon is that haunting is felt. I want to use this affective, erotic experience of haunting to think about what gets included within our frames when we talk about literacy and literature, and how we attend not only to what is there but the conditions of arrival for those things. This will involve playing with what Katie King calls "scoping and scaling" (2011, 3), moving the frame and focus around in order to push my dulled habits of attention into something sharper. It will also involve trying to focus on what happens at the margins of the stories that my liberal humanist education has never stopped telling: stories about what literacy and literature are, about what those things do, and ultimately about what it means to be a human being.

Beloved crucially connects Sethe's habits of attention to love, and thus I want to understand what I do in these pages as an act of what Cesare Casarino calls "philopoeisis":

> In the end, it will be a question of witnessing whether one's first love—which has remained one's true love all along—can rise from its own ashes, not as the eternal return of the identical love or as the eternal return of a different love, but rather as the eternal return of the love of the same and of loving that thing such as it is. And here the thing itself will bear the paleonymic name of *literature*. And the love of the thing, that is, the love of literature, will bear the untimely and neologistic name of *philopoeisis*. (2002, xiv)

It is my love for literature—although, as Casarino suggests, the thing that I love may come to look very strange to me, and to literary scholars—that impels me to love it "as it is." It is here that what Morrison calls dullness and sharpness become crucial, for I will argue that literature, when it is understood as one of the humanities, is rather severely restricted. And my desire to attend to it, my inescapable love for it, emerges from a sense that it gets under my skin (and not only my skin) in ways that outstrip how we in liberal humanist institutions of education talk about the value of literature most of the time today.

Let me dwell for a moment longer on "thing," since that word appears in both Morrison's fiction and Casarino's affectively driven method of literary reading. In *Networked Reenactments*, Katie King, in a context not terribly far removed from this book, writes, "'Things' is a useful word here: its etymology stresses that things are processes as well as subjects and objects, that they are simultaneously the location for dispute and the subjects of dispute as well as the outcomes of dispute" (2011, 2). In this precise sense, literature is the thing that demands my attention here: it is at once a problem, a dispute, a location, a process, and an outcome. Indeed, to the extent that there is a method here beyond "scoping and scaling," it is to constantly be suspicious of attempts to close and foreclose the meaning of "literature" and of "reading." If at any time those start to seem settled, a new shift in focus and framing should render any solidity blurry, or porous.

How does one attend to a thing, then? King writes, "To see the whole territory we pan out and up for a satellite view, or we come in closer and closer to see the very particular street patterns, maybe even to detail the backyard of a specific house, the parking lot of a particular building. We move the orientation point around with our mouse, cursor, finger, or whatever, to shift *scope and scale*" (2011, 4). She is obviously playing with the techno-possibilities of Google Earth as a way of reconfiguring methods of feminist interpretive practice, where interpretation is a question of attention. As Sara Ahmed reminds us, "There is a politics to how we distribute our attention" (2008, 30). While some of what I do in this book is consonant with what literary scholars have long called close reading, I also seek other distributions of my attention, backing up and trying to get a wider view. Indeed, *Animate Literacies* engages what Franco Moretti (2005) has called "distant reading," in order to suggest that his protodigital humanities models are still not distant enough (in that he continues to let the human fill the whole frame). Toward this end, in chapter 10 I zoom way out to propose a literary ethology that sees literature as one tiny version of a much wider field of animal/animate literacies.

King weaves her methodological attunements to the production of affects, which is another way of saying that she operationalizes Ahmed's thesis on the politics of attention. She writes,

Denaturalizing and *feeling* our own movements among knowledge worlds and distributed memberships, among authoritative and alternative knowledges and politics, we find ourselves drawing on a wide culturally altering sensorium and an individual and collectively cultivated set of affects. *Feelings* are ways of perceiving ourselves under satellite view, not in the god's eye or only under surveillance, but in a humbling inclusion as agencies ourselves, only too partial and uncertain among political opportunities and exigencies in various knowledge worlds. (2011, 7)

Feelings then are not some kind of affective supplement to knowledge, but a kind of knowledge. They may even be the only sure proof we have that we are moving among knowledge worlds. I go into much more detail about the affects of literacy in chapter 11, "What Happens When I Read?," zooming in below the level of a reading mind encountering a signifying text in order to see reading as a distributed event happening in multiple systems that make up a body always in contact with a complex and swirling ecology of actants that always affect it (often without any conscious registration).

King also reminds me that in the movement that is this book, I am entirely enmeshed within the object (or really, dispute) I am trying to track: my perspective is resolutely partial, entangled, situated. Indeed, this entanglement between my self and literature is such that I could not exist as I am without it. This necessitates that at times I write about my own affective experience with literacies and attend to how my experiences may enable certain kinds of generalization without becoming universal.[6] This comes into sharpest focus in chapter 12, "The Smell of Literature," and 13, "Pleasures of the Text." Moving from the account of literacy as primarily affective in chapter 11, I dwell, some might think idiosyncratically, on two ways in which the affective scene of reading is much wider, and weirder, than most humanists will typically allow. In the course of focusing on the olfactory and erotic dimensions of literacies, I insist that not only would granting these more attention allow us to have a more complex conception of the pleasurable affects of literacy, such a move also enables the construction of more interesting, and materialist, accounts of the profoundly unequal access to literacies in our contemporary world. The complex politics of literacy become legible precisely through shifting from literacy events to literacy situations. Ahmed is helpful here again. She writes, "Attention involves a political economy, or an uneven distribution of attention time between those who arrive at the writing table, which affects what they do once they arrive (and many do not even make it)" (2006, 32). I come back to this parenthetical statement much later in the book. For now, this claim allows me to highlight how my own position as a professor of literature—someone who reads and writes for a living, and who is paid to disseminate ideas and methods that emerge from and around a particular field or disciplinary apparatus—makes this book possible in that it entirely structures my attention. Even as I strain to shift my focus and to hold open my sense of what literature is, I write in and toward a particular set of fields and their traditions.

Even as those traditions have "primed" my attention (as Brian Massumi might say), they cannot entirely circumscribe my love for literature.

In *Proust and Signs*, Gilles Deleuze writes that "to fall in love is to individualize someone by the signs he bears or emits" (2000, 7). Love is, to use a distinction from Roland Barthes's *Camera Lucida*, about "punctum," not "studium" (1981, 25–27). We love what pierces us, pricks us, gets under our skin. This is never a question of a generality (let's call it the idea of literature) but something individual or singular (the material fact of corporeal, affective encounters between myself and a host of other agencies and entities in acts of erotic signification). Deleuze goes on: "Love is born from and nourished on silent interpretation" (2000, 7). Interpretation bears love and continues to nourish it. Love then emerges from questions, from a gap between what one thinks one knows and a singularity from which we cannot divert our attention. In this sense, when interpretation and love are comingled, interpretation cannot have as its goal the total elucidation of an object. The point is not the end, as it were, but the task. I interpret literature not to understand it, or to present readings of it as if those were things that could be accomplished, but to "stay with the trouble" that is literature, to use Donna Haraway's (2016) beautiful phrase.

Theorists of feminist science studies and standpoint epistemology have long insisted that our perspectives are necessarily partial and embedded within the situations we wish to study. There is, of course, an ethics to this (and, as I argue later in the book with some help from Audre Lorde, an erotics). Haraway writes, "Positioning implies responsibility for our enabling practices. It follows that politics and ethics ground struggles for the contests over what may count as rational knowledge" (1991, 193). Knowledge, then, emerges out of necessarily interested, "passionate" (191), and partial perspectives that are ineluctably shaped by ethical and political orientations. It is also true, within these discourses, that *"we are a part of that nature that we seek to understand"* (Barad 2007, 67). So, I am in no way outside of either literature or the larger world in which that thing appears as a singular activity, and my engagement with it is shot through with a politics that orients me to it in particular ways, and that structures how I attend to literature's relations to a host of human and nonhuman entities entangled with it.

In Karen Tei Yamashita's novel *Tropic of Orange*, a homeless man who may or may not have previously been a surgeon stands on an overpass in Los Angeles conducting a symphony emerging contingently from the movements of the city on and around the highway system. The narrative consciousness tracks how this conducting is simultaneously a kind of "recycling" and a "mapping" (Yamashita 1997, 56–57). I want to quote at length one of the passages where this man, Manzanar, thinks of the city:

> But what were these mapping layers? For Manzanar they began with the very geology of the land, the artesian rivers running beneath the surface, connected and divergent, shifting and swelling. There was the complex and normally silent web of faults—cracking like mud flats baking under a desert sun, like the crevices of aging hands and faces. Yet, below the surface, there was the man-made grid of civil utilities: Southern California pipelines of natural gas; the unnatural waterways of the Los Angeles Department of Water and Power, and the great dank tunnels of sewage; the cascades of poisonous effluents surging from rain-washed streets into the Santa Monica Bay; electric currents racing voltage into the open watts of millions of hungry energy-efficient appliances; telephone cables, cable TV, fiber optics, computer networks.
>
> On the surface, the complexity of layers should drown an ordinary person, but ordinary persons never bother to notice, never bother to notice the prehistoric grid of plant and fauna and human behavior, nor the historic grid of land usage and property, the great overlays of transport—sidewalks, bicycle paths, roads, freeways, systems of transit both ground and air, a thousand natural and man-made divisions, variations both dynamic and stagnant, patterns and connections by every conceivable definition from the distribution of wealth to race, from patterns of climate to the curious blueprint of the skies. (57)

Manzanar provides here a "mapping" that bespeaks the sort of love for a thing I try to enact in Animate Literacies. There is a palimpsest of layers, with different historical, geological, and political imbrications, and it is only by devoting a kind of attention "ordinary persons" do not allow themselves that one can see, and hear, and feel the web of these relations. Love has to stay with what is rank, decaying, politically oppressive. If one is to love literature "as it is," to use Casarino's phrase, then one cannot enter with a predetermined desire to see only those parts of it that fit into a neat, idealistic vision of what it is and what it does. Literature and literacy are sources of enormous erotic and political possibility, yes, but they have only come to be what they are by partaking of dehumanization and a staggering amount of violence, both intrahuman and with respect to the more-than-human world.

Attending to literature, loving it, requires that I shift my perspective in as many ways as I can to sense its myriad connections to what is often left out when people define literature, and it means staying with its ghosts: with its emergence within a social formation that produces and violently enforces a particular vision of what it means to be human, one that renders most humans inhuman or ahuman or less-than-human. It means figuring out how to love literature even when it has been—and continues to be—directly implicated in this violence. At a moment when the value of literature is very much in question, those of us who think there is something in it worth staying with (as I do) owe it to ourselves, to each other, and to the dispute I continue to call *literature* to attend to it in all its messiness. This will turn out to be, I should think, both horrifying and joyful.

4

HUMANIZING ASSEMBLAGES I: WHAT IS MAN?

I want to scale up from the scene of pedagogy in *Beloved* to offer a more general account of what I call *humanizing assemblages*, since this concept enables us to see how the statist capture of literacy articulates the more-than-human milieu of literacy situations with the intrahuman politics of imperialist modernity. The historian Lynn Hunt offers an account of how particular literacy practices, state apparatuses, and conceptions about what it means to be human became tightly bound up with each other in the eighteenth century. While I argue that we need to significantly expand her theory in several ways, its simplicity makes it a perfect *Ansatzpunkt* for conceptualizing humanizing assemblages. Taking for granted that the "human" of human rights philosophy and law is the dominant conception today, she builds the case that it was produced through the reading of epistolary novels. More specifically, she claims that reading novels engendered cognitive reconfigurations of human brains in ways that heightened empathy, which in turn made it possible to think of the human as an abstract universal that was nevertheless emotionally sutured to liberal subjects. Laconically, she writes, "New kinds of reading (and viewing and listening) created new individual experiences (empathy), which in turn made possible new social and political concepts" (Hunt 2007, 33–34).[1]

While I think one can reasonably offer accounts of the emergence of the modern human(ist) subject that don't focus on the novel, the novel as a specific case allows for some generalization.[2] First, there is a complex feedback loop here between literacy practices and state apparatuses. While the state is not anything simple or unified, there is clearly a state investment in literacy practices, concretized in the state sponsorship of schools.[3] And these subjects, who come into being by passing through such educational assemblages, come to have investments in the state.[4] The word "investment" here indicates some measure of psychic attachment or attention paid, and it also underscores specific material configurations of resources. In fact, I would see these two senses of investment as inseparable as they both involve distributions of energy within a system in relation to something external that affects it. Investment is thus a way of characterizing the activity of bordering as it occurs where subjects and the state come into frictional contact.[5]

The conditions of possibility for what Ian Watt (1957) has called the "rise of the novel" included the invention of the printing press and the large-scale manufacture of paper and ink, the existence of at least intranational routes for the circulation of commodities, and the emergence of specific buildings for holding books for either sale (the bookseller) or lending (the library). If the novel is a material object made by machines from plant fibers and inks, and implicated in networks of distribution that involve innumerable nonhumans, then one has to conclude that the human which is produced by novel reading is, at least in part, the effect of these nonhuman agencies.[6] The rise of the novel also necessitates a readership for novels, something that in the eighteenth century was possible only because of differential access to time, money, and education: in the budding capitalist economy, it was primarily wealthy, European women who had the money to buy books, the time to read them, and the education to make slogging through often long, realistic accounts of the lives of individuals a pleasurable thing to do. From this it would make sense to conclude that the human that comes from wealthy Europeans reading novels would, as a concept, bear the traces of the intrahuman and more-than-human relations that make it possible. In other words, while this human would loudly proclaim its universality, it is, in fact, highly particular.

Sylvia Wynter's writings offer an account that is somewhat similar to Hunt's, but has three additional virtues. First, she locates the emergence of this particular version of the human, which she calls "Man," in relation to a larger history of modernity and its entanglements with Western imperialism, capitalism, and racial slavery, as well as the linked emergences of modern science and more secular worldviews in the West (or, as we are more likely to say today, the global North).[7] Second, Wynter gives an account of how literature constructs selves that is attentive to what Haraway (2008) would call "natureculture" systems, systems that cannot be thought of as either natural or cultural because those are not separate or separable things. Third, Wynter considerably extends the connections Hunt proposes among literacy, states, and the human by not restricting the work of humanization to novels, and by refusing to take for granted any monolithic and universal version of "the human," foregrounding instead "genres of being human" (Wynter and McKittrick 2015, 31).

Wynter proposes that "it is we who are the function [of literature]. It is as specific modes of imagining subjects of the aesthetic orders which literature's figuration-Word weaves in great feats of rhetorical engineering that we come to imagine/experience ourselves, our modes of being" (1984, 50). Indeed, this account links aesthetics to affects, and opens onto the problem of how humans come to feel themselves (and others) as human. Wynter's account is, in some ways, an extension and elucidation of this claim by Frantz Fanon, in *Black Skin, White Masks*: "Reacting against the constitutionalist tendency of the late nineteenth century, Freud insisted that the individual factor be taken into account through psychoanalysis. He substituted for a phylogenetic theory the ontogenetic perspective. It will be seen that black man's alienation is not an individual question. Beside phylogeny and ontogeny stands sociogeny" (1967, 11). Sociogeny names how material-discursive assemblages—including engendering, colonization, and racialization—produce differential modes of human being. These are not forces that act after the fact on humans (culture added to nature), but are part of the milieux in which those humans take shape through assemblages of humanization (I would say that they adhere in the literacy situation). In "Towards the Sociogenic Principle," Wynter refers to this as "our present culture's . . . definition of what it is to *be*, and therefore of what it is *like to be* human" (2001, 31).[8] That is, modes of being human become, quite literally and corporeally, part of our being, and determine how we think and feel about ourselves and the world around us.[9]

By tracing the relations between European colonial ideology, the rise of modern science, the construction of nation-states, and transformations in educational institutions that form the earliest experiments with the humanities, Wynter elaborates how the "study [of literature] was . . . intended to 'humanize' by enabling the 'contemplation of Man in his Works'" (1984, 46). This study made possible "an utterly new way of feeling, of imagining Self and World" (33). This sociogenic function of literature operates to shape a human's affective and "cognitive mechanisms" or what Wynter elsewhere calls, drawing on systems theory, its "autopoietic" movement through the world. The crucial thing for me is that she locates this theoretical account of humans as biocultural creatures (to use Samantha Frost's phrase) within a history of modernity that attends to the coloniality of its emergence and endurance. Put differently, the transmission of violence across generations occurs precisely through naturecultural practices and specific material and corporeal becomings.[10] Literacy education in statist schools is one instance of this more general operation of humanizing assemblages.

For Wynter, the human imagined by the humanities (or the *studia humanitatis*) beginning in the fifteenth century in Europe was a highly specific, historically contingent version of the human, one she calls "Man, which overrepresents itself as if it were the human itself" (2003, 260). The synecdochic logic here, by which a specific version of being human comes to be overrepresented as the human itself, is a crucial feature of the colonial diagrams running through modernity.[11] Building on work by Aníbal Quijano, Walter Mignolo, and Howard Winant, Wynter argues:

> If . . . race . . . is a purely invented construct . . . , it was this construct that would enable the now globally expanding West to replace the earlier mortal/immortal, natural/supernatural, human/the ancestors, the gods/God distinction as the one on whose basis all human groups had millennially "grounded" their descriptive statement/prescriptive statements of what it is to be human, and to reground its secularizing own on a newly projected human/subhuman distinction instead. (2003, 264)

That is, as the modern concept of the human emerges, one that circulates in cultural productions such as literature and which, therein encountered, actually reconfigures the cognitive/corporeal systems of readers and listeners, it is inextricably racialized. Explaining this insight, Alexander Weheliye writes that "there exists no portion of the modern human that is not subject to racialization, which determines the hierarchical ordering of the Homo sapiens into humans, not-quite-humans, and nonhumans" (2014, 8).

This differentiation and hierarchical ordering of various genres of being human, where only one gets to count as fully human, occurs through what Weheliye calls "racializing assemblages": mechanisms for socio-genically producing the fully human in dialectical relation to what Judith Butler calls its "constitutive outside" (1993, 8).[12] Taking up Derrida's pale-onymic concept of "writing itself, in its nonphonetic moment" (1978, 25), and weaving it together with what Frantz Fanon calls "epidermalization" and Butler's concept of gender performativity, I would generalize to argue that a crucial aspect of humanizing assemblages is writing race and gender into or as the body (even when race and gender disappear into preindividual logics of investment and control that nevertheless articulate highly gendered and racist distributions of resources and bodies).[13] Some of this might happen as writing on the body (the branding and whipping of black slaves, makeup and body modifications that are distinctly gendered[14]), using "the body as inscriptive surface."[15] But while Stuart Hall argues that epidermalization is "literally the inscription of race on the skin" (cited in Browne 2015, 97), I want to heed Weheliye's and Butler's warnings not to imagine some unmarked biological body prior to humanizing's inscriptions of race and gender. That is, as a biocultural creature whose becoming and flourishing are sociogenic, the human is always being written, being performed according to operative but not necessarily physically given scripts. Indeed, this statist literacy descends from bodies as such to "a never-ending modulation of moods, capacities, affects, and potentialities, assembled in genetic codes, identification numbers, ratings profiles, and preference listings, that is to say, in bodies of data and information (including the human body as information and data)" (Clough 2007, 19).

Among other things, thinking about race and gender as practices of writing the body (where, as Butler has long argued, there is no "author"[16]), and practices of reading the body (as information), opens up the possibility of conceptualizing Man as the diagram around which assemblages dispersed throughout the social milieu are oriented.[17] Being able to navigate this milieu requires particular forms of racialized and gendered literacies, or what Berlant calls "literacy in normativity" (2011, 52): we have to learn to read our bodies and the bodies of others as having a race and a gender in order for those bodies to be legible as human in Man's overrepresentation.[18] As I underscore more clearly in the coming pages, these literacies directly involve questions of movement, mobility, and the social organization of space.[19] One could think here of how bodies are segregated in gendered bathrooms (which, right now in the United States, is a site of dispute with regard to the state) as a banal instance of how these literacies determine everyday life.[20] Jim Crow segregation and the ubiquitous "white" and "colored" signs provide another example. Simone Browne agues that "it is the making of the black body as out of place, an attempt to deny its capacity for humanness, which makes for the productive power of epidermalization" (2015, 98). Referring to how gender performance is linked to apparatuses of humanization and dehumanization, Butler writes that "it is not enough to claim that human subjects are constructed, for the construction of the human is a differential operation that produces the more and the less 'human,' the inhuman, and the humanly unthinkable. These excluded sites come to bound the 'human' as its constitutive outside, and to haunt those boundaries as the persistent possibility of their disruption and rearticulation" (1993, 8). The human, then, cannot appear or be produced without a simultaneous, but often disavowed, production of these constitutive outsides. As Lisa Lowe argues, "the operations that pronounce colonial divisions of humanity—settler seizure and native removal, slavery and racial dispossession, and racialized expropriations of many kinds—are imbricated processes, not sequential events; they are ongoing and continuous in our present moment, not temporally distinct nor as yet concluded" (2015, 7). Importantly, the operations of humanizing assemblages cannot occur except via emergence from more-than-human literacy situations. Becoming sensitive to the outside of humanizing literacies, to the situation, involves becoming being haunted and learning to attune to the material presence of histories of violence in literacy situations and their affective tonalities.[21]

Thus, we have to say that humanization and dehumanization cannot be decoupled because humanizing assemblages produce both in the same machinations. Indeed, it allows me to clarify that the human is nothing other than a political concept, one that is linked to ideas in biology, history, philosophy, and literature to be sure, but which is fundamentally porous and resistant to closure. And yet, when the modern, Western, imperialist version of Man becomes global, and is violently overrepresented as the human, this border policing—by the nation-state first and foremost—is necessary in order to secure the very border of the political. Indeed, one of the things that this modern version of human, Man, reinscribes from older Western conceptions of the human is that the human alone is, to use Aristotle's phrase, the political animal. Humans, and humans only, are political subjects capable of political deliberation and political action. Nonhumans may be objects of political action, but may not participate, for they have no rationality, language, agency, sense of temporality, and so on. There has been no shortage of qualities held up as the defining difference between humans and non-, in-, or less-than-humans, and I dwell on several of them in the rest of this book, but there has always been some insistence on specifying a trait that would qualitatively establish human exceptionalism. Thus, humanizing assemblages are configured precisely to generate and police these borders between the human and non, those capable of participating in the political and those excluded.

While I don't necessarily disagree with Dominic Pettman's (2011) claim that thinking of the human as a bounded entity is an error, I think casting Man (and, indeed, any other mode of being human) as a fiction is more helpful. Fiction is, etymologically, related to the Latin verb *fingere*: to make. A fiction, then, is something constructed, produced. It is not, in this sense, the opposite of reality. Man is a fiction that is written in and as bodies through diffuse humanizing assemblages that function in modalities of both discipline and control.[22] "The assemblage," Jasbir Puar writes, "as a series of dispersed but mutually implicated and messy networks, draws together enunciation and dissolution, causality and effect, organic and nonorganic forces" (2007, 211). Rather than a straightforward production of the human through domination or ideological interpellation, assemblages of humanization draw into their operations resources, institutions, and relations that span the entirety of human societies and extend far beyond the human. Such assemblages and their messy, even contradictory, effects (and affects!) enable us to see how so many people, even those who must endure violent dehumanizations, would still abide by Man and the (nation) state formations to which it is linked. What this way of thinking about power offers us, then, is a way of attuning to how omnipresent humanizing assemblages are while still foregrounding both their unevenness and the spatiotemporal interstices where delinquency is possible. Indeed, delinquency and failure always accompany the operation of assemblages as, at the very least, virtual possibilities.[23]

If I want to insist that we see the human (Man) as a fiction, then, it is both to highlight the contingency of this history and to let that contingency animate our imaginations for the future.[24] We have been compelled to be human in particular ways—often through the subtle machinations of state power and biopolitical modes of governmentality—but that does not change the fact that while this fiction modulates our attunement to the world, it does not, in fact, exhaust the world and its messy possibilities. There are, as black, brown, indigenous, postcolonial, queer, and feminist thinkers have been insisting for decades, countless people who have never been allowed access to being recognized as fully human. These genres of performing the human—and their aesthetics, literacies, and corporeal practices—offer alternative ways of performing humanity and engaging the political. This is why, instead of simply claiming to be against dehumanization in order to stake our political hopes on less violent forms of the same old humanist logics of inclusion, we might practice what Julietta Singh (2017b) calls "dehumanism": a dwelling with (aesthetic, corporeal, political) the dehumanized in order both to call into question Man's purported universality and to experiment with alternative fictions.

Didier Debaise, explicating Whitehead's philosophy, writes that "the sole aim, the sole goal of a 'society,' is to maintain its historic route, the movement of its inheritance, the taking up, the transmission of the acts of feeling that comprise it. . . . For living societies, to be interested means 'orienting themselves,' 'choosing,' 'searching': essentially it is a matter of an activity in relation to a specific environment" (2017, 73).[25] The modern project linking states, capitalist economies, colonial formations (both distant and settler), ecologically devastating modes of resource extraction and production, and assemblages of (de)humanization tends toward maintaining this "historic route." What we might then call Man's inertia exists precisely because it is interwoven with so many facets of contemporary life (it informs so many societies), and most of us have been educated not to attend to it at all. But Wynter's writings on genres of being human call us to feel the possibility of orienting ourselves toward the human differently, of learning to attune to Man as a fiction, and one that is always being remade historically as part of its maintenance. I want to insist that although the transmission of Man-as-the-human is enfolded into our lives in ways that we sometimes struggle to sense (it adheres in the literacy situations that make up our lives), its transmission through assemblages also gives Man a particular fragility. We need to learn to seize on ways of reading and writing the human differently that disrupt and re-articulate the energies that go into its maintenance. If Man provides coordinates around which everything must be oriented, then what I call *bewilderment* names any disorientation with respect to Man.

This finally allows me to track back to *Beloved*'s dispersed pedagogy. The lesson, remember, is that Sethe is, as a black slave and as a woman, part human but part animal: not fully human. She has characteristics of both, and Mrs. Garner defines "characteristics" as "a thing that's natural to a thing." I would like to dwell for a moment on how *Beloved* challenges the lesson that Sethe learns from Schoolteacher and Mrs. Garner. The difference in humanness between Sethe and the white pupils is absolutely not something natural. I quote at length:

> Whitepeople believed that whatever the manners, under every dark skin was a jungle. Swift unnavigable waters, swinging screaming baboons, sleeping snakes, red gums ready for their sweet white blood. In a way, he [Stamp Paid] thought, they were right. The more coloredpeople spent their strength trying to convince them how gentle they were, how clever and loving, how human, the more they used themselves up to persuade whites of something Negroes believed could not be questioned, the deeper and more tangled the jungle grew inside. But it wasn't the jungle blacks brought with them to this place from the other (livable) place. It was the jungle whitefolks planted in them. And it grew. It spread. In, through and after life, it spread, until it invaded the whites who had made it. Touched them every one. Changed and altered them. Made them bloody, silly, worse than even they wanted to be, so scared were they of the jungle they had made. The screaming baboon lived under their own skin; the red gums were their own. (1987, 234)

Here, what whitepeople call "nature" is always already culture. There is no nature divorced from intrahuman politics. But also human culture is always already nature, shaped by nonhuman agencies (the jungle grows and spreads on its own). From *Beloved*'s dispersed pedagogy, we learn that grappling with naturecultures involves tracking both nonhuman agency and the politics of colonialism and white supremacy. We also learn that the version of the human operative in the humanizing machine of Schoolteacher's lesson (what Wynter calls "Man") is a fiction that can only be narrated at considerable cost. In Judith Butler's terms, "If there are norms of recognition by which the 'human' is constituted, and these norms in-code operations of power, then it follows that the contest over the future of the 'human' will be a contest over the power that works in and through such norms" (2004, 13). The powers that give rise to the human cannot, therefore, be themselves human. This seems to be precisely Morrison's lesson, and in reading it, being affected by it, we may also feel, through the performative force of Morrison's narrative as we read it in a book, that other fictions are not only possible, but necessary.

We could say that humanizing assemblages inescapably produce dehumanization as a kind of exhaust. The thing about exhaust, from an ecological perspective, is that it transforms the ecosystem into which it is released, and can, over time, make the flourishing of that system impossible: this is, after all, the basic claim of most mainstream environmental activism addressing pollution and the production of greenhouse gases. Work on the human from black, brown, indigenous, postcolonial, feminist, and queer perspectives not only highlights how this unsustainability of Man functions (that is, that humanization cannot function without dehumanization), but also creatively affirms this crisis as the basis for rearticulating other ways of being human. Indeed, if Singh's (2017b) dehumanism links the posthumanist to the decolonial, we could say that the political project is not just decolonizing the human, but decolonizing the literacies that materially enable particular genres of being human. Importantly, other genres of being human are also not simply human inventions, for they rely on complex networks of nonhumans for their existence. If we take seriously the claim, made by many indigenous thinkers, that humans are part of the land, and land is a "mode of reciprocal relationship" (Coulthard 2014, 60), then we have to affirm, with Eve Tuck and Marcia McKenzie, that "decolonization is not just something that humans (may) do; it is (primarily) something that the land does on its own behalf" (2015, 71).

5

SLAVERY, THE HUMAN, AND DEHUMANIZATION

Having argued that novels produce empathy in readers, thereby enabling a specific version of the human to become the dominant political concept in the eighteenth century, Lynn Hunt goes on to note that "capitalizing on the success of the novel in calling forth new forms of psychological identification, early abolitionists encouraged slaves to write their own novelistic autobiographies, sometimes partially fictionalized, to gain adherents to the budding movement" (2007, 66). Focusing now on one of these narratives—*The Narrative of the Life of Frederick Douglass, an American Slave, Written by Himself*—will allow me to concretize the arguments from the previous chapters about how Man, the imperialist nation-state, literacy, and affect converge. To do this, I focus both on Douglass's own narrative (which, in part, opens onto a wider field of questions about the politics and materiality of literacy which I take up in chapters 6 and 7), but also on how Douglass's text is framed by interpretive statements by white abolitionists. This framing tends to rein in if not undercut Douglass's creative conceptual linking of literacy, the state, and the human, and his intense interest in education as the accumulation of affects that generate the need for corporeal experimentation. Because this framing has proven so crucial to how Douglass's *Narrative* is often read as a celebration of the link between literacy and humanization, I want to begin with it.

The preface to the narrative, written by William Lloyd Garrison and published along with the *Narrative* in 1845, addresses readers clearly imagined as largely white, Christian, and Northern:

Mr. DOUGLASS has very properly chose to write his own Narrative, in his own style, and according to the best of his ability, rather than to employ someone else. It is, therefore, entirely his own production; and, considering how long and dark was the career he had to run as a slave,—how few have been his opportunities to improve his mind since he broke his iron fetters,—it is, in my judgment, highly credible to his head and heart. He who can peruse it without a tearful eye, a heaving breast, an afflicted spirit,—without being filled with an unutterable abhorrence of slavery and all its abettors, and animated with a determination to seek the immediate overthrow of that execrable system,—without trembling for the fate of this country in the hands of a righteous God, who is ever on the side of the oppressed, and whose arm is not shortened that it cannot save,—must have a flinty heart, and be qualified to act the part of a trafficker "in slaves and the souls of men." I am confident that it is essentially true in all its statements; that nothing has been set down in malice, nothing exaggerated, nothing drawn from the imagination, that it comes short of the reality, rather than overstates a single fact in regard to SLAVERY AS IT IS. (1997, 6–7)

Despite the rhetorical flair of this passage, its arguments are quite simple. First, it is spectacular that Douglass has written such a document given his "dark" career as a slave.[1] Second, a reader has two possible affective responses to the narrative: a tearful, heaving, afflicted, painful response and a response that lacks these qualities. The former response aligns the reader with the abolitionist cause; the latter response aligns the reader with slavery. Affect here directly correlates to political stance. Third, after this Manichean division has taken place, Garrison proclaims his confidence in the text's truth. What is the paratactic relation between the truth of the text proclaimed twice and the emotional responses described between those proclamations?

Could it be that the political aim of abolition runs a curious risk here of being contaminated by fiction or what Garrison calls "the imagination"? Garrison qualifies his link between emotional response and political allegiance by insisting that such emotional responses to this text arise from the true content of the narrative, not its form as narrative. It seems that Garrison understands the logic Hunt describes, namely, that abolition as a social movement can use existing novel-reading practices for a political end. This use requires first that the political field and the practice of novel reading do not collapse into each other. Not all emotions arising from reading novels are directly translatable to political action, so Garrison wants to paratextually and proleptically prime the reader for one of two responses.[2] And Garrison pitches his pedagogical address to readers suggesting that their affective response is not a result of narrative form (which is what Hunt argues is at stake) but a response to the truth of "SLAVERY AS IT IS." This truth, however, is secured by three linked synecdoches: the truthful description of the institution of slavery stands in for the narrative as a whole; every character within the narrative is taken to stand in for either "the man-stealers" or "their down-trodden victims"; and Frederick Douglass as an individual stands in for all black male slaves.[3] That is, what Garrison calls truth is not strictly speaking some quality of the text, but something produced in the synecdochic reading practice he imagines and pedagogically insists upon in his preface.[4]

Garrison's pedagogical framing urges that identifications be formed in adherence to a socially constructed binary opposition. Garrison's political worldview splits the world into two groups—"man-stealers" and their "downtrodden victims"—according to their relation to, precisely, "man," which cannot be understood apart from the state. Garrison writes, "Let it never be forgotten, that no slaveholder or overseer can be convicted of any outrage perpetrated on the person of a slave, however diabolical it may be, on the testimony of colored witnesses, whether bond or free. By the slave code, they are adjudged to be as incompetent to testify against a white man, as though they were indeed a part of the brute creation" (1997, 9). Here the law, "the slave code," recognizes two types of persons differentiated by their capacity for testimony: whites and blacks.[5] The former are legal subjects with rights of trial while the latter are "incompetent" as though brute (even when free). That is, their incompetence in producing a type of utterance—testimony—is equated with their animality. The verb "adjudge" registers the particularly political nature of this "incompetence." In Garrison's formulation, white men have defined the limits of the political—and therefore the limits of the human—according to the limits of their racial identification. This limit is delimited by incompetence, an inability excluding some from the political realm because this ability or competence is declared itself to be politics. According to Garrison, the existence of the *Narrative*—which he reads as a certain kind of testimony to "SLAVERY AS IT IS"—proves that Douglass, black man and former slave, is competent. Douglass's literacy is proof that slaves are capable of literacy and therefore human. Slavery, by denying the slave education and literacy, dehumanizes blacks and should be abolished. Moreover, his *Narrative* comes to be a particular kind of evidentiary testimony functioning outside the restricted realm of the state's judicial apparatus but with respect to exactly the same concerns and structures (that is, the anticipated result of readers' identification is precisely mobilization toward the legal abolition of slavery).

The very link between literacy (linguistic competence) and the human that enables the dehumanizing logic of the US antebellum state is thus here preserved and asserted, and Garrison demands that sympathetic readers recognize black slaves as potential human beings according to the readers' existing understandings of what it means to be human. That is, Garrison does not see Douglass's narrative as a challenge to the modern, imperialist conception of the human, nor does he think such a challenge is required of his readers. In fact, his logic is not substantively different from Mrs. Auld's analyzed later; he simply moves Douglass back into the category of the human. Here we have to recall Paul Gilroy's claim that "using the memory of slavery as an interpretive device suggests that this humanism cannot simply be repaired by introducing the figures of black folks who had previously been confined to the intermediate category between animal and human" (1993, 55). We need, instead of a reading practice that would find in Douglass's narrative confirmation of the necessary link between literacy and humanity, one that disentangles them and "works toward the abolition of Man" (Weheliye 2014, 4) and toward the creative production of experimental forms of humanity outside of (and in antagonistic relation to) imperial state power.

Taking off from the insight that "humanity has held a very different status for the traditions of the racially oppressed" (Weheliye 2014, 8), I want now to examine how Douglass's narrative of humanization proposes a subtle critique of how humanization and dehumanization are structurally coupled, and his flight thus represents not a simple search for integration into the existing mode of being human called "Man," but a dissolution and reconfiguration of Man, proleptically gesturing toward "the radical reconstruction and decolonization of what it means to be human" (Weheliye 2014, 4).

In attending to the *Narrative*'s knotting together of slavery, literacy, and the human, I focus for the most part on what might be called quotidian details rather than the moments of extreme physical violence that punctuate the narrative. In doing so, I follow Saidiya Hartman's queries in *Scenes of Subjection*: "What does it mean that the violence of slavery or the pained existence of the enslaved, if discernable, is only so in the most heinous and grotesque examples and not in the quotidian routines of slavery?" (1997, 21). Hartman's study forces a consideration of the ways descriptions of such scenes of violence—whippings and beatings, scenes at auction, rapes, and forced singing and dancing—produce a kind of empathy or identification that is, finally, dehumanizing. As she puts it, "Those shackled to one another do not document the disparities of the human condition or, most obviously, the violation of the natural liberty . . . but merely provide an opportunity for self-reflection" (35). That is, when (mostly) white readers are confronted with descriptions of the brutalized black body, what emerges is often not an identification with the enslaved so much as an opportunity to dialectically consider their own freedom.[6]

The structure of the *Narrative* is the rhetorical figure of chiasmus. Just before narrating his fateful fight with Mr. Covey the slave-breaker in chapter 10, Douglass writes, "You have seen how a man was made a slave; you shall now see how a slave was made a man" (1997, 47). This chiasmus is able to work only because the text has already put into place a world governed entirely by a series of interrelated and mutually reinforcing binary oppositions. Henry Louis Gates Jr. rightly signals the governing role played by the human/inhuman binary in Douglass's *Narrative*: "Douglass's narrative strategy seems to be this: He brings together two terms in special relationships suggested by some quality that they share; then, by opposing two seemingly unrelated elements, such as the sheep, cattle, or horses on the plantation and the specimen of life known as slave, Douglass's language is made to signify the presence and absence of some quality—in this case, humanity" (1991, 89). Before getting into the specific role that literacy plays, I want to dwell on this binary opposition between human and animal that governs the narrative and conceptual movement of the text.

In chapter 8, when Douglass is between ten and eleven years old, his master dies and he "is immediately sent for, to be valued with the other property" (1997, 35). It is this scene of valuation, or reckoning his worth as a commodity among other commodities, that prompts his feelings to rise up "in detestation of slavery" (35). That is, the external valuation produces a particular political affect, one that will mingle with the affects produced in his literacy education in order to enable specific forms of imaginative and corporeal action.

The scene of valuation works according to a flattening of distinctions, something that, as Marx has detailed, is precisely what is enabled by the emergence of exchange value. While use values are incomparable and singular, exchange value abstracts specific materialities in order to render everything commensurate via the sign of money. Douglass writes, "We were all ranked together at the valuation. Men and women, old and young, married and single, were ranked together with horses, sheep, and swine. There were horses and men, cattle and women, pigs and children, all holding the same rank in the scale of being, and were all subjected to the same narrow examination. . . . At that moment, I saw more clearly than ever the brutalizing effects of slavery upon both slave and slaveholder" (35–36). Douglass's rhetorical strategies here subtly argue that slavery as an economic-political-cultural system operates entirely according to binary oppositions but that it also, in highly specific ways, collapses those very distinctions and in doing so undercuts its own claims to conceptual coherence. That is, the legal and political existence of slavery relies upon a rigid, legally enforced distinction between human persons and inhuman chattel. This distinction appears in and as what W. E. B. Du Bois calls "the color line." To be white is to be a man; to be black (even by a drop) is to be property. In rendering the black slave a commodity, slavery animalizes or brutalizes her or him, which is to be taken quite literally: slavery makes animals out of those Douglass recognizes as human.

Born from these scenes of dehumanization, Douglass's *Narrative* proposes a richly ironic conception of the human. On one side, we can cluster Douglass's studied account of how slavery purportedly dehumanizes black humans by treating them as chattel in racializing assemblages that make the social formation of the United States prior to Emancipation possible and that continue, in reconfigured form, into the present. On the other side, we can gather a range of critiques of this system, critiques that tend toward one of two poles, which I can schematically call the rehumanization of the slave, and the total dehumanizing effect of slavery as an institution (both of these critiques are operative in *Beloved* as well). I deal with the second of these more directly in chapter 6, taking up how slavery requires slaveholders to be educated in order to treat slaves as animals, an education that can only operate, on Douglass's account, by shutting down their "simple" human souls and, in effect, rendering the slaveholders inhuman. This is what Douglass means in the passage above: there is something brutal about not recognizing distinctions between humans and cattle.

The rehumanization of the slave is more complex, in part because it can very easily be misread (as it is in Garrison's preface). When Douglass's *Narrative* insists that the slave really is human, it does not do so according to the same concept of the human that is operative in slavery as component system of imperialist modernity. From the perspective of the dehumanized, the human is always felt and lived differently than for those whose humanity is never in question.[7] Fred Moten offers a spur to this line of interpretation when he argues that "what is sounded through Douglass is a theory of value—an objective and objectional, productive and reproductive ontology—whose primitive axiom is that commodities speak" (2003, 11). First of all and most obviously, Moten is underscoring the highly specific quality of slaves as speaking commodities, and reading their utterances in relation to Marx's somewhat strange fantasy of what would happen if commodities could speak (thus demonstrating the need for a thorough rethinking of the idea of commodity grounded in the material facts of slavery). But this insight can also enable a rereading of the *Narrative* as suggesting that a range of things which aren't human—sheep, horses, books, boards, bricks—have a kind of agency or affective capacity to communicate and act. What this allows, then, is a conception of the human in Douglass's text that rejects both its specific racialized form as concretized by state and economic institutions and a specific ontological postulate of humanism which would see agency and communicativity as uniquely human capacities. Translated back into Wynter's terminology, Douglass desires to be human, not to be Man.

Chapter 10, the longest chapter of the *Narrative*, dramatizes the chiasmatic movement from slave to man for Douglass via physical violence between himself and Covey. Shortly after the incident I am about to analyze, Douglass declares that "Mr. Covey succeeded in breaking me. . . . The dark night of slavery closed in upon me; and behold a man transformed into a brute" (1997, 45). The broken/unbroken binary here is crucial, for it functions to signal both the specific site of biopolitical struggle between Covey and Douglass and to rhetorically affirm Douglass's continuity with the oxen. Covey, who has a reputation as a "nigger breaker" (42), breaks slaves like some men break work animals. Eventually, Douglass resists Covey's "breaking" through physical resistance, often read as a literalization of Hegel's master/slave dialectic.

I am interested in how the chapter begins by narratively—and thus educationally and affectively—situating that fight. In the language of Brian Massumi's affect theory, I am struck by how Douglass is primed for the fight. The chapter begins with Douglass being sent to gather wood with a team of "unbroken oxen." As Douglass led them, "the oxen took fright" and bolted, eventually upsetting the cart. That is, unbroken oxen do not simply do as they are expected. Despite being brutes or cattle, these nonhuman animals exert agency that is disruptive and unanticipatable. Douglass then spent "one half of the day" righting the cart and disentangling the oxen from the trees (which also exert a kind of agentic capacity in disrupting Douglass's plans).[8] Just as Douglass was about to get the oxen and cart back through the gate, "the oxen again started [and] rushed through the gate, catching it between the wheel and the body of the cart, tearing it to pieces, and coming within a few inches of crushing me against the gate-post" (43). This second disruption of Douglass's movement (oriented, of course, by Covey's commands) was even more extreme, and this event caused Douglass to have to report to Covey, upon which "he ordered [Douglass] to return to the woods again immediately" (43), where he tore "three large switches" from a gum-tree and "rushed at [Douglass] with the fierceness of a tiger . . . cutting [him] so savagely as to leave the marks visible for a long time after" (43).

The passage performs a number of crucial conceptual moves. First, Douglass's realistic mode of narration reveals that nonhuman objects (trees, fences, posts) actively participate and intervene in human reality, including functioning as part of a literacy assemblage that transforms Douglass's own body into a surface for script that very materially writes his inhuman status.[9] Second, it restates the inhumanity of the slaveholder, figuring Covey as both "savage" and like a tiger. Third, without making it explicit, it suggests that the physical fight that follows between Covey and Douglass is possible, in part, because of Douglass's learning from the oxen that no matter how much humans want to think oxen are mere commodities, they can act in unexpected and disruptive ways. That is, while Douglass's hand-to-hand combat with Covey proves his manhood by staging an almost straightforwardly Hegelian battle for recognition, it can be read as issuing from what I am tempted to call an animal capacity for disrupting human work. Read from within the logic of a particular kind of humanism (such as the one offered by Garrison in his preface), this may sound like I am siding with the slaveholders in seeing Douglass as less than human. Against this logic, I am trying to trace how Douglass may be instead offering a fugitive, furtive reconceptualization of the human, one that does not need a dialectical distanciation from animality to operate, and which can, in fact, affirm a vital link—at once ontogenic, affective, and political—between humans and other animals, and which has some attunement to the fact that both are constantly affecting and being affected by a host of other agencies both vital and nonvital.[10]

To begin to unfurl this alternative conception of the human, we could think about Tavia Nyong'o's analysis of one of Douglass's articles in the *North Star*, in which Douglass depicts a scene on Broadway in New York where white ladies had as "appendages" both "black horses" and "black servants." According to Nyong'o, "Douglass's comparison of black servants to black horses was pointed. What he described here was the shared reification of black people and domestic animals. They were both treated as objects of labor and conspicuous consumption" (2009, 127).[11] This both restates and slightly extends the link in the *Narrative* between Man's practices of breaking animals and slaves and the non-Man, even animal "starting" that resists and disrupts those practices in unexpected and unanticipatable ways. By positioning the comparison in relation to what Marxists call reification—which should always be serially connected with dehumanization, brutalization, objectification, and so on, which serve as assemblages for producing the fully human—Nyong'o allows me to align Douglass with recent work in animal studies by Donna Haraway and Nicole Shukin that sees animals and (some, most) humans as coimplicated in various kind of oppression and exploitation.[12] That is, the expropriating mechanism of capitalism—including the primitive accumulation that continues to mark the present—materially joins humanimal and nonhuman animal labor, thus enabling us to imagine new ways of thinking the political that might seize on and actualize this already given coimplication. As Che Gossett puts this, "Black radical imaginings of abolition provide us with a theoretical infrastructure to reconsider world formative relations of life" (2015, n.p.).

To put this in the most straightforward terms possible, it is only when the very borders of the political are drawn for and around the fully human Man that being a thing, an object, an animal, and so on carries with it the violent and devastating consequences we witness in—and indeed as—Western imperial modernity. Thus, while we may find common cause with Garrison and other whites' pragmatic misreading and misunderstanding of Douglass's text in efforts to render slavery illegal by playing the game of the nation-state, we are being led toward asking a much larger question. Stefano Harney and Fred Moten articulate the question thus: "What is, so to speak, the object of abolition? Not so much the abolition of prisons but the abolition of a society that could have prisons, that could have slavery, that could have the wage, and therefore not abolition as the elimination of anything but abolition as the founding of a new society" (2013, 42). We need to seek, then, not simply the elimination of practices of dehumanization, objectification, thingification, and reification. We need different ways of conceptualizing and practicing the human that don't come into being through those assemblages.[13]

6

LITERACY, SLAVERY, AND THE EDUCATION OF DESIRE

In *Narrative of the Life of Frederick Douglass*, chapters 6 and 7 narrate how Frederick learns to read and write, respectively. Chapter 6 finds young Frederick entering the service of a woman who "had never had a slave under her control previous to [himself]" (Douglass 1997, 28). Dealing with this novice, Mrs. Auld, Frederick finds that his "early instruction was all out of place" (28). This locution presents education, or at least "instruction," as something tied to a specific place or milieu: education is always about orientation, causing us to consider "how bodies come to 'have' certain orientations over time and that they come to be shaped by taking some directions rather than others and toward some objects rather than others" (Ahmed 2006, 58). Instruction that orients one in a particular milieu can disorient in another.

For Frederick, what is uncanny about Mrs. Auld is her "kind heart." Her manner of interacting with the slaves is remarkable, and "the meanest slave was put fully at ease in her presence" (Douglass 1997, 29). This affective presence orients Frederick toward his earliest literacy lessons. Mrs. Auld "very kindly commenced to teach me the A, B, C" (20). As soon as Frederick can "spell words of three or four letters," a phrase that underscores the materiality of language as much as it marks developmental progress, Mr. Auld intervenes:

> Just at this point in my progress, Mr. Auld found out what was going on, and at once forbade Mrs. Auld to instruct me further, telling her, among other things, that it was unlawful, as well as unsafe, to teach a

slave to read. To use his own words, further, he said, "If you give a nig-ger an inch, he will take an ell. A nigger should know nothing but to obey his master—to do as he is told to do. Learning would spoil the best nigger in the world. Now," he said, "if you teach that nigger (speaking of myself) how to read, there would be no keeping him. It would forever unfit him to be a slave. He would at once become unmanageable, and of no value to his master. As to himself, it could do him no good, but a great deal of harm. It would make him discontented and unhappy." (29)

Mr. Auld's discourse on slavery and education, meant to justify the ces-sation of Frederick's reading lessons, proves entirely true. Frederick, upon hearing this speech, understands "the pathway from slavery to freedom" (29), a path he follows in chapters 10 and 11 following no small amount of discontent. We see again, then, something similar to the scene in *Be-loved* when Sethe overhears Schoolteacher's lesson: these words, a lesson for Mrs. Auld on which Frederick eavesdrops, reorient him both toward the political entanglements of literacy practices and toward his own future, fig-ured materially as a path. This path is, of course, the figure of the chiasmus.

Chapter 7 finds Frederick attempting to continue his education, having lost Mrs. Auld as a teacher. The loss was a difficult one, for Douglass "had no regular teacher," and had "to resort to various stratagems" to learn (31). Before narrating these stratagems, which I take up in chapter 7, Douglass reflects upon the education Mrs. Auld is receiving at the same time. Be-cause "she at first lacked the depravity indispensable to shutting me up in mental darkness . . . it was at least necessary for her to have some train-ing in the exercise of irresponsible power, to make her equal to the task of treating me as though I were a brute" (31). The "depravity" necessary for whites to abide slavery requires "some training." The training is in "the exercise of . . . power," and this power structures the way she must treat slaves as "brutes," beings toward whom humans have no responsibility.

The distinction between human and animal or inhuman is required in order to sustain the peculiar relation between white master and black slave: "In the simplicity of her soul she commenced, when I first went to live with her, to treat me as she supposed one human being ought to relate to another. In entering upon the duties of slaveholder, she did not seem to perceive that I sustained to her the relation of a mere chattel, and that for her to treat me as a human being was not only wrong, but dangerously so"

(31). Mrs. Auld's "duties" arise only when she enters a specific cultural and economic role, "slaveholder."[1] Reorienting to this role requires training, and specifically a new distribution of people into roles relative to her role as slaveholder. This redistribution relegates some of those she previously "supposed" were human beings to the role of "chattel" or "brutes" over whom she has "irresponsible power." That is, the training doesn't actually alter the parameters of Mrs. Auld's ethics: humans are still to be treated as humans, brutes to be treated as brutes.[2] Rather, the training consists in moving some humans from the category human to the category of brutes. This is, in part, what Douglass refers to as "the dehumanizing character of slavery" (19).

After studying this change in Mrs. Auld's relation to him, Douglass declares, "She was an apt woman; and a little experience soon demonstrated, to her satisfaction, that education and slavery were incompatible with each other" (31). The lesson Mrs. Auld learns has to be read two ways. First, it restates the gist of Mr. Auld's earlier speech. She has learned her lesson and now knows that slavery cannot function if slaves are educated because such education makes them unmanageable. At the same time, although this is conceptually a very different claim, slaves cannot be educated because they are not human beings, and only human beings can be educated. Educating slaves is (paradoxically) both dangerous and impossible, hence the incompatability of education and slavery. But second, her declaration disavows the lesson that has just been narrated by Douglass. If Mrs. Auld has to be trained to think of Douglass and his fellow slaves as "mere chattel" in order to enter her duties as a slaveholder, then education most certainly is compatible with slavery. Moreover, slavery requires education. It requires that slaveholders be educated to dehumanize. This second reading undercuts the meaning of the first by throwing into relief a curious presupposition: only when education is synonymous with humanization can it be said that education and slavery are incompatible. Douglass and the Aulds have not only different educational experiences, but different understandings of what education is: its scope, its functions, its ties to the concept of the human.

Upon learning to read, Douglass procures a progymnasmata containing abolitionist speeches. Douglass writes, "What I got from [the abolitionist] Sheridan was a bold denunciation of slavery, and a powerful vindication of human rights" (33).[3] In a rather straightforward way, learning to read is what allows Douglass to discover "human rights," which allow him to recognize his own humanity, thus authorizing new kinds of corporeal and political action (escape from slavery, antislavery activism). "Human rights" as Douglass learns of them reading Sheridan prompt the slave to "learn to write" in an education that allows for the existence of *Narrative of the Life of Frederick Douglass*.[4] That is, *Narrative of the Life of Frederick Douglass* narrates its own conditions of possibility, and these conditions grow out of an educational encounter with the idea of "human rights" appearing in a found book, understood with the aid of a stolen literacy education. This theft is, as Saidiya Hartman underscores, always a question of movement and orientation: "Stealing away defied and subversively appropriated slave owners' designs for mastery and control—primarily the captive body as the extension of the master's power and the spatial organization of domination" (1997, 69).

Having read this book, Douglass relates, "The reading of these documents enabled me to utter my thoughts, and to meet the arguments brought forward to sustain slavery; but while they relieved me of one difficulty, they brought on another ever more painful than the one of which I was relieved" (33). This new difficulty arises from the reading of the documents, which is to say that Douglass's "pain" emerges from an encounter with a text. Sheridan's text changes how he understands himself and his relation to the world in such a way that Douglass can write: "As I writhed under it, I would at times feel that learning to read had been a curse rather than a blessing. It had given me a view of my wretched condition, without the remedy. It opened my eyes to the horrible pit, but to no ladder upon which to get out. In moments of agony, I envied my fellow-slaves for their stupidity. I have often wished myself a beast" (33). Learning to read is "a curse" that brings "moments of agony." In a social formation that has bound the human to particular literacy practices, Douglass's formulation sounds bewildering. But if we remember Aparna Mishra Tarc's argument that "language forcibly humanizes us according to particular forms of logos and cultural norms" (2015, 10), then it's much harder to disavow "the violence of literacy."[5] For Douglass, literacy produces terrible affects, and these affects redirect his attentions, his actions, his desires.

The specific cause of this agony seems to be that Douglass recognizes himself as a human being with rights but cannot gain such recognition from others because most people have been educated under slavery to consider blacks "brutes" or "mere chattel." Douglass is caught in an intermediate position between human and brute, and the agony this position produces is directly related to desire. Douglass has, upon learning about human rights, the desire to be a fully recognized human being. The inability to gain such recognition in a world governed by the binary opposition of human and beast entangled with a state apparatus engineered to sustain slavery leads Douglass to "wish himself" a beast, which is to say he desires to feel included in one of the categories opposed in the binary instead of being in between. When coupled with the racializing assemblages of the imperialist state in modernity, humanizing education operates by superimposing the human/animal binary on the binary white/black in such a way that whiteness and humanness are in harmony while blackness resides uneasily between humanness and animalness. This is precisely what Alexander Weheliye means when he refers to "race, racialization, and racial identities" as "ongoing sets of political relations that require, through constant perpetuation via institutions, discourses, practices, desires, infrastructures, languages, technologies, sciences, economies, dreams, and cultural artifacts, the barring of nonwhite subjects from the category of the human as it is performed in the modern west" (2014, 3). What W. E. B. Du Bois calls "the color line" signals the intersection and divergence of the twinned humanizing and dehumanizing tendencies of education. We can specify that for a young Frederick caught between these two tendencies, this tension "cannot be consciously thought out. It must be dynamically unfolded: experimentally and innovatively acted out" (Massumi 2015, 107).

The solution to this agonizing in-betweenness for Douglass is simple: "I would learn to write" (1997, 34). The freedom to move could be augmented if Douglass could produce written documentation, forged of course, suggesting that a white master had given him permission to run errands. This calls to mind Simone Browne's analysis of written passes as technologies of surveillance. This system "relied on the notion that the slave could be known through a written identification document" (2015, 52). This specific literacy practice underscores how "in the slave plantation system, the restriction of the mobility and literacy of the enslaved served as an exercise of power. The racializing surveillance of the slave pass system was a violent regulation of black mobilities" (53). Indeed, Douglass's *Narrative* begins to suggest that literacy and mobility are inseparable, thus ushering us toward conceptualizing literacy as, in the first instance, a problematic of spatiality, orientation, and forms of circulation and traffic among a range of bodies and things. This literacy situation is thus captured by Man and inserted directly into the (de)humanizing logics of the imperialist state and what Hartman (1997, 72) calls "the appropriation of space consequent to everyday practice" during slavery, but as I shall attend to more and more in the course of this book, this capture cannot exhaust literacy, which subtends and overspills the state's restriction of it.

After learning more from the poor boys, Douglass writes, "I wished to learn how to write, as I might have occasion to write my own pass" (1997, 34). Writing—a material note—therefore appears as a catalyst for altering his orientation in social and physical space. Writing would also enable Douglass to intervene in the larger political sphere in a way that could enable a recognition of his humanity (and, perhaps, the humanity of other slaves). That is, by writing Narrative of the Life of Frederick Douglass he will, to return to Hunt's formulations, communicate an interiority indexed to the real person Frederick Douglass that can, by virtue of its narrative form, compel readers to identify with this character and thus rehumanize the black slave. The ability to write is what Douglass thinks will allow him to overcome being caught between humanness and animalness. It can do this because writing an autobiographical narrative indexically proves the author's "interiority," which is to say, his humanness. To be recognized as human, Douglass must write.[6] He must write to prove that he is not a brute and should not be treated as such. His desire to be human is, then, also the desire to write. It is the desire to gain recognition as a human being by learning to write, and by writing to let the reader identify with the narrative's main character. The desire to be a beast, we now see, is the desire not to write and even the desire not to know that one could write. But, drawing on the relations in Douglass's writings taken up in chapter 5 between himself and the oxen, and between black slaves and black horses, we can also say that the desire to be a beast signals the anticipatory affirmation of his animal ability to start: to resist, to disrupt, to reconfigure the world as it is. Writing, for Douglass, is not about pleasure in the first instance, or self-expression, or any other quality that my liberal humanist education has put forward in its favor.[7] It is a necessity born from cruel affects produced in a milieu of omnipresent racialized violence, and a desire to move more freely, to reorient himself in social and political space by attending to and exploiting moments that prime his body—always in relation to a range of other things and beings affecting him—to act in disorienting ways. As Manning argues, "desire is movement, it is the body in movement" (2006, 36).

Becoming literate is, for Douglass, able to make him human only by running a circuit through readers who must be the kind of readers capable of identifying with him as the subject of the narrative and subsequently recognizing his humanity. This politics of recognition, as Glen Sean Coulthard has forcefully argued in the context of indigenous struggle in Canada, "rests on the problematic background assumption that the settler state constitutes a legitimate framework within which Indigenous people might be more fully included" (2014, 36). Indeed, while it might be pragmatically necessary as a means of securing new forms of mobility, aspiring toward legal (and socially widespread) recognition of human personhood does not sufficiently call into question "the normative status of the state-form as an appropriate mode of governance" (36).

When Douglass learns to read, through an education linking literacy to the human, he uneasily recognizes himself in the conception of the human he finds in his book. This aligns with what Coulthard, drawing on Fanon's critique of Hegel, calls for: "that those struggling against colonialism must 'turn away' from the colonial state and instead find in their own *decolonial praxis* the source of their liberation" (2014, 48). As Douglass affirms himself as human in a society that refuses to recognize him as Man, Douglass is made to suffer an agony that must be lived through, "experimentally and innovatively acted out" (Massumi 2015, 107). This acting out takes Douglass from fight to flight to writing, and underscores the rhizomatic links among those three. In this corporeal acting out, we can begin to discern what Fred Moten calls "an embodiment [that] is also bound to the (critique of) reading and writing, oft conceived by clowns and intellectuals as the natural attributes of whoever would hope to be known as human" (2003, 12). This hope, as Moten calls it, animates Douglass's fugitive relation to literacy, the state, and to the conception of the human crystalizing around their entanglements. Douglass is only pragmatically or strategically interested in using literacy to have his status as Man recognized by the state: his *Narrative* simultaneously undertakes to dissolve that Man in critique and to construct an alterative human praxis and literacy in his flight. Returning to my argument from chapter 5, Douglass does not perform literacy or humanity in tune with how whites in the antebellum United States do.

7

WHAT IS LITERACY?

After Mrs. Auld underwent instruction to become a proper slaveholder, "nothing seemed to make her more angry than to see [Frederick] with a newspaper" (Douglass 1997, 31). It is not, here, Frederick's ability to read that is troubling—for that is, at this point, barely developed—but the materiality of the paper that causes concern. Mrs. Auld does not want Frederick spending time with marks on paper, for this dwelling of not-quite-human with printed marks constitutes, in and of itself, a threat. Getting slightly ahead of myself, I want to say that it is the agentic, affective potential of print that troubles Mrs. Auld and captivates Frederick.

Frederick begins to "always take [his] book with [him]" (32) as he goes about the town. By bringing this object along with some bread, and by "going about one part of [his] errand quickly," he is able to "convert . . . little white boys . . . into teachers" (32). As Frederick puts it, careful to avoid details that would get the boys into trouble, he gave bread to the hungry boys in return for "the more valuable bread of knowledge" (32). Despite the lack of detail here, what is clear is that Douglass understands that learning to read requires the material support of printed text, time for lessons, and literate persons able to guide his budding ability to decode the marks.

Young Douglass seizes on this possibility when he is in Durgin and Bailey's shipyard, where he sees builders marking boards with letters used to indicate which side of the ship they are destined to become. This, too, functions as a kind of eavesdropping, for Douglass effectively trespasses the boundaries of the intended audience of those marks in order to spend enough time with them that he is "able to make the four letters named" (34). With these letters in hand/head, he sets about challenging boys to games to prove that he can "write as well" as them, something they disbelieve owing to the racialization of literacy. This surreptitious, fugitive literacy education makes use of whatever materials Douglass can find: "During this time, my copy-book was the board fence, the brick wall, and pavement; my pen and ink was a lump of chalk" (35). Here I want to mark a crucial difference from *Beloved*, where Sethe's labor made the ink that enabled whitepeople to become fully human; instead, here the dehumanized Douglass takes up lumps of chalk in order to become human. The difference between the durability of these materials will come into focus later.

I want to think, now, about these materials and the ways that literacy events presume and include a host of nonhuman matters. But before beginning to scan across histories of literacies, two more general axioms have to be quickly sketched. The first was implicit in chapter 6: that literacy and its materiality are never separable from intrahuman social and political hierarchy. In Douglass's time, this involves thinking about the ban on slave literacy. Even following the official end to slavery in the United States and the nominal extension of voting rights to black Americans, many states adopted literacy tests at the polls that had the calculated effect of disenfranchising blacks. Such measures operated precisely by equating humanity with literacy. I return to these matters later in order to consider how institutions of learning—schools—institutionalize and operationalize these inequalities around literacy practices.

Second, and as a result of the first, I want to keep my attention on Katie King's question, "What counts as writing?" (cited in Vaccaro 2015, 285). This involves attuning to "the gathering of materials" and "the multiple meanings associated with a language and practice" (285). Putting these together, I will try to ask what literacy is without presuming in advance that I know how or where to sense its limits, and without losing sight of how any delimitation of it is implicated in intrahuman political relations.

I want to start by asking a question that receives an even more circumscribed answer: What is literature? As René Wellek and Austin Warren note in *Theory of Literature*, this question is "rarely answered clearly," although they immediately propose that "one way is to define 'literature' as everything in print" (1942, 20). They quickly reject this, however, since it risks becoming indistinguishable from "the history of civilization," thus "crowding out" literary studies.[1] Thus, they propose limiting literature to simply the "great books," which allows them to underscore the necessary relation between literature as concept and pedagogical institutions (21). But this too proves too wide, as "great books" come in several genres, which leads them to distinguish between "literary," "everyday," and "scientific" uses of language (22). While the second two are connected with literacy, they are not "literary" or "imaginative." While they fairly easily cordon off scientific language, the distinction between the everyday and the literary proves more complex. While some "quantitative" differences are suggested, and while the distinction is more clear when considering pragmatics, they ultimately locate the difference in "referential aspects": "The statements in a novel, in a poem, or in a drama are not literally true; they are not logical propositions" (25). Thus, literature becomes the particular set of language taking shape in one of three genres (the novel, the poem, the play) that "refers" to reality in a way that involves some kind of imaginative or tropological swerve from "logic."

David Damrosch, taking up the slightly more Goethean question of what counts as "world literature," gives a similar, but crucially more pointed, definition. To become world literature, something must be "read *as literature*" (2003, 6). That is, the distinction between literature and other language lies not, strictly speaking, in the text but in its mode of circulation, dissemination, and interpretation. Accordingly, world literature is "not an infinite, ungraspable canon of works but rather a mode of circulation and of reading, a mode that is applicable to individual works as to bodies of material, available for reading established classics and new discoveries alike" (5). "Literature" names not a thing or a set of things, but a mode of attention that is concretized in material ways.

If Wellek and Warren's definition of literature as inclusive of only literary language proved decisive for setting up and maintaining the educational institutionalization of literature as an object and a discipline (more on this shortly), by the end of the twentieth century it was under serious strain from within the spaces at universities tasked with disseminating literature. Under pressure from an emergent cultural studies that seized upon an expanded sense of the text and semiotics, fields of literary study had to reckon with the fact that, as Charles Bernheimer puts it in his 1995 statement on the state of comparative literature, "literature's identity, its difference from the nonliterary, cannot be established according to absolute standards"; instead it must be "historicized" (1995, 15).[2] This is, of course, the moment at which departments of literature began increasingly to offer courses on film and media studies, cultural studies, and popular culture. Rather than focusing on strictly literary production, anything and everything becomes a text that can be read and interpreted.

The anxiety prompted by this move "from work to text" (to use Barthes's [1977] phrase) is greatly exacerbated by the emergence of digital media and their seemingly virtual, but highly material, texts.[3] James O'Donnell writes,

> We live in a historical moment when the media on which the word relies are changing their nature and extending their range to an extent not seen since the invention of movable type. The changes have been building through the twentieth century, as the spoken word reanimated communication over telephone and radio, and as the moving image on film and television supplemented the "mere" word. The invention and dissemination of the personal computer and now the explosive growth in links between those computers on the worldwide networks of the internet create a genuinely new and transformative environment. (1998, 9)

Among other things, this digital anxiety is helping to usher in a new sense of how humans and literacy relate, and I want to spend the rest of this chapter sketching it in such a way that I can claim that the supposedly new developments are, in fact, discernible throughout the history of the human-literacy assemblage. In *How We Think*, N. Katherine Hayles takes up the everyday use of internet communications in order to argue that "embodiment then takes the form of extended cognition, in which human agency and thought are enmeshed within larger networks that extend beyond the desktop computer into the environment" (2012, 3). That is, the link between a corporeal human person and an environment is part of cognition. Persons do not think about environments as something outside of themselves: the assemblage person/environment thinks.

This way of conceptualizing the person, cognition, environment, thinking cluster owes much to the interdisciplinary Macy Conferences on cybernetics in the early twentieth century, and which have provided much of the theoretical impetus for so-called "posthumanist" theory.[4] The goal of these conferences was "to formulate the central concepts that . . . would coalesce into a theory of communication and control applying equally to animals, humans, and machines" (Hayles 1999, 7). While the conferences produced theories of cybernetics (or systems theory) and helped inaugurate research into artificial intelligence, one of their most important advances was to see humans "primarily as information-processing entities who are *essentially* similar to intelligent machines" (7). At stake in Hayles's account of this shift in thinking the human person as "essentially" similar to both machines and animals (although Hayles doesn't devote the attention to the animal side of the cybernetic triangle that Cary Wolfe's work does) is a new theory of how environment, bodies, and information are entangled. She notes that "consciousness, regarded as the seat of human identity in the Western tradition long before Descartes thought he was a mind thinking, [is] an epiphenomenon . . . an evolutionary upstart trying to claim the whole show when in actuality it is only a minor sideshow" (3). That is, "the Western tradition" constructs itself based on a synecdochic understanding of thinking and cognition, taking a "minor" part of it—consciousness—to be the whole. This has enormous consequences for reconceiving of not only literature but also language and literacy, especially when combined with a shift in attention to the materiality of language. Hayles writes that "normally, narrative fiction leaps over the technologies (printing press, paper, ink) that produce it and represents the external world as if this act of representation did not require a material basis for its production" (216), and she spends considerable attention reading literary texts that reject this leap. The upshot of both of these moves—decentralizing consciousness and insisting upon attending to the materiality of literacy practices—helps me scale back to see just how limited the conception of Man's relation to literacy in Western, imperial modernity is.

As I have argued, nation-states were highly invested in linking the human and literacy in order to differentiate the fully human persons given special legal status from the in- or a- or not-quite-humans excluded from partaking in (its sense of) the political.[5] There were differing ways of accounting for this capacity that varied across slavery, colonial, genocidal, and gendered contexts, but in many cases what was at stake was holding up a highly specific version of what it means to be a literate human—the kind of human Wynter calls Man—and rendering all beings who act or think or perform differently nonhuman, reducing them to various kinds of things (to play on Aimé Césaire's concept of "thingification"). Donna

Haraway's work offers a powerful rejoinder to this insistence upon drawing a border around Man and its supposedly unique capacities and literacies. She writes, of work arising from "recent scientific comparative evolutionary interdisciplines," that "people can stop looking for some single defining difference between them and everybody else and understand that they are in rich and largely uncharted, material-semiotic, flesh-to-flesh connection with a host of significant others. That requires retraining in the contact zone" (2008, 235).

Literacy, then, is a contact zone: one in which an animal, including a human animal (which I argue is not a selfsame, bounded biological entity let alone a disembodied liberal individual with a halo of consciousness), is entangled with a host of matters within the literacy situation. The human, to use Karen Barad's (2007) term, is something "intra-active," emergent: it does not exist in or apart from an environment that animates it, and it "becomes with" a host of others, as Haraway would say. Indeed, we will have to see human language as becoming with a range of other languages, ones that are not human: "Signs are not exclusively human affairs. All living beings sign. We humans are therefore at home with the multitude of semiotic life" (Kohn 2013, 42).[6]

Let me focus on the materials caught up in literature. In Robert Darnton's influential study that jump-starts "book history" as a field, he proposes a circuit model of communication as "a way of conceiving the production of texts as a multifaceted enterprise encompassing social, economic, political, and intellectual conditions" (Finkelstein and McCleery 2005, 12). Darnton argues that "by unearthing those circuits, historians can show that books do not merely recount history; they make it" (cited in Finkelstein and McCleery, 22). This formulation both enlarges the conception of the book as a material object caught up in circuits not only of communication but of material power (in a manner similar to what Ian Watt offers about the rise of the novel), but also begins to gesture toward what I see as the crux of the matter: taking books (and other materialities) as not just historical objects, but as things that directly participate in making history. Without books and their agential participation in the world, there could be no human in the modern sense. Indeed, returning once again to Hunt's account, human cognition as we know it—which involves the production of what she calls "empathy"—is the effect of an intra-active entanglement of a human being and literary text. It is not enough then to say that novel reading produces the human: we also have to account for how Man is the highly specific effect of particular cominglings of material objects and their animacies with a particular kind of biocultural creature called the human within what I call the literacy situation.

Although historians of the book can claim that "the book is a product of human agency (despite the importance of technological innovations and impersonal forces)" (Howsam 2015, 6), I am precisely interested in these "impersonal forces" as they give rise not only to books but to various ways of being human. It might be helpful, then, to quickly track backward, for the book as an object supposedly consisting of bound paper with marks on it is itself something that cannot be easily conceptually restricted. Although one could, in a gesture Haraway would endorse, go back to "Stone Age" practices of "recording transactions with knots on strings" (Kurlansky 2016, 4), or even to the cave paintings from Lascaux and Chauvet, which may be up to thirty thousand years old, it's become customary to treat writing as beginning with the cuneiform inscriptions on those Assyrian tablets found in "the earliest libraries [which] consisted of clay tablets kept on shelves" in Assyria (Attar 2015, 17).

Cuneiform inscription on clay involves specific materialities. Wet clay tablets were made and "the writing tool . . . seems to have been a cut reed. Pressing straight down vertically would produce a circular impression in the soft material. Pressing down at an angle would yield a fingernail-shaped impression" (Kurlansky 2016, 6). The material properties of clay, and the available reeds, entangled with the human body to create a set of enabling constraints for the emergence of a particular script, one that was intra-active with an economy devoted to the circulation of commodities within a social formation. These tablets were "the world's primary writing material for three thousand years" (9).

Slightly later libraries in Egypt are filled with papyrus rolls. Papyrus plants "were most valued as writing material" (Kurlansky 2016, 9). The plant "was tall, with a bushy tuft of leaves and flowers on top. In its most favorable growing conditions, the Nile delta, it grew to sixteen feet high, with stalks as thick as two inches" (9). Only in particular growing conditions—a general phrase indicating an ecosystem's relation to geology and climate—does papyrus make sense as a possible material for writing. Using this plant as a surface for inscription involved a technological transformation: outer layers of the plant were removed, and inner layers were unrolled, laid flat, and pounded out. Since the resulting writing surface was porous, it needed sizing, or coating in a substance that would keep ink in place. With papyrus, the plant's own sap served this purpose (and the Romans would later use flour and vinegar). It is virtually impossible here to fail to notice how much this plant and its highly specific materiality enabled writing.

Where clay tablets and papyrus enabled writing to endure because of their specific properties, thereby enabling humans to leave marks on surfaces that could circulate and exist longer than individual lifetimes (in, say, libraries), wax tablets allowed what Kurlansky calls "casual writing" (2016, 12). These were "easier to write on and easier to erase than other writing media" in the ancient world, and it led to the invention of the codex, which Kurlansky calls "the forerunner of the book" (13) since, instead of being unrolled (as a scroll made of papyrus would be), it consists of pages through which one turns.

Wax, then, gave way to paper. "Paper is made of cellulose fibers that are broken down and mixed with water until they are so diluted that they are barely visible. The liquid is then scooped up onto a screen and allowed to drain, which leaves a very thin layer of the randomly woven fibers—paper—behind" (Kurlansky 2016, 29). As Kurlansky notes, "some historians think that the idea of papermaking came from felting, a practice that pre-dated weaving and entailed beating wool until it mashed into a thick, fibrous mat" (29), suggesting that paper's emergence as a writing technology is inseparable from other practices of human entanglement with nonhuman matters and agencies. Indeed, the scholarly (in)attention to this prior entanglement has everything to do with gender and race. As Vaccaro (2015, 274) notes, although craft—including felting—is "increasingly recognized as a theoretical process and method," it was "maligned in Renaissance hierarchies of liberal and mechanical arts" since it "evokes the remunerative, utilitarian, ornamental, and manual labor and laborers—the feminine, ethnic, and 'primitive.'"[7]

For a long time, paper was made from flax, hemp, and cotton, but in the nineteenth century, industrial production made it possible to produce it from wood. Although these experiments were not immediately successful, the process would come to dominate global paper production by the end of the nineteenth century, in part owing to the unrelenting deforestation of North America under the joint watch of corporations and nation-states. After trees are felled from their (at that time) natural growth in forests, logs are transported to mills and "quickly stripped of bark and chipped, and the chips are reduced to mush by the chemicals in the digester. Dyes are added at this stage of the process . . . [and] chemicals are added to make some kinds of paper more compatible with certain kinds of printing and to make paper more opaque. Georgia clay is one of the common additives used" (Kurlansky 2016, 279).

While this production has become commonplace, its initial emergence was not only contingent, but the result of a multispecies encounter. In the late 1600s, René-Antoine Ferchault de Réaumur, a man fascinated with insects, noticed that "wasps gathered wood particles from weathered old barns or fenceposts and built ingeniously designed waterproof homes with domed shaped roofs of thin, light, overlapping paper" (Kurlansky 2016, 248). Recognizing the agency of the wasps, "it occurred to Réaumur that these remarkable natural engineers had a better way of making paper than people did" (248–49). Here, decaying human objects, already constructed of felled trees, provide raw material for wasp engineering, which in turn is borrowed by a human to reconfigure book making.

Without going any further into the (to me) fascinating history of the materiality of writing practices leading up to the book, it's possible to note several crucial factors. One, the raw materials that form the surfaces on which humans write emerge from agencies quite removed from human agency. Whether the geological agency that forms clay, or the plant agencies that, within particular distributed networks of agency called ecosystems, create papyrus plants or trees in forests, without those other agencies there would be no writing. And once removed from original context and fabricated for human use, those things continue to exert a kind of agency both in offering particular material affordances for inscription, but also, although this is much harder to track here, offering particular affective resonances. Clay and papyrus and paper don't feel the same, and they prime writers for different kinds of corporeal engagements that are abstracted out in the general term "writing."

What animates the book then? Trees. Sunshine. The labor of wasps. A whole back history of clay and papyrus and wax and wool, none of which can be thought of as simply or merely human. When humanists treat the history of the book as a matter of what humans do among themselves, they can do so only by practicing a curious but ubiquitous form of inattention to these animacies. Giving up on this inattention, shifting the scope of our analysis from just the human part of literacy to its larger, more entangled, multispecies flourishing, involves having to work against the ways that Western, imperialist humanism often "prevents us from detecting (seeing, hearing, smelling, tasting, feeling) a fuller range of the non-human powers circulating around and within human bodies" (Bennett 2010, ix). Instead, with Jane Bennett and other new materialist thinkers, we may take it as axiomatic that "things . . . act as quasi agents or forces with trajectories, propensities, or tendencies of their own" (viii).

This is to say that literacy is a matter of affect, and that affect cannot be restricted to something human. As Seigworth and Gregg conceptualize it, "Affect arises in the midst of *in-between-ness*: in the capacities to act and be acted upon" (2010, 1). While humans are used to thinking of writing as a kind of action upon surfaces, we need a manner of attention that also attends to how those surfaces act upon us, and how literacy events (whether writing or reading or teaching) are only possible because of a trail of other affective encounters among heterogenous agencies and matters in the literacy situation: "Feeling, as such, is the primordial form of all relation and all communication" (Shaviro 2009, 63). Indeed, unless one restricts the frame to the merely human, it's difficult to know how far back and how dispersed in space one can draw a line around a literacy event. Which means: we are not in a position to define literacy.[8]

When Douglass constructs a fugitive classroom throughout the city, he is less using a variety of materials and other people, although his agency in this is obviously enormously important, than he is participating in contingent, fleeting, and ad-hoc appearances and disappearances of literacy contact zones. The fence, the brick, the pavement, the chalk, his book, the boards at the shipyard: these are things with affective force, things that have propensities and tendencies of their own. They enter into Douglass's literacy education, and they animate it, but they are not exhausted by it. Literacy links a human to fragile, diffuse, ever-shifting multispecies and multiobject networks.

Thus, the human of modernity—Man—which maintained its consistency due to a complex entwining of state power, literacy practices, and a variety of assemblages that constitute subjects, is a fragile thing. Any version of the human is. In "learning to appreciate how the human is also the product of that which lies beyond human contexts" (Kohn 2013, 15), we can learn to affirm alternative possibilities for performing the human, and performing literacy and literature. As part of the project of "decolonizing language," Eduardo Kohn puts forth the proposition that "life is constitutively semiotic" (9). What this requires us to think is not even simply "the languages of man" as Walter Benjamin (1996a) puts it, but "language as such." It means asking, with Elizabeth Grosz, "what would a theory of language, signification, or the trace look like that did not, through logocentric techniques, privilege not only the human but a particular kind of (European, masculine, upright, and erect carnivorous—a carnophallogocentric) subject and discourse?" (2011, 14). I am drawn to the force of this question, and I think its force is most propulsive if we resist the urge to answer it, except provisionally and propositionally. Indeed, I think we have to give up on the idea that language or literacy are anything other than modes of activity, contact, and mingling. Language is not ontological, but ontogenic.[9] Since "we are, in fact, open to the emerging worlds around us" (Kohn 2013, 15), when other agencies and matters necessarily continue their constitutive practices of entangled self-organizing, we shift too. And given the horrors attending the emergence and maintenance of Man, this inevitable shifting is cause for wonder, and for affirmation.

8

HUMANIZING ASSEMBLAGES II: DISCIPLINE AND CONTROL

Beginning in the eighteenth century, for Foucault, "the disciplines became general formulas of domination" (1977, 137). Discipline—operationalized in different modes in schools, prisons, the military, and industrial production facilities—involved the invention of technologies or assemblages capable of producing "docile bodies": "A body is docile that may be subjected, used, transformed and improved" (136). What Foucault calls transformation and improvement is what I have been calling humanization. This is explicit in Immanuel Kant's 1803 *On Education*, where he claims both that "man can only become man through education" (1960, 3) and that "discipline changes animal nature into human nature" (2). Kant's frequent references to Savages in this account remind us that such humanizing discipline cannot function without a simultaneous production of the inhuman or less-than-human as Man's constitutive outside.

This production of the human at the level of control of impulses, attentions, and movements—which have to be not extinguished but reoriented—also operates at the level of the scholarly production of knowledge. There is a long history of how domains of knowledge have been delimited and segregated, going back at least as far as Plato's *Republic* and its insistence on the necessity of particular forms of mathematical training and his deep suspicion about the pedagogical uses of literature, and even in Plato some of Socrates's remarks demonstrate that these divisions take place in relation to a concept of what it means to be human.[1] But this "de-partmentalization" of knowledge undergoes a particular intensification during modernity, one that passes a particular threshold between the fourteenth and sixteenth centuries and takes on its present form, more or less, in the nineteenth.[2] To give the briefest possible sketch, I want to quote Richard Norman's précis in *On Humanism*:

> The Italian word "umanista" was coined, probably in the late fifteenth or early sixteenth century, to denote a scholar or teacher of the *humanities*—the disciplines of grammar, rhetoric, poetry, history and moral philosophy. These studies were referred to by the Latin label *studia humanitatis*, a phrase which implies a contrast between the study of "humanity" and the study of divinity, of natural philosophy, and of vocational disciplines such as law and medicine. The humanists of the fourteenth to the sixteenth centuries, in Italy and other European countries, were in particular interested in the study of the classical literature of ancient Greece and Rome, finding in it an ideal of human life which they wished to receive. . . . The first use of the corresponding abstract noun "humanism" is in German. The word "Humanismus" was similarly used in an educational context, in early nineteenth-century Germany, to refer to the traditional classical education built around the humanities. (2012, 8–9)

What we see is that different objects (the human, the divine, nature, various vocations) require not only different methods of study but different institutional configurations. As part of the production of what Wynter calls "Man1" (the newly secular vision of Man appearing during early modernity), the studia humanitatis operationalizes the modes of attention and study that pertain to the understanding and production of Man. In the nineteenth century, as the research university emerges as a factory for knowledge production and as public schooling appears as an apparatus for fabricating Man on a mass scale, the humanities are de-partmentalized over and against the natural sciences and the human sciences (this is part of the appearance of what Wynter calls "Man2"). This involved, as Foucault demonstrates in *The Order of Things*, a "general redistribution of the *episteme*," one that produces "man as an empirical entity" (1994, 344). That is, over a period of a few hundred years as the fiction of Man is taking shape at the intersection of state power and institutionalizations of knowledge (including literacy), it comes to seem increasingly durable, tangible, and real in part because its reality is built into the material configuration of institutions and their disciplinary divisions.

While the word "discipline" offers a shorthand for seeing intimate connections between the production of particular kinds of subjects in assemblages like schools, prisons, and hospitals on the one hand, and the articulation of distinct fields of scholarly activity on the other, following Deleuze, many scholars have insisted that discipline no longer holds the dominant role in the capitalist and statist capture of energies, potential, and creative movement. In "Postscript on the Societies of Control," Deleuze (1992, 3) argues that the disciplines Foucault describes in such detail that functioned between the eighteenth and early twentieth centuries have gone into crisis, by which he means that power no longer takes the body (with an identity, say) as its privileged point of transfer. Instead, the biopolitics of control have turned toward the population (Foucault 1978) in ways that disaggregate the body into preindividual capacities, affects, systems, and movements. To understand how Man is currently articulated as *homo oeconomicus* (Wynter 2007), we have to account for how Man functions today less as a particular entity than a diagram at work in dispersed assemblages that articulate bodies in processes of becoming and distribute these informatic bodies in space in large measure by controlling their movement and speed.[3] Man is subtly recomposed from an ideal representation guiding disciplined improvement as its telos into a diagram that cuts through dispersed assemblages that machinically produce the human/inhuman/less-than-human divisions in the social. There is no relation here of exteriority, then, between large-scale systemic state racisms and microaggressions dispersed haphazardly throughout the social field. Rather than a stable system of divisions among races, genders, sexualities, and other coordinates, power's dispersal is such that the work of articulating Man over and against its many constitutive outsides happens in disconnected, contradictory, and often largely invisible ways. Indeed, my argument is that these assemblages of (de)humanization have taken on a largely affective character. Without downplaying the effects of law, school policies, state demographics, and medical regimes, I want to argue that the question of who or what counts as human—Do I? Do you? Do they?—is most immediately a question of affect.

This shift from discipline to control foregrounds the biopolitics of affect: "A life coincides with its affective potential, for better or worse" (Massumi 2015, 186). Recalling Wynter's (2001) claim that Man is articulated in relation to a normalization of what it feels like to be human, the direct investment in bodies, movements, and capacities that function above, below, and alongside the level of the subject (Protevi 2009, 4). Man, here, is no longer a representation held up as a model for the docile body to asymptotically mime (ecce homo), so much as a logic underwriting a complex network of investments, strategies, blockages, and intensifications. If affects are largely prepersonal and form part of the situations from which subjects retroactively construct identities, then we have to suggest that the operations of power today seek to articulate masteries of the population that condition the emergence of identities instead of operating to manipulate already formed persons.[4] Massumi calls this "ontopower" and argues that "it does not cause in any traditional sense. It conditions. It reconditions the field of emergence, in order to modulate and orient what becoming unfolds from it" (2015, 240). Ontopower operates precisely at the level of the literacy situation, conditioning relations such that some events are more likely than others to emerge.

Take, for example, the United States, which today has the world's largest prison industrial complex (Davis 2016), incarcerating more than a quarter of all prisoners worldwide. While Foucault saw the disciplinary prison as an assemblage that operated on the soul of the prisoner to remake her as a different kind of person, the contemporary prison is better understood as a way of modulating investments in bodies and capacities in relation to economic calculations. Increasingly, either prisons in the United States are directly for-profit enterprises, or prisoners are contractually obliged to provide labor for corporations as a way of offsetting the costs incurred by the state to detain them. While the documentary The Thirteenth underscores the ways in which this system emerges from the Thirteenth Amendment to the US Constitution—which made slavery illegal except in cases of criminality adjudicated by courts—this system functions according to rather different modes of power and investment.

This prison system is entangled with contemporary practices of schooling and their data-driven management of students as information. Modeled after the US federal "three strikes" guidelines for sentencing, US schools have operationalized the distribution of students along a continuum stretching from those who must be invested in to secure their movement through elementary, secondary, and higher education and into the kind of neoliberal self-management expected of homo oeconomicus, to students whose cases render them unfit for schooling and subject to the carceral system. This school-to-prison pipeline (Laura 2014) pursues the social death of populations precisely in the name of maximizing their economic potential. The ways in which populations are distributed in schools and funds are differentially invested in those schools (subject to federal standards because of policies like No Child Left Behind and Race to the Top) signals the operations of what Michelle Murphy calls "the economization of life," which names "the practices that differentially value and govern life in terms of their ability to foster the macro-economy of the nation-state" (2017, 6). The economization of life enables a translation of disciplinary assemblages of racialization to forms of control and investment that avoid the language of race almost entirely: "The economization of life was performed through social scientific practices that continued the project of racializing life—that is, dividing it into categories of more and less worthy living, reproducing, and being human—and reinscribed race as the problem of 'population' hinged to fostering the economy" (Murphy 2017, 6).[5] This is Foucault's "biopolitics of the population" (1978, 139) plugged into the invention of the economy as a macroeconomic object of speculation and intervention, the fostering of which became, throughout the twentieth century, "the primary purpose of states" (Murphy 2017, 7). That is, although Murphy doesn't put it this way, we can see the articulation of population and economy as possible only on condition of a statist capture of literacy, redirecting more-than-human energetic and material networks toward the task of reading the social body almost solely in terms of maximizing profitability and control.[6]

I think it is crucial that Murphy analyzes the role that social sciences played in the biopolitical control of populations in relation to a new felt reality of the economy. This foregrounds how disciplinary literacies (social scientific methods of producing meaning) are materially and affectively linked to corporatist states. Jack Halberstam, summarizing Foucault, has written that disciplinarity "depends upon and deploys normalization, routines, convention, tradition, and regularity, and it produces experts and administrative forms of governance" (2011, 8). He notes that the disciplinary apparatus of the university is now at a "crossroads" facing two futures: "The university as corporation and investment opportunity and the university as a new kind of public sphere with a different investment in knowledge, in ideas, and in thought and politics" (8). I return, in the final chapters of *Animate Literacies*, to the future of universities and the study of literacy more broadly. Here, I want to note that in the university as corporation, excellence is the watchword of administrators (Readings 1997) and the work of thinking is reduced to metrics of scholarly production, citation, and social media circulation (so-called "altmetrics") that can be used to calculate the value-added labor of professional researchers.[7]

It is this model of the university that Roderick Ferguson theorizes in *The Reorder of Things*, arguing that when confronted with radical demands that the university redistribute access to populations marginalized by disciplinary modes of racialization that restricted access, the university invented means to incorporate difference through "management . . . evolving ways in which institutions could use rather than absolutely dismiss the demands of minority activists" (2012, 58). Ferguson argues that this dramatically reconfigured the biopolitics of the university's relation to Man: "The interdisciplines [women's studies, ethnic studies, and so on] would not jettison a concern for the positivities long associated with man. Instead, the agencies and processes of life, labor, and language would be subjected to an unprecedented scrutiny that sought to determine their constitution through historical particularities rather than transhistorical universalities. This new biopower would take as its representative the subject constituted through difference" (2012, 34). Ferguson here sees minority challenges to the disciplinary restrictions of Man (such as the student strike at the City University of New York in the early 1970s) as being innovatively co-opted into the calculation of diversity and the institutional reconfiguration of Man—now always marked by the particularities of race, gender, class, sexuality, ability, and nationality—as a nexus of distributing probable accumulations and dispossessions (credits, degrees, fellowships, research chairs, debt, and so on).

Education, in this context, takes the disciplinary function of surveillance that Foucault saw at work in the panopticon and the examination and plugs it into the control of affect at a preindividual level. It is no surprise then to see considerable and often extremely contentious public debate in the United States right now about safe spaces and the feelings of students. Jasbir Puar writes that "specific to a Deleuzian model of control societies is an emphasis on affective resonance, on how surveillance technologies activate, inflect, vibrate, distribute, disseminate, disaggregate: in other words, how things feel, how sensations matter as much as if not more than how things appear, look, seem, are visible, or cognitively known"

(2007, 129). In this context, the emergence, especially since No Child Left Behind, of an enormous apparatus of testing and surveillance has to be understood not as a disciplinary means of correcting the docile body, but as a mechanism of rearticulating the student as the object of cloud computing and differential investment of state resources. The student here is primed for constant anxiety relative to ever-shifting assessment strategies and reformed curricula that carry the force to significantly control access to future schooling and shape the kinds of economic positions students might hope to occupy. Indeed, the temporo-spatial rhetoric of "left behind" in relation to a set of annual targets for improving test scores always disaggregated by population suggests that students have become what Patricia Clough calls "machinically assembled bodies" (2004, 11).[8] The disciplining and control of the body in relation to a social-material plane oriented around Man as the overrepresentation of the human works precisely on these machinically assembled bodies, and power intervenes by conditioning the situations—always more-than-human—from which subjects temporarily emerge in events. Or, put differently, while a subject is the object of disciplinary operations, prepersonal literacies constitute the field of biopolitical control.

Politics is always, as Sara Ahmed (2008) reminds us, the politics of attention, and this is precisely what is at stake in this book's attempt to attune to the literacy situations from which literacy events emerge in order to reimagine the politics of education as always a question of the prepersonal affective relations that can and do condition the emergence of subjects invested in (by) states, but which can also condition more errant and delinquent events and pleasures.[9] Part of this investment has to do with the production of identities as back-formations that get caught up in "inscribed habits of inattention" (Boler 1999, 16). That is, thinking solely in terms of identity—which does have, I think, a crucial role to play in critiques of existing systems of control—makes it extremely difficult to attend to the messy, uncertain, shifting processes of becoming that are, today if not always, directly the scene of politics. Shaviro writes that "the subject cannot be given in advance; it must always emerge anew, in an unforeseeable way, as it is precipitated out of the metastable transcendental field. What's basic . . . is not the individual, but the always ongoing, and never complete or definitive, process of individuation" (2009, 81).[10]

Wynter's argument that the human is not a noun but a verb, a praxis, helps to underscore this point: that Man is not a stable thing—even at the level of representation or mythology—so much as it is an operational logic that links assemblages of subjectivization in ways that orient machinically assembled bodies in social and material space. That is, the orientation of energies, capacities, and attention toward Man happens at a preindividual level. It is also highly unstable.[11] This has important consequences for how we enact educational encounters in classrooms and other sites of study, and it suggests that taking seriously the politics of literacy requires that we shift the scale of our attention away from delimited readers (with identities) encountering texts understood as signifying structures, and toward the swirling scene of encounters among energies, entities, and disaggregated systems that I am calling the literacy situation. Indeed, literacy is not a skill a subject can have so much as a condition of material existence and becoming. We should speak less of literate subjects (a quantum in the economization of life, literally calculated as part of the Human Development Index) than of literacies that, jacked into state apparatuses of control, enable subjects to crystalize through the complex relations of more-than-human agencies and entities dispersed widely throughout both space and time.

Taking seriously Halberstam's provocation that "we may, ultimately, want more undisciplined knowledge, more questions and fewer answers" (2011, 10), I want to call for wandering away from disciplinary knowledge, in an academic sense, to account for the politics of literacy that are caught up in schools. Disciplinary knowledge works precisely through the construction and policing of borders (between objects, methods, subfields, etc.) and this border work informs the politics of perception of the scholar even when he or she attunes to the more-than-human situation. Andrew Pickering offers an analysis of how this works in the sociology of scientific knowledge (SSK), a field that sees and feels but cannot account for nonhuman agency in the sciences within its disciplinary regime. He writes that SSK "is grounded in the traditional humanism of sociology as a discipline, inasmuch as it takes the human subject to be the center of action. Whenever SSK detects a tendency for the action to be located elsewhere—a decentering of the human subject . . . any trace of nonhuman agency is immediately recuperated by translating it into an account of nonhuman agency that is attributed straight back to human subjects" (Pickering 1995, 25). This is precisely the move I found in the field known as history of the book in chapter 7: When scholars recognize the material influence of nonhuman agency, the disciplined response is to factor it out, refer it back to human agency. Discipline, in the contemporary academic institutionalization of knowledge, cannot help but find Man everywhere because Man is structurally inseparable from its epistemic attunement to the world.

This is seldom conscious or explicit precisely because it happens at the preindividual level of perception and attention. We might see it as a more diffuse version of a problem of Enlightenment knowledge production Edward Said diagnoses in *Orientalism*. Said writes that

> the determining impingement on most knowledge produced in the contemporary West (and here I speak mainly about the United States) is that it be nonpolitical, that is, scholarly, academic, impartial, above partisan or small-minded doctrinal belief. One can have no quarrel with such an ambition in theory, perhaps, but in practice the reality is much more problematic. No one has ever devised a method for detaching the scholar from the circumstances of life, from the fact of his involvement (conscious or unconscious) with a class, a set of beliefs, a social position, or from the mere activity of being a member of a society. (1979, 10)

That is, by pushing Said's diagnosis beyond his own humanist frame, we can argue that the fact of feeling oneself to be human and taking that humanness for granted is always operative in the way thinkers approach (and indeed produce) their objects.[12]

In an explicitly posthumanist account of disciplinarity drawing on systems theory, Cary Wolfe has argued that disciplines "may be profitably thought of as subsystems [of a larger system called education] that follow the same systemic logic, which both produce and depend on their own elements for the autopoiesis (journals, conferences, research groups, protocols of advancement and recognition, etc.)" (2009b, 111–12). This reference to systems theory allows Wolfe to posit that disciplines operate according to discourses (in the Foucauldian sense) in order to "reduce and process the overwhelming complexity of an environment that is by definition always already exponentially more complex than any particular system itself" (112). In Wolfe's account, there can be no specificity to our knowledge without such systemic, autopoietic reduction. This reduction, in fact, allows disciplines to "constitute their objects through their practices" (108). In an important way, this rhymes with Karen Barad's account of how an apparatus functions in a phenomenon when research—or conceptual thinking—takes place.[13] In these abstract terms, it's difficult to imagine a better conception of what an academic discipline is. But what gives me pause, in light of Gauri Viswanathan's critique of English and even a sketchy account of the history of the modern disciplines, is how this formulation doesn't tie back into a critique of how these disciplines are the products of imperial assemblages of humanization.[14] That is, while I am entirely willing to grant that every particular study must involve an orientation toward what I think is misnamed an object of inquiry, it does not follow that those orientations must or should be determined by the disciplinary structures such as have been articulated in relation to Man.

Samantha Frost's Biocultural Creatures offers me a way of shifting ever so slightly away from a cybernetic account of disciplines toward an energetic one. Building on the general postulate that all matter is energy, Frost devotes considerable care to how membranes between cells function, because those cells make possible a relatively stable, yet always active, shifting, and moving entity called "the body." She writes, "In between the conceptual options of a smear and a hermetically sealed container is the porous body. What makes a living body distinct from its environment are not the substances of which it is composed . . . but rather the activities and processes that occur within and by means of that body" (Frost 2016, 75). This account allows her to think about any membrane "in terms of the chemical transitions and transactions it makes possible" (67). While I am obviously shifting up in scale several levels very quickly, in this account, there is not quite a system called education containing subsystems that all function autopoietically, but rather a mass of always moving energy that is differentiated at sites that aren't borders in a rigid sense so much as zones of complex traffic and contact. Disciplines, I might then be able to say, are always touching and being touched by other disciplines, being affected by them.[15] Their borders aren't given, but always emergent (however stable they seem). In fact, the borders between disciplines are nothing but energy. And rather than continue to devote energy to shoring up the knowledge practices that body us as scholars by orienting everything we do toward Man, it seems to me we can redirect this energy, or, more precisely, our energies can be redirected, for it is not clear that the energies of the nonhumans caught up in disciplinary assemblages with us are oriented in that direction anyway. Movement in other directions is not only possible, then, it always has to be reined in.

This is because discipline, ultimately, is a mode of mastery, as Julietta Singh has argued: a particular, colonialist relation between a subject and some fractured or fragmented object where this differential is extended in time.[16] Scholars are forced to master their attentions in order to master bodies of knowledge, and universities materially support this activity when the scholars' mastery (already double) can feed into state or corporate mastery over the land and/or the wider population. This means that when we practice disciplined knowledge production, whatever our politics, we scholars have our energies, attentions, and perceptions captured by institutions that are calibrated to the project of humanization and its dehumanizing exhaust. What we need, then, is not more disciplinary knowledge but ways of attuning to the more-than-human political situation that, from the perspective of disciplines, become errant, delinquent, and failed. We have to learn to attend more precisely to how we are affected by literacy situations, and to follow those affects into uncertain and uncontrollable relations.

9

BEWILDERMENT

While I have no desire to downplay the omnipresence of discipline and control, I would argue that these seize on and capture energies, capacities, movements, and affects that circulate and make up the political stuff of planetary life. As I lay out in more detail in chapter 15, there is a statist capture of literacy that modulates and directs literacy events, but that always comes after the fact, as it were, of open-ended, always shifting, more-than-human entanglements in literacy situations. At the threshold between situation and event, then, are modes of disciplining and controlling attention and attunement. In this chapter, I want to sketch a way of attuning to literacy situations that allows the unpredictable affects generated in literacy situations to become events. I call these affective events *bewilderment*, and in the coming chapters I sketch both methodological approaches to the study of literature and literacy that affirm becoming bewildered, and ways of thinking about the politics of study—in classrooms and beyond—that articulate bewilderment as a directly political phenomenon enabling dispersed, fugitive, and ephemeral dislocations and disorientations that move us away from Man. In proposing bewilderment as an affective event, one that pulls the swirling more-than-human entanglements of literacy situations into events that register to the perceptual and attentive apparatus of the human persons involved, I am inspired by the use of the word "bewilderment" in two late nineteenth-century literary texts: Bram Stoker's *Dracula* (published in 1897) and Kate Chopin's *The Awakening* (1899).

In *Dracula*, as the Crew of Light in London struggles to understand what has happened to their friend Lucy (who has been bitten by Dracula), there is a moment when Dr. Seward, a psychologist in charge of a mental hospital, records in his diary an exchange with his former professor, Dr. Abraham Van Helsing. The exchange turns on the relation between literacy, disciplined knowledge, and affect. Van Helsing hands Dr. Seward a newspaper article describing children being "decoyed away" and found with "small punctured wounds on their throats" (Stoker 2003, 203). Upon reading this, Dr. Seward notes that "an idea struck" him, causing him to "look up" at Van Helsing. What we see in this locution is that ideas arrive from outside the subject, although their precise location cannot be specified, and they condition particular forms of corporeal response, in this case a movement of the head, shoulders, and eyes. As this literacy event sets Dr. Seward into motion, Van Helsing asks what he "makes of it," a phrase that signals how meaning is something produced and constructed within literacy events in a relations between a reader—who is, as I argue in chapter 10, an ensemble of systems more than a coherent self—and a material text that only appears within specific relations of extraction, production, and circulation, all of which are impossible without nonhuman agencies. Dr. Seward replies, "Simply that there is some cause in common" (203), a response that frustrates Van Helsing for its narrowly disciplinary, scientific quality.

Van Helsing tells Dr. Seward, "You are clever man, friend John; you reason well, and your wit is bold; but you are too prejudiced. . . . There are things old and new which must not be contemplate by men's eyes" (204). Van Helsing, as representative of the most advanced science in Europe, then launches into a critique of narrow scientific, disciplined rationality and its rigid empiricism. Among other things, he discusses hypnotism, comparative anatomy that short-circuits anthropocentric distinctions between "men" and "brutes," and new discoveries in "electrical science." After nearly two full pages of Van Helsing's lecture, Dr. Seward notes, "Here I interrupted him. I was getting bewildered; he so crowded on my mind his list of nature's eccentricities and possible impossibilities that my imagination was getting fired. I had a dim idea that he was teaching me some lesson" (205). While there is a growing—"dim"—awareness that something from this lecture may come to congeal into a cognitive "lesson," Dr. Seward is more than anything aware of an affective experience: "getting bewildered." Before there is cognition, then, there is an exposure to a set of relations that disorients, and in disorienting sets part of the self into motion: "my imagination was getting fired." What spurs imagination, then, is the affective experience of bewilderment, which becomes event precisely in the relation between a disciplined attentive apparatus (Dr. Seward's scientifically trained mind) and a messy, unknowable set of relations that are always swirling around him and affecting him, even though he doesn't consciously register it.

In order to amplify this concept of bewilderment and extend it beyond contexts in which academic discipline are involved, I want to look at a moment in Kate Chopin's novella *The Awakening*. Edna Pontellier, a wife and mother dissatisfied with the limits and routines of her wealthy North American lifestyle at the turn of the twentieth century, is at a beach resort in Louisiana. Her husband is off seeing to the demands of the capitalist accumulation that makes this confining life possible, and Edna begins, without being consciously aware of this, to have particular feelings for another man, a younger-still novice capitalist named Robert. At the beginning of chapter 6, we read:

> Edna Pontellier could not have told why, wishing to go to the beach with Robert, she should in the first place have declined, and in the second place have followed in obedience to one of the two contradictory impulses which impelled her.
>
> A certain light was beginning to dawn dimly within her,—the light which, showing the way, forbids it.
>
> At that early period it served but to bewilder her. It moved her to dreams, to thoughtfulness, to the shadowy anguish which had overcome her the midnight when she had abandoned herself to tears. (Chopin 1993, 14)

The passage begins with a disconnect between Edna's conscious sense of herself and the world and some vague, diffuse force that pulses around and within her, a force that orients her action in the world. This force is then figured as a kind of light, one that is at once a question of knowledge (showing) and of power (forbidding).[1] Most crucial for me is how this nonconscious or preconscious state affects her: it "moves" her, which is to say that it concerns precisely her orientation. This light bewilders her: estranges her from the world of custom, convention, and civilization to which she is habituated. It makes her feel like she doesn't know where she is or is going. It disorients her. And this disorientation, this becoming lost, this bewilderment moves her. An affect here circulates around and within her, and its effect is some kind of movement from where she is to an elsewhere.

This elsewhere is, first, "to dreams," which signals a kind of reverie that, to stay within her exact moment, we could read in terms of wish fulfillment, but which I would prefer to link to the productive as if that is the sine qua non of animal play according to Brian Massumi.[2] This "as if" opens up, to anticipate a fuller account of Massumi's theory, a margin for maneuver, some play in the situation in the sense engineers might use that term. Second, bewilderment moves her "to thoughtfulness." This reveals something extraordinarily important: that when one knows one's way, one is relieved of the burden of being full of thought. Habit becomes unthinking, and the only way to be moved to think is to lose one's way. Finally, Chopin ties this dreaming and thinking to "shadowy anguish." This is the pain of not knowing, a pain that is again indexically tied to power (abandonment), and a power situated precisely within her split subjectivity.

I want to propose that Edna's split subjectivity is an effect of being oriented toward Man. In different ways, Freud's and Nietzsche's philosophies of the subject presume and describe the self-splitting within the human that is a precondition of becoming Man. This splitting—or what Nietzsche calls "self-vivisection"—separates the human animal into parts and subjects one part to the other.[3] That is, this splitting is part and parcel of the disciplinary work of humanizing education, for it separates the necessarily animal condition of corporeal possibility for living from the purportedly human aspects of the creature that have to be developed and strengthened in the course of an educational regime.[4] This split self is the disciplined self, the self that surveils itself, that subjects itself. As I have been arguing throughout this book, this disciplined self has been even further disaggregated in the shift from disciplinary to control societies: "Control is a biopolitics that works at the molecular level of bodies, at the informational substrate of matter" (Clough 2007, 19). While such a shift in the circulation and operation of power can be historicized as Deleuze (1992) suggests, where discipline is surpassed by control by the end of the twentieth century, I think it is important to insist that the human body is, and always has been, a multiplicity. That is, it is not really the disaggregation that is new so much as the inability to map onto the body a unity, whether biological or psychic.[5]

Bewilderment produces anguish but also dreams and thinking, and all of this happens at a remove from any unified sense of self. Indeed, bewilderment as an affective experience may be best understood as any event where the self, always becoming in processual relation to myriad entanglements with nonhuman forces and agencies, registers its emergence in and from a world in flux that always exceeds control. In trying to affirm this bewilderment now as a necessary mode of disorientation, I want to underscore this affective link between a joy of the "as if" and a particular pain. Getting lost is, for those of us whose lives are so often lived within the habitual spaces of cities, houses, and institutions, always caught up in what Franco Moretti (1982) calls, in his reading of *Dracula* and *Frankenstein*, "the dialectic of fear": an admixture of fear and loathing, desire and repulsion.

I want to propose now that this particular affective state of disorientation—bewilderment—might be the most productive way to open up possibilities for moving away from being Man toward other, incipient and furtive, ways of performing the human. Instead of orienting all of the educational movement toward Man, what we need today is an education that does not know where it is headed.[6] While Man has become the most important orienting point in the diagram running through the Western imperialist state's humanizing assemblages, it is crucial to remember that humans have been differentially positioned relative to this Man by the state and its de/humanizing assemblages, and I want to caution against taking Man as a thing one can finally be. It is, as I have already argued, a fiction, one that describes what particular entities are, but like any fiction it is both constructed (etymologically, it is something made) and necessarily a partial representation of what is. Man is a selective, highly disciplined/controlled conception of what it is to be human, and it should not be mistaken for the human as such. It functions as an orienting telos that directs our energies, attentions, and capacities in particular ways, and over time, thanks to what Wynter calls the "sociogenic principle," this can come to seem and feel simply like how things are. But we are, or can be, different and otherwise. And indeed, I think there is an important political lesson to be learned by thinking that in actual fact no one is Man, although some have been granted recognition as such by the imperialist state.

Nyong'o and the other contributors to the "Queer Inhumanisms" issue of GLQ are highly attentive to how many versions of posthumanist theory sidestep this differential relationship to the human. He writes:

> Posthumanist theory has tended to present the decentering of the human as both salutary and largely innocent of history. Up until the present time, we are told in one version of this philosophical fable, we have incorrectly centered the human. Now we can, and must, correct that error, if only (paradoxically) to save ourselves. It is in anticipation of such tales that black studies has repeatedly asked: have we ever been human? And if not, what are we being asked to decenter, and through what means? (2015, 266)

This set of questions highlights precisely the difference between what Wynter calls "Man" and the human, and indicates the necessity of that distinction for a political-educational praxis of bewilderment. Man, in the account I'm providing, is the point around which social, political, and geographical space is oriented, and (to anticipate the questions I ask in chapter 10) it functions as a point of reference for de/humanization as a problematic of orientation and movement. "We" are not oriented toward Man in the same ways, and any critical account of Man's function has to begin by tracking that differential positioning.[7]

This allows me to say that the "wild" at play in bewilderment is not a place per se, but an affective disorientation from where one finds oneself in relation to Man, one that sets any person moving away from the only place we are told matters. As Nyong'o puts it, "Wildness pulls focus away from the human, bringing into sharper relief a background of a pulsing, vital, even queer materiality" (2015, 258). In becoming bewildered, we shift our focus, then, away from a virtual horizon that requires ever more disciplined movement and attention, and toward an attunement to what looks, when we gaze upon Man, like the background: a whole material world that is always already here, and of which we are a part.[8] This is precisely what I call the *literacy situation*: an omnipresent, more-than-human scene of affective collisions and communications among entities and agencies.

Jack Halberstam has noted that "the path to the wild beyond is paved with refusal" (2013, 8), in particular the refusal to be oriented toward Man and its politics, its disciplinary restriction of our attentions. "Listening to cacophony and noise," Halberstam writes, "tells us that there is a wild beyond to the structures we inhabit and that inhabit us" (7).[9] Refusing Man, then, is inseparable from an affirmation, a different kind of attunement, a different orientation to the world. Or, more precisely, different orientations in the plural, for one of the most violent, horrific features of Man is its totalitarian drive toward unity, unification, universality.

Bewilderment may be tentatively understood then as movement away from Man's discipline in any direction. Intellectually, it is antidisciplinary. It prefers questions to answers, or it asks questions it fails to answer.[10] Politically, it is antisettlement, or, to use Stefano Harney and Fred Moten's language, it is fugitive, resisting "the perfection of democracy under the general equivalent" (2013, 57) and any smooth operation of political governance, since "governance is the extension of whiteness on a global scale" (56). Bewilderment seeks out "knowledge of freedom . . . (in) escape, stealing away in the confines, in the form, of a break" (51). Harney and Moten insist, therefore, that the map of Man is superimposed on a different cartography, one where "borders fail to cohere, because the movement of things will not cohere" (94). Bewilderment names not a flight away from any particular space or place then, and it certainly does not figure the wild as out there in some utopia; it refers to any process of attuning to what is always already here, in and around us, and which exerts an affective pull on us away from Man.[11]

After sketching a beautiful moment of bewilderment—feeling "lost but alive and unvanquished in their displacement" in a John Ashbery poem (2011, 33), Lauren Berlant asks the difficult question, "Why do some people have the chops for improvised unknowing while others run out of breath, not humming but hoarding?" (2011, 37). If bewilderment names an affective state of dis-ease that puts things into motion, then we have to think about how this deterritorializing motion can, to stay with Deleuze and Guattari's terms, easily become reterritorialized by Man. Chopin's novella depicts just this. After her feelings for Robert moved her, Edna was clearly "not herself," or rather "she was becoming herself" (Chopin 1993, 55). This leads first to a disinclination to spend time in her house doing what is expected of her as a wealthy woman (one whose legal status approximates property more than person), and an increasing proclivity to hang out with Mademoiselle Reisz, a musician who lives by herself (we might say that she has a room of her own). It is Mademoiselle Reisz who figures for Edna both the general sense of a response to the situation and the difficulty of it. Narrating it after the fact to another man (not her husband, and not Robert), Edna says, "When I left her today, she put her arms around me and felt my shoulder blades, to see if my wings were strong, she said, 'The bird that would soar about the level plain of tradition and prejudice must have strong wings. It is a sad spectacle to see the weaklings bruised, exhausted, fluttering back to earth'" (79). I will return to the importance of birds in chapter 10. My point for the moment is that Mademoiselle Reisz figures a productive movement following bewilderment as flying, as becoming-bird. But she also figures Man and its assemblages as a crushing gravity, one that produces (in a Spinozist phrase) sadness. This subjunctive figuration immediately precedes Edna's flight from her husband's house to one of her own, which is dubbed by everyone around her the "pigeon house" (81). That is, while Edna begins something like a process of becoming bewildered, she ends up shut up in a cage, a domesticated, confining space that replaces unknowing and freedom with, to return to Berlant, a kind of hoarding (of property). Unsurprisingly, Edna's sadness doesn't abate.[12] In a social formation that restricts women's movement—social, legal, corporeal, and locomotor—the difficulty of sustaining bewildered flight is considerable. Perhaps more than anything, the novella thus dramatizes the precarity of an individual bewilderment, one that doesn't tap into and build off the movement of other bodies suspended together in the affective situation.[13]

Something else appears in the pages of Douglass's Narrative. Very early in the book, Douglass dwells upon the songs sung by the slaves, "the words to which to many would seem unmeaning jargon, but which, nevertheless, were full of meaning to themselves" (1997, 19). In these literacy events—songs—you have a bifurcated text that both signifies and does not signify. That is, they serve as a means, to anticipate chapter 10, of constructing a territory in which movement—imaginative and political, if not yet in fugitive corporeality—becomes possible through a literacy event ephemerally marking a limit in order to carve out a space of action within the violently policed limits of state-sponsored slavery. These songs critique the world as it is—Douglass writes, "To those songs I trace my first glimmering conception of the dehumanizing character of slavery" (19)—but they also create. The vibrations produced by vocal cords, pulsating through the air in the fields, touch some ears differently than others, and for some listeners ("many") they are asignifying. But for some the others, they are "wild songs, revealing the highest joy and the deepest sadness" (18). The sonorous materiality of these songs enables affects to circulate, and in so doing, a collective bewilderment sets us, enabling a shared, distributed relation to the world as it is—the one violently yoking everyone to Man—that is at once critical and imaginative. Hartman argues here that "what Douglass yearns for is dangerous music and dangerous thought" (1997, 47). Against the universality of Man and its will to preserved legibility, these songs sound and dissipate, their only record being the affectively charged bodies of those in their wake.

While the directions in which we flee will be myriad, and while the specific situations that set us moving (which make us "start" like the oxen in Douglass's *Narrative*) will be radically contextual and different for each of us, Sylvia Wynter has very pointedly argued that desire to move way from being Man can serve as a crucial reference point for collating our always intersectional and differential politics, needs, and aspirations. She writes:

> The argument proposes that the struggle of our new millennium will be one between the ongoing imperative of securing the well-being of our present ethnoclass (i.e., Western bourgeois) conception of the human, Man, which overrepresents itself as if it were the human itself, and that of securing the well-being, and therefore the full cognitive and behavioral autonomy of the human species itself/ourselves. . . . The correlated hypothesis here is that all our present struggles with respect to race, class, gender, sexual orientation, ethnicity, struggles over environment, global warming, severe climate change, the sharply unequal distribution of the earth's resources . . . —these are all differing facets of the central ethnoclass Man vs. Human struggle. (2003, 260–61)

Our struggles converge then not in some singular vision of a better world, or even a shared sense of being wronged. Rather, they converge in refusal to be Man, in refusal to discipline and control ourselves in the ways so many institutions—but the imperialist state and its educational apparatuses above all—insist. This is why despite the fact that becoming bewildered will happen in myriad unanticipatable ways, at unplannable times, it provides a furtive, fragile, fleeting event in which we can recognize, together, that we just don't want to get fucked up by Man anymore, and we are already moving in other directions.

10

TOWARD A LITERARY ETHOLOGY

The relation between bewilderment and recalibration of attunement toward the material world that is around us (and is us!) is sounded often in Samantha Frost's *Biocultural Creatures*, which emerges from the political theorist's eighteen-month leave from teaching to take courses in the biological sciences in order to be able to work more cogently across disciplinary lines. She writes, of the convergence between scientists and humanists who are institutionally segregated, that "for us to engage with one another's work through this moment of convergence seems to present an opportunity for each kind of critique to be thrown back on its assumptions, to discover new modes or perspectives for thinking, to become bewildered only to perceive a novel pattern or unexpected set of connections" (Frost 2016, 19). Working across—or, better, against—disciplinary boundaries is bewildering, and this, as Chopin's novella figures, is an affective state that moves us to think, both about what we think we know and about what has to be assumed or not called into question for what we think we know to make sense. Disciplines, it turns out, allow us to leave a lot unstated, unquestioned. Traditional approaches to literature and literacy focus on the relation between a reader (understood primarily as a knowing mind) and a text (understood as a set of signifiers and not necessarily a material object or ensemble of objects). This chapter and the next propose two different attempts to wander away from this approach to literature and literacy. Here, I zoom out, situating literature and even human literacy in a much wider set of animal literacies. In chapter 11, I zoom in, exploring how reading affects the systems of the reader without becoming necessarily conscious. Both of these chapters, along with the two that follow them, offer an account—expansive but not exhaustive—of what I call the *literacy situation*.

In this chapter, I propose the concept of an ethology of literacy practice. I want to think about this chapter's work as a kind of antidisciplinary nest weaving, creating a particular space for dwelling within literacy that appears only because of a repetitive movement that builds with found objects. As Erin Manning notes, "Ethologies are not about knowledge as end points but about accumulation and difference" (2006, 144). I will turn around literacy again and again, borrowing what concepts I can, in order to feel it differently. Unlike scientific practices that move an object (an animal, an event, a reaction, a process) from its natural conditions of emergence to the controlled setting of the laboratory, in calling this *ethology*, I want to try to see what literacy looks and feels like in the thick web—or mangle—of its appearance as a contact zone among a whole host of animating entities of different kinds, situated at different levels of scale, and participating across a vast range of proximities.[1] It is not a wild method, but a bewildering one.

There has been some pressure on the narrow, liberal humanist restriction of literacy (to a particular proficiency in reading and writing in received standard written variants of major languages) from what is often called the new literacy studies. These researchers tend to see literacy as a social process, one that is less about abstract meaning relations than about specific, contextual, social relations. Arguing that literacy is not simply a thing, but derives instead from "aspects of a specific ideology" (in a given social formation), Brian Street argues that while states might want to conceive of literacy as a narrow "technical skill," it is, rather, "a form of political and ideological practice" (1984, 110). Many of the researchers associated with this movement expand what counts as literacy by thinking of it as multimodal, encompassing a range of semiotic practices. Indeed, they argue that "literacy *events* are activities where literacy has a role. Usually there is a written text, or texts, central to the activity and there may be talk around the text. Events are observable episodes which arise from practice and are shaped by them" (Barton, Hamilton, and Ivanic 2000, 8). While this research has considerably widened the understanding of literacy in ways that are crucial for my analysis here, it also ends up methodologically restricting literacy to a human concern, a concern that adheres in its adoption of methods from anthropology. Borrowing from anthropology—which seems to study the human in a web of human relations—researchers end up only observing what humans do.[2] To the extent that objects appear, they are (as in book history, as in the sociology of scientific knowledge) factored out as agentic participants.

I want to use the concept of the literacy situation to expand beyond this anthropological understanding of literacy by insisting that nonhuman agency animates any literacy event, and that attending to these events requires attuning to what affects are at play that aren't, strictly speaking, observable (in empiricist ways) and which participate outside of customary frames (as I put it in chapter 2). Laurent Berlant writes that "a situation is a genre of living that one knows one's in but that one has to find out about, a circumstance embedded in life but not in one's control" (2011, 195). Most people, including literary and literacy scholars, know quite well that nonhumans (books, paper, ink, glue, light, chairs, desks, computers, etc.) are part of literacy situations, but the disciplinary frames condition an immediate factoring out of these agencies. This is, as Berlant implies, a defense mechanism against feeling out of control. The literacy situation is primarily a matter of affects, or sensations, as Alfred North Whitehead might say.[3] In order to understand literacy as an affective contact zone, we have to find methods for grappling with it that don't simply derive either from literary studies or from the so-called "human sciences" since both ultimately presuppose the human as both an object and the only conceivable subject position from which knowledge can emanate.

This antidisciplinary thrust is inextricable, for me, from the political impulse to turn away from Man (as Coulthard, riffing on Fanon, would say). In looking to ethology, I am not merely seeking to take an existing discipline and use it to rethink literacy practices. Indeed, there are already researchers pursuing human ethology in ways that don't particularly interest me. The main reason is that this discipline, qua discipline, has been structured by a presupposed orientation toward Man.[4] In order to dislodge ethology from Man, then, I want to underscore and privilege the blurriness, the porosity, the activity of bordering, and I want to seek ways to understand difference that would not fall back into humanist impulses toward ordering it. I want a disorderly, bewildering ethology, one that will treat humans, nonhuman animals, and nonvital objects as active participants in literacy even as I attune to the differing animacies involved. It is helpful to begin then by refusing precisely the border between humans and other animals insisted upon and policed by Man.[5] The human is a kind of animal, one that has capacities that are directed, augmented, and stifled when it becomes Man (or is forced to approximate Man), and in the effort to understand this creature's difference from other beings (and to begin to catch a semblance of what it can do), it is necessary to resituate it horizontally with respect to other animals instead of virtually differentiated from them in some kind of rupture.

In casting this project as ethology, I'm also spurred on by Susan McHugh's call for a "narrative ethology," one that "emphasizes embodied relations of agency and form as distinct from, say, the content through which ethological, fictional, and all other narratives get sorted and shelved as the political problems of representation. This formulation affirms the ways in which ethology and fiction alike proceed from the complicated operations of affect, and leads to an ethics premised on feelings honored as concrete, intense, and shared" (2011, 217–18). McHugh foregrounds precisely the refusal of sorting that enables a redirection of attention away from Man, and it also primes us for a shift from a focus on representation to a focus on affects and feelings as, precisely, the scene of touching that makes literacy itself a political problematic.

In A Thousand Plateaus, Deleuze and Guattari write that "not only does art not wait for human beings to begin, but we may ask if art ever appears among human beings, except under artificial and belated conditions" (2002, 320). This formulation is, no doubt, polemical and deliberately counterintuitive, which is to say: it is an attack upon Man and its restriction of art to a human capacity. For Deleuze and Guattari, art is not primarily about a host of things that Man likes to link it with—particular disinterested ideas about aesthetic form, or artistic intention, or the institutionalized canonization of things as art—but is a question of territory (320–23). Art is inseparable from a politics of spatialization and movement.[6] Drawing from, among other sources, Messiaen's analyses of bird songs and their refrains, Deleuze and Guattari write, "*We call a refrain any aggregate of matters of expression that draws a territory and develops into territorial motifs and landscapes*" (323). Art, then, does not simply arise in space; it draws and maps territories. It animates politics.

While I will narrow my focus shortly from art in general to practices that can be understood within a narrower, but extremely blurry, frame called "literacy," I want to note how the feminist ethologist Vinciane Despret takes up a similar set of concerns in *What Would Animals Say If We Asked the Right Questions?* Picking up on Étienne Souriau's use of the verb "to instaurate" with respect to how a work of art appears, which means "to follow a path," Despret writes, "To insist on the fact that the artist is not the cause of the work and that the work alone is not its own cause; the artist carries responsibility, the responsibility of the one who hosts, who collects, who prepares, who explores the form of the work" (2016, 121). That is, Despret rejects a vision of animacy that would insist on locating art in the artist as intention, and rejects reducing the cause of art to the art object itself in either a transcendent or materialist mode. Instead, art emerges from hospitality, collection, exploration. This is, of necessity, a question of contact among a range of animacies, and the cause of art cannot be located outside of this confluence. In Barad's (2007) terms, we might say that art is always "intra-active" and that both work and artist(s) appear only in and through this "instauration," which is itself a mode of what Deleuze and Guattari call "territorialization."

Despret also crucially ties this artistic instauration to love, and the example that allows her to weave this claim is a bird's nest. Following this weave will take me from art as a problem of spatiality to literacy by following a path of instinct. By returning to Souriau again, Despret paraphrases to say "the nest is a work of love" before quoting: "A creator of love: the work mediates" (2016, 121). That is, the "work of love" is a pregnant double genitive where the double direction signals precisely what Barad calls "intra-action," or what Souriau calls "mediation." Art is always and only between, in touching. The nest and the bird "compear" in and as love.[7] To understand love in this way is to move toward "a theory of instinct that, far from mechanizing the animal and returning it to biological determinism, instead offers, in a speculative mode, much more fruitful analogies" (122).

I want to dwell on instinct here, for it has often been used, as Despret suggests, to differentiate the human from other animals, usually according to a binary opposition to something like intelligence. This binary opposition is rejected in the evolutionary philosophy of Henri Bergson, who instead sees them as mutually included tendencies.[8] Weaving together Bergson with Deleuze, Gregory Bateson, and Georges Simondon, Brian Massumi conceptualizes instinct as precisely the resistance to any biological determinism, one that, in fact, makes possible animal play, which, in his account, "creates the conditions for language" (2014, 8).[9] This is so because play, as Bateson argues, involves a logic of "similar but not same," a difference that introduces "noncoincidence," a precondition for any form of semiotics. Play, for Massumi, always involves both abstraction and a conditional mode, two things that remove play from the serious work of living and create a particular kind of excess: "The aesthetic yield is the qualitative excess of an act lived purely for its own sake, as a value in itself, over and against any function the act might also fulfill" (10). Play is, strictly speaking, "useless" (11), and yet it makes possible this excess that introduces into the world of determined necessity what Massumi calls "a margin of maneuver" (13), or, more simply, "it opens the door to *improvisation*" (12). That is, play, which Massumi locates precisely in animal instinct (which is always already entangled with intelligence), creates the possibility of invention, creation, and the active, vital, corporeal movement that remakes the world as something other than what it is: "Creativity and instinct are inextricably entwined" (91). Massumi's account of animal play as the site of politics includes a resituating of language in that zone, where it is understood as something not simply human: "The prehuman, preverbal embodied logic of animal play is already essentially language-like. . . . Human language is essentially animal, from the point of view of the ludic capacities it carries" (8).

I want to suggest that we can understand even literature in the very restricted sense of fiction recognized as literary art in terms of animal territorialization. Pascale Casanova's *The World Republic of Letters* suggests as much, but without this leading her to see literature as part of a wider field of animal practices. She argues that "literature is invented through a gradual separation from political obligations: forced at first to place their art in the service of the national purposes of the state, writers little by little achieved artistic freedom through the invention of specifically literary languages" (Casanova 2004, 45–46). This is, in an obvious way, simply raising to a higher power the shift from what is to what could be that is, for Massumi, the gesture of play. This suggests that play will function at many levels, caught up in movements of de- and reterritorialization as apparatuses of capture—such as the nation-state or the school—in effect confine, restrict, and redirect play toward the aims of Man: language emerges from animal play; this language is then folded into logics of the state, and, drawing on their animal capacities, writers must then revolt by creating new language that can play at a higher level.

Casanova essentially defines literature as a form of cultural capital: a "unit of measurement for everything that is or will be recognized as literary" (2004, 15). This capital is unthinkable, like the capital analyzed by Marx, without circulation: "This capital is therefore embodied by all those who transmit it, gain possession of it, transform it, and update it" (15). Literature, as a kind of capital, circulates, and its circulation effectively instaurates (to return to Souriau's phrase) writers and readers but also "publishers, editors, critics, and especially translators" (21) as it moves. This movement, where material objects (books in particular in Casanova's account) circulate among a wide variety of institutions and bodies, creates what she calls "world literary space": "territories whose sole value and sole resource is literature, ordered by power relations that nonetheless govern the form of the texts that are written in and circulate through these lands" (4).

Literature, which in Casanova's account is the most privileged and human version of a literacy practice, can thus easily be reconceived as an animal practice of territorialization. Casanova, of course, does not say this, and her refusal of it allows me to underscore, again, just how potent Man's discipline is. Casanova writes, "Trying to make sense of a space of such gigantic complexity means having to abandon all the habits associated with specialized historical, linguistic, and cultural research, all the divisions between disciplines—which, to some extent, justify our divided view of the world—because only by going beyond those boundaries will it be possible to think outside conventional frameworks and to conceive of literary space as a worldwide reality" (5). The project is, to be sure, transdisciplinary, but Casanova's refrain of "all" masks the extent to which she is willing to go beyond only disciplinary boundaries that already presume a distinction between human and inhuman. Nowhere does she propose thinking about literature as a subset of a wider phenomenon of animal practices, for instance, nor does she attend to the animacies of any nonhuman participant in literature. To repeat a claim from earlier in this book, then, Casanova's model of distant reading does not get enough distance from literature, since it is still oriented toward and around Man. Thus, we have to back up, widen our frame.

But first, one more crucial lesson from Casanova. Writers write, for her, to join and move in this "world literary space," one that is structured by profound inequalities and systems of domination, which appear precisely because this space is always already entangled with "the political history of states" (2004, 35). Casanova, in fact, couldn't be more clear: "The birth of literature grew out of the early political history of nation-states" (35). This relation means that as I track literacy events, even those which are the most literary, I have to attune to the particular forms of domination at work, since literacy as a problematic of space and territorialization cannot be separated from the political question of how bodies (human and non-) are oriented in those spaces.

This means that I have to think not only about what bodies do in particular spaces—a question that requires me to think about how particular configurations of objects in and as space affect the bodies that move through them—but also what Sara Ahmed calls the "conditions of emergence or . . . arrival" in that space (2006, 38).[10] Ahmed's example, in the opening pages of *Queer Phenomenology*, is a perfect place to begin: the writer's table. After working through a more traditionally phenomenological account of how a table appears to her perception, Ahmed asks about "what is behind the table," which means thinking about "what must have already taken place for the table to arrive" (37). This involves, in one sense, an account of a table that works against commodity fetishism, seeing it as an object of human labor, where that labor (in logging, milling, carpentry, retail, and transportation among all those events) is sedimented in the object. Ahmed works through Marx's conception, queering it toward seeing how objects can affectively act: "The writing table thus 'tends toward' the writer. An action is possible when the body and the object 'fit'" (51). This "fit" involves particular material corporeal tendencies and relations, but those are in turn inseparable from larger histories of capitalist exploitation, genderings of social formations, and modes of ecological expropriation. Ahmed asks, then, not just after the table but after "the tools of writing: inkwell, books, pencils," and also paper: "How does the 'matter' of the paper matter?" (26).

In Ahmed's extensive reading (extensive in the sense that it pushes perception far beyond humanist frames), the simple fact of someone sitting at a table to write draws us into having to think about the gendered conditions of philosophy and economics that make it possible for some bodies (and not others) to have "a room of one's own" and the materials and time necessary to write.[11] Those materials—the table, the paper, the ink, the pencils—also involve exploitative extraction and expropriation of labor and natural resources along linked circuits of production and transformation. And the writing involves having an education, which enables one to be able to write in the restricted sense of alphabetic literacy, something that happens in a wider educational system that is, as I have been arguing, a humanizing assemblage in that this literacy comes to be defined in such a way that having it opens up certain forms of orientation—including social mobility—to some bodies, while either denying it outright to some bodies (as was the case in the United States during slavery) or using it as a mechanism of assimilation to Man with others.[12] Even when and if one has the literacy to write, and the room, and the time, and the materials, when one sits down, one is affected by every object present and everything that happens as one arrives to sit down, and everything that happens to or touches them before that. Indeed, this larger affective situation creates the conditions of possibility for the emergence of the human.

Although there have been a range of ways in which literary scholars have refused to see writing as simply the expression of authorial consciousness—from Freud's unconscious motivations, to Gertrude Stein's fascination with automatic writing, to William S. Burroughs's experiments with drugs and aleatory cutting, to deconstructive fascination with the neutral, to cybernetic experiments with autopoiesis—none of these accounts, at least on their own, comes close to attending to the enormous complexity of forces and affects that Ahmed's account summons (chapter 11 attends to this complexity). There is, in any event of animal literacy, then, a whole host of agential participants involved in the situation that animates it: an animal body, a surface of inscription, a method or tool of inscription, and a diffuse and always singular set of conditions that are constituted by a very large, but not infinite, set of objects, systems, and relations. Literacy names the site at which this meeting, this touching, takes place, and it extends far beyond the generation or circulation of meaning in events as conceived by humanists to the circulation and touching of entities and bodies in situations.

I want to suggest that we conceive of animal literacy in the following way: some animals take up various materials—processed trees, dyes, tools made from a dizzying array of things, computers fashioned from fossilized remains of prehistoric animals and mineral deposits extracted from the earth by complex assemblages of other technologies and human labor, and so on—in order to make marks. While we pressure the ways in which purportedly human activities associated with literacy must be rethought as animal practices, we also have to widen our net, as it were, to engage marking practices of nonhuman animals as literacy practices or events. Could we not think the spider weaving its web or the bird weaving its nest, to use obvious examples, as kinds of writing, ones that are always already caught up in multispecies assemblages? Among human animals, these marked surfaces or objects are then circulated in networks of exchange that involve human animals, nonhuman animals (the postal service on horseback, carrier pigeons, etc.), and machines. At some point and in particular spaces, these marked surfaces are taken up by other animals who spend their time with them. Sometimes they are solitary, but often they come together in groups. And even when the animal is the only one of its kind present, there is always a collectivity of entities in the situation animating the event.

Since the emergence of print literacy at least, the ways that these animals make, circulate, and spend time with these marks appears as a crucial factor in social hierarchization. That is, in order to have time to make and spend time with these marks, certain animals have to be exempted from the compulsion to produce and work in ways that serve the immediate biological and material needs of their animal communities. Proficiency with the marks, that is, tends to follow upon and confer a certain privilege. When, during modernity, state formations begin to invest in compulsory schooling as a result of their commitments to biopolitics and the enforcement of Man as the only permissible way of performing humanity, a basic ability to understand and manipulate these marks becomes a point of differentiation between those admitted into the human community of animals and those consigned to the outside via dehumanization. Slaves, natives, women, the subaltern, the poor—all these animals are marked as different, inferior, based in part on their (socially enforced and produced) illiteracy according to a particular and state-enforced conception of literacy which is restricted and restricting. While literacies form the material and affective milieu in which any human (or other entity) takes shape, it is only statist literacy that makes some humans Man.

Before zooming in on the ways that literacy animates human subjects and politics at the pre- or subindividual level in chapter 11, I want to consider an example of a nonhuman animal literacy practice that, I argue, requires us to conceptualize literary ethology as always entangled with ecology. Despret offers an account of an orangutan named Watana who is especially gifted at tying knots, a practice that (as even humanist historians of the book would acknowledge) must be included within the conceptual orbit of what counts as a literacy event. Despret writes:

> In controlled and filmed conditions, the experimental device consists of offering her some material for knotting and bricolage: rolls of paper, cardboard, pieces of wood, bamboo tubes, string, rope, laces, gardening stakes, and bits of cloth. As soon as the material is provided, Watana begins to knot, using her hands, feet, and mouth. She assembles and knots two ends of string, then makes a series of knots and loops, passes the loops through one another, and inserts bits of cardboard, pieces of wood, or bamboo. She creates a necklace with two strings, puts it around her neck, then throws it up in the air several times. Afterward she collects it and carefully unties it. (2016, 157)

Although this event happens in "controlled conditions," Despret notes that orangutans do "weave nests in the wild," thus returning us to the literacy event from the beginning of this chapter. What this longer description of Watana offers us though is an empirical description of the complexity of the work, the love involved in literacy, and the play between a particular animal and the nonhuman agencies of the various materials.[13] Although working from a more restricted sense of what "play" means than Massumi, Despret offers up that "these forms indicate that the pleasure [for Watana] is not just for play but that they're meaningful, that they express an *act of generating forms*" (157). The playful, meaningful generation of forms that happens when a confluence of animating entities come into contact: this is a literacy event.

I want to briefly underscore "generating" here, for it allows Despret to signal how ideas about what counts as literacy have tended to disavow both animal literacy practices and the practices of human women. She is interested in Watana's untying of the knots, since "untying the knots is just as important as the tying itself" (Despret 2016, 157). This observation leads Despret to write, "Like the problem that archaeology faces with the discoveries of women's inventions—collection baskets or baby slings—the artifacts of animals have left very few traces, which hardly honors the fact of their having a role in history, or even having a history itself" (157). Obviously riffing on Hegel's famous restriction of "having history" to mean having preserved, written history, Despret signals how a particular presupposition about what to include within histories of literacy ends up working in tandem with a masculinist and eventually statist and imperialist conception of literacy: the marks must endure.[14]

This presupposition has enormous, if barely perceptible ecological consequences.[15] As I traced in chapter 7, scholars have tended to see the historical shifts in writing technologies from knots, to clay, to papyrus, to wax, to paper, and most recently into binary code stored in cyberspace in terms of differential abilities to endure and circulate in some kind of fixed, legible form. Unsurprisingly, given how much logging, petroleum-driven processing, and chemical transformation and fixing is involved with paper, the widespread use of paper-based print literacy, which is a condition of possibility for the violent machinations of Man's humanizing assemblages in Western imperialist modernity, is part and parcel of Man's becoming a "geological agent" in the Anthropocene.[16] That is, the material, ecological costs of producing Man (and not just being human, as Sylvia Wynter powerfully insists) quite literally transform the geology of the Earth in ways that threaten to make Man's civilization, if not human existence itself, extinct.

There is a perverse fetishization growing today—bound up with what Christopher Breu (2014) calls "avatar fetishism"—which is inseparable from the rise of green capitalism on the one hand and the digital humanities on the other. It sees a turn away from paper toward virtual literacy as an ecologically sensitive alternative.[17] Jussi Parikka, in *The Anthrobscene*, tries to track what has to be disavowed for this fetishistic fantasy to be sustained. He writes in order to "remind ourselves of the environmentally disastrous consequences of planned obsolescence of electronic media, the energy costs of digital culture, and, for instance, the neocolonial arrangements of material and energy extraction across the globe" (Parikka 2014, 6). In digital literacies, we may be able to pretend there is less materiality than with paper, but this ignores how the immaterial print of binary code is only there thanks to (1) devices that require enormous amounts of non-renewable metals and substances that have to be extracted in ecologically damaging and politically neocolonial assemblages, and which will endure in landfills after their three- to five-year usefulness for tens of thousands of years; and (2) the enormously harmful extraction and processing of fossil fuels that make computers, and all other aspects of our highly petroleumized world, possible: "Cloud computing is still to a large extent powered by carbon emission–heavy energy production" (29).

Staying with this trouble, it is virtually impossible to imagine a way for literacy to be maintained as it is customarily thought within imperialist humanism and its humanizing assemblages that is in any way ecologically sustainable. Literacy in this restricted sense then is not simply a site where intrahuman violence of racial, gendered, and (neo)colonial hierarchization takes place; it also participates in the humanist destruction of the Earth as a site of human and nonhuman flourishing.

Unless.[18] Watana's unweaving, and Despret's situating it in relation to a host of ephemeral practices associated with female creativity, reminds us that literacy and its pleasures do not necessarily have to take shape in permanent ways, ways that endure, that can be preserved in libraries so that they can take on importance for Man's history of itself. We might begin to move away from Man, then, by looking toward other pleasures than writing for posterity. We might attune to and affirm furtive, fugitive, ephemeral literacy events, events that cannot be captured by Man and the state, and which refuse precisely the drive toward temporal endurance that structures what Tavia Nyong'o calls "the pedagogical temporality of the nation-state" (2009, 163). There might be, then, a wild literacy that refuses capture and, thus, other possibilities for performing the human far outside of the grasp of the state.

11

WHAT HAPPENS WHEN I READ?

Throughout *Animate Literacies*, I have practiced methods of literary analysis that are the default mode of attention in humanist literary studies, but I have also tried to pull back the frame of my focus significantly in order to see those literacy events as embedded in a wider field of literacy practices not only among humans (entangled with imperialist state formations) but among nonhuman animals, and to attune to how those events rely upon and emerge from the direct, but seldom noticed, participation of a range of material, nonhuman agencies. In this chapter, I want to zoom in to the preindividual level of corporeal systems and affective encounters that happen largely outside of conscious awareness. I thus propose different but complementary ways of conceptualizing the literacy event as suspended within a much wider milieu I call the *literacy situation*. This literacy situation happens, we could say, "beyond, beneath and beside" the literacy event (Sedgwick 2003, 8). The first part of this chapter maps accounts of why literary reading matters, especially as part of political projects that are explicitly decolonial, feminist, queer, and Marxist. I find these accounts generally persuasive, but also unhelpfully abstract, which prompts me to zoom in below the level of the subject to attune to the pre-personal scene of affective encounters in the literacy situation. I argue that it is in this situation, and not primarily in the events that emerge from it, that the politics of reading adhere. At stake in this chapter is a more precise, but still necessarily open-ended and blurry, account of what it means to say that we can become bewildered through literacy events.

It makes sense to begin, I think, with one of the better statements on what humanistic close reading has to offer: Edward Said's *Humanism and Democratic Criticism*. As one of the founding scholars of postcolonial studies, Said's career was spent analyzing the ways that Western European cultural and intellectual production was always complicit in modernity with the imperial mission of Western nation-states. And yet, Said discerns in the humanism that was coemergent with modern imperialism a kind of counterforce to the more violent and colonialist tendencies. Summoning the secular project of humanism (associated with Wynter's Man₁), Said argues that, "schooled in its abuses by the experience of Eurocentrism and empire, one could fashion a different kind of humanism that was cosmopolitan and text-and-language-bound in ways that absorbed the great lessons of the past . . . and still remain attuned to the emergent voices and currents of the present, many of them exilic, extraterritorial, and unhoused, as well as uniquely American" (2004, 11). That is, Said sees something in humanism's form of attention to literacy events (it is "text-and-language-bound") that enables it to be repurposed from Man and its empire toward other, more "cosmopolitan" politics. The key, for Said, is the insistence upon the human: "The core of humanism is the secular notion that the historical world is made by men and women, and not by God, and that it can be understood rationally according to the principle formulated by Vico in *New Science*, that we can really know only what we make or, to put it differently, we can know things according to the way they were made" (11). In this account, what makes humanism humanist is the secular view that the world is made by men ("world" is etymologically related to the human), which means that anything manmade that exists can be critically known and thus remade by them.

This vision is, in different forms, part of the DNA of Marxist, feminist, postcolonial, antiracist, and queer critique. It is this that authorizes our interest in scouring archives past and present for the signs of the world's contingency—it doesn't need to be this way—and for the strategies developed by others in order to resist what Said (2004, 22) calls "the state of affairs" in the world today. My interest is less in abandoning this general thrust than in drawing on those same modes of politically driven critique in order to suggest that this vision need not—and indeed should not—be restricted to the human, nor can it be grasped by treating the subject as the default unit of analysis.[1] For Said, humanism's "purpose is to make things available to critical scrutiny as the product of human labor, human energies for emancipation and enlightenment, and, just as importantly, human misreadings and misinterpretations of the collective past and present" (22). While it would be silly to deny that some of the energies that make up our world can be referred to humans, Said's focus here is both synecdochic and symptomatic of Man's restriction of attention.

I want to move from the abstract level of polemical statement in favor of humanistic attention to what I call the *middle level* of a reader and a text by returning to the linked but divergent accounts of Lynn Hunt and Sylvia Wynter discussed in chapter 4. In Hunt's account, the kinds of reading practices associated with the emergence of the novel in the eighteenth century make possible "new emotions" (empathy) that in turn give "human rights . . . political content" (2007, 21). The key, for her, is how the form of these texts (mainly epistolary novels) enabled readers to "empathize across traditional social boundaries between nobles and commoners, masters and servants, men and women, perhaps even adults and children. As a consequence, they came to see others—people they did not know personally—as like them, as having the same kinds of inner emotions. Without this learning process, 'equality' could have no deep meaning and in particular no political consequence" (40). Novels then represent feelings (what Hunt calls "interiority") and reading them generates feelings. One particular kind of feeling—empathy—translates into the political conception of equality, which is the real, material, affective content of the abstract belief in human equality proposed in human rights discourse. Hunt uses two different phrases to think about how novels do this: "brain changes" (33) and "identification" (42), and I will take each of these up in more detail.

But first, I want to review Wynter's argument about sociogenesis as a way of reconfiguring and slightly shifting Hunt's claim. In tracking how literature sociogenically interfaces with the human in a postfeudal political landscape in Europe, Wynter writes that "these new [secular] systems would thereby effect an ongoing evolutionary shift at the level of the aesthetic processes of co-identification, which would accompany the evolutionary processes of human epistemology" (1984, 51). Wynter's language posits aesthetic texts as part of the evolutionary development of the human, as one of the contributing factors—along with genetics and the environment—that inescapably shape the corporeal and political becoming of the human. We might say that she sees humans as what Samantha Frost calls "biocultural creature[s]," which means they "become what they distinctively are through the habits that culture them" (2016, 5). For the human at least, this culturing includes aesthetic, or literary, texts. The problem, for Wynter, is that, as these texts circulate ideas about what it is to be and "be like" a human after 1492, they overrepresent a highly particular and restricted version of this human—Man—as the human.[2] It matters enormously then which texts we read and how we read, for these literacy events end up bioculturally shaping the ways we are embodied by the world and the ways we embody it.[3]

This means that while Hunt is not wrong per se about the relation between reading, changes in cognition, and politics, she does not attend enough to how the version of human operative in eighteenth-century French and English epistolary novels is Man, not the human as such. And in taking that version of the human as simply "the" human, the human rights law that emerges in Western Europe and the United States is inescapably, structurally inseparable from the post-1492 history of imperialism that generates European colonization and the transatlantic slave trade. Remembering this—or, to return to the early pages of this book, becoming haunted by it—allows a less celebratory and more suspicious account of the work done by literacy as it is entangled with state apparatuses. It means remembering, as Gayatri Spivak puts it, riffing on Derrida's *pharmakon*, that "literacy is a poison as well as a medicine" (1997, 483).

Dwelling more on the process of identification can help to underscore both literacy's function as pharmakon and the complexity of the event. By drawing on Diana Fuss's feminist and queer rethinking of the Freudian concept of identification, it's possible to see Hunt as privileging one of the possibilities for identification, but downplaying its other possible directionalities and forces. For Fuss, "identifications are mobile, elastic and volatile" (1995, 8), not unidirectional and simply generative as Hunt seems to suggest. While identification can take the form of a relation that recognizes commonality (I am like another) it can also signal the attachment to an ego ideal (what I hope to be like) or a desire to have, possess, or even consume: "*every* identification involves a degree of symbolic violence, a measure of temporary mastery and possession" (9). That is, identification involves violence.

The process of identification doesn't just operate by linking an existing self to an imagined or imaginary other that occupies an as-if relation to reality. Identification actually remakes the reading self. That is, the interiority that serves as the middle term between self and other is generative in both directions: reading makes a reader imagine herself as having the kind of interiority that she simultaneously recognizes in the other. Something like this is implicit in Hunt's claim about "brain changes": reading corporeally, affectively changes the reading self. Before getting to the neuroscience of this, I can put it as Fuss does: "Identification is the detour through the other that defines a self" (1995, 2). It does this, in part, by "operat[ing] as a mark of self-difference, opening up a space for the self to relate to itself as a self" (2). That is, it functions only at the site where a literacy event splits the self. This splitting of the self from itself, as I have argued, is generated in the humanizing assemblages that produce Man.

So identification can do what Hunt says it does only through a kind of violence. Reading novels as a humanizing practice necessitates the splitting of the self and the rewriting of the self as it exists in another mode. It is precisely here that we see the generative violence of the shift from human to Man at stake in Wynter's theorization. But, thankfully, this identification turns out to be more fragile than Hunt allows. Fuss insists upon "the astonishing capacity of identifications to reverse and disguise themselves, to multiply and contravene one another, to disappear and reappear years later [that] renders identity profoundly unstable and perpetually open to radical change" (1995, 2). This is so, in the most basic way, because for identification to function as the always ongoing motor of a self's sustenance, "a subject . . . must bear the traces of each and every encounter with the external world" (3). That is, because a self is porous, "leaky," and open to the alterity of texts and the world, it is always being renegotiated and reconfigured (Manning 2013).

Taking identification's multiplicity, complexity, and uncertainty into account renders the stability of any human's identification with Man fragile.[4] And it reveals a very particular site of political possibility, one that Wynter (1984) seizes upon in her call for new ceremonies that would move us away from Man and toward the human by engaging different narratives about what it is and what it is to be like a human. Drawing on Judith Butler's Bodies That Matter, Fuss argues that "Butler's comments on disidentification go even farther in encouraging a reconceptualization of the political, laying out the theoretical groundwork for a politics of affiliation fully cognizant of the sacrifices, reversals, and reparations involved in every identity formation" (1995, 7). Two things follow from this concept for me. The first is that instead of a literacy event drawing together a human and a novel automatically leading to an identification for the reader that would suture her to Man, we can imagine these events producing disidentifications with Man. Second, while I entirely support Wynter's call for new narratives of what it means to be human that offer alternatives to Man, disidentification also allows us to think not just about what is read, but how reading transpires. That is, there exist modes of disidentificatory literacy that can read even, say, eighteenth-century novels against the grain.

Let me give a brief, and perhaps obvious, example. Mary Shelley's 1819 novel *Frankenstein* stages, in almost melodramatic fashion, a scene of literacy in which a creature identifies with Man but cannot be recognized as Man. This staging is, in a displaced form, a way of signaling how Shelley, as a woman and a writer at the beginning of the nineteenth century, was consigned to less than fully human status. When Frankenstein's monster, after offering a fascinating account of his own fugitive literacy education, encounters Milton's *Paradise Lost* and Goethe's novel *The Sorrows of Young Werther*, his account to Victor Frankenstein of "the effect of these books" turns entirely on Man.[5] He says, "As I read . . . I applied much personally to my own feelings and condition. I found myself similar, yet at the same time strangely unlike the beings concerning whom I read, and to those whose conversations I was a listener. I sympathized with, and partly understood them, but I was unformed in mind; I was dependent on none, and related to none" (Shelley 2012, 89). The monster's awareness of his loneliness as the only one of his kind is here in constant tension with the identificatory work of Man in the classics of Western literature. Like the women, slaves, and colonized produced as constitutive outsides by humanizing assemblages, the monster senses that while he may well approach all the attributes of the fully human person in terms of cognition, literacy, and emotional development, he will never be recognized as Man. The structural doubling of humanizing education—which takes the human as a particular creature dialectically distinguished from its constitutive outsides and as a telos of *Bildung*—politically seizes upon the prior understanding. Monsters, no matter how humanly they behave and even are, are still monsters.

I return to Shelley's novel in chapter 14 because it provides a fascinating case for considering many of the questions raised in *Animate Literacies*.

What I'm interested in here is the fact that so many feminist and queer readers of this novel identify not with Victor as representative of Man (something that the novel's form, as Hunt reads it, would enable), but with the monster. Jack Halberstam, in *Skin Shows*, argues that "the novel is not about the making of a monster[;] its subject is the construction of humanness" (1995, 43), a construction that is, in fact, monstrous. Indeed, Halberstam's reading of the novel is premised on precisely what I'm calling a disidentification with Man that corresponds to an identification with the inhuman monster. He writes, "The monster, in fact, is where we come to know ourselves as never-human, as always between humanness and monstrosity. Just as, for the monster, paradise is always lost in *Frankenstein*, so, for the reader, humanity—humane treatment of others, justice, etc.—is always beyond our reach" (37). In a similar vein, trans theorist Susan Stryker writes, "Like the monster, I too am often perceived as less than fully human due to my embodiment; like the monster's as well, my exclusion from human community fuels a deep and abiding rage in me that I, like the monster, direct against the conditions in which I must struggle to exist" (cited in Barad 2015, 392).[6]

Reading does not have predictable effects, or, as Stryker's reading signals, affects (not everyone in every context will have their reading generate rage). J. Hillis Miller has written eloquently about this unpredictability:

> What happens when I read, when I *really* read, which does not happen all that often? What happens is something always fortuitous and unpredictable, something surprising, however many times the book in question has been read before, even by me. One way to define this unexpected quality of true acts of reading is to say that they never correspond exactly to what other readers tell me I am going to find when I read that book, however learned, expert, and authoritative those previous readers have been. Another way to describe what is unpredictable about a genuine act of reading is to say that reading is always the disconfirmation or modification of presupposed literary theory rather than its confirmation. What happens when I read a particular book never quite fits my theory (or anyone else's) of what is going to happen. You can never be sure what is going to happen when someone in a particular situation reads a particular book. Rather than thinking of all those books on the shelf as the sure and safe repository of the values of

Western culture, the army of unalterable law ranged in rows, it might be better to think of them as so many unexploded bombs that may have who knows what result when they get read by the right (or the wrong) person at the right (or the wrong) place or time. A book is a dangerous object, and perhaps all books should have warning labels. Strange things happen when someone reads a book. (1990, 20–21)

At the time of writing this, he was a professor of comparative literature at Yale and one of the preeminent critics of the so-called "Yale School" that is credited with bringing deconstruction to the American academy. That is, this is a person who spent most of his time reading and was indeed enormously famous for doing just that, and yet even for him "really" reading is a rare occurrence. This opens up a set of questions about attention and attunement. Additionally, he tends to pitch this unexpectedness as a question of how one interprets a book in relation to traditional scholarship, but his explosive metaphors at the end suggest that reading has effects that cannot be restricted to the cognitive or intellectual. Finally, the passage suggests an ambivalent relation to "Western culture" as both the only imaginable horizon of one's reading, and as a tradition that might become exploded through the contact zone of reading, which is always situational, corporeal, unexpected.[7]

Gayatri Spivak is interested in something similar in *Death of a Discipline*, where she imagines reading "as transgression of the text" (2003, 55). Indeed, for her reading comes to be far less about generating interpretations or even learning to disagree with traditions that circulate in the academy than about a particular set of affects and effects. I will come back to her text later because it offers one of the most compelling formulations I have come across of how literacy, the human, and nonhumanist forms of community emerge, but I want to signal here two things she offers as effects of reading. First, it can "perhaps rearrange our desires" (23). This might take many forms, of course, but one that is implicit and rhizomatically articulated throughout her book is that it can undo our desire to be Man.[8] Second, it can generate an affective shift from fear of uncertainty associated with Man's fetishization of planning toward an acceptance and even affirmation of this uncertainty: "Let literature teach us that there are no certainties, that the process is open, and that it may be altogether salutary that it is so" (20). Not only is reading itself an uncertain process, but enabling a particular openness toward and even politically driven affirmation of this uncertainty is, perhaps, one of literature's most crucial effects.

But how can literature enable this? Or, put differently, how can we account for the open-ended, unexpected ways in which literacy events can lead to what Elizabeth Grosz (2011) calls our "becoming undone"? I want to suggest that in order to really understand this, we have to widen our frame beyond the human by zooming in to the role of nonconscious processes of the humanimal body and the animacies of the nonhumans which collide with that body in the contact zone of literacy. The starting point here is a basic recognition of what Hayles calls "the posthuman view," which "considers consciousness, regarded as the seat of human identity in the Western tradition long before Descartes thought he was a mind thinking, as an epiphenomenon, as an evolutionary upstart trying to claim that it is the whole show when in actuality it is only a minor sideshow" (1999, 2–3). What we have to cultivate, then, is attention not just to conscious events of meaning generation, but also to "the forms of materiality that resist, exceed, and exist in tension with the cultural and the linguistic" (Breu 2014, 3). "Beyond, beneath and beside" the conscious work that most humanists take as the scene of humanistic literacy is a whole swarming, networked, distributed, and mind-bogglingly complex world of movement, affect, and touching (Sedgwick 2003, 8).

This involves, as Christopher Breu has poignantly argued, learning "to fully attend to the materiality of our bodies." To do this, "we need to insist on the ways in which the materiality of language (as well as the forms of subjectivity shaped by language) and the materiality of the body not only interpenetrate and merge but also remain importantly distinct and sometimes form in contradiction to each other" (2014, 9). To begin to sketch such an attunement, then, requires a caveat: that as I look to neuroscience and other sciences to learn how to attune this wider confluence of agencies, I cannot forget the lesson of so much theory associated with the cultural turn: that these discourses too are discourses, not literal presentations of facts that are free from either political entanglement or the distorting, blurring, constraining effects of human languages.[9] We need here a kind of interpretive agnosticism, since, as Eve Sedgwick reminds us, "the line between words and things or between linguistic and nonlinguistic phenomena is endlessly changing, permeable, and entirely unsusceptible to any definitive articulation" (2003, 6).

To begin to zoom in now, I want to think fairly straightforwardly about what happens to a human brain when literacy events transpire. Maryanne Wolf argues, like Hunt, that "when reading takes place . . . th[e] individual brain is forever changed, both physiologically and intellectually" (2007, 5). The latter is, of course, what has always mattered to humanists like Said, so I focus on the former. Wolf builds her account of the complexity of reading through a single example: reading a 233-word excerpt from Marcel Proust's *À la recherche du temps perdu*. Instead of simply describing this, she asks the reader to read the passage as quickly as possible and then retroactively tracks back to draw out what just happened without, for the most part, the reader being consciously aware of it. I want to quote at length:

> In response to this request [to read Proust quickly], you engaged an array of mental or cognitive processes: attention; memory; visual, auditory, and linguistic processes. Promptly, your brain's attentional and executive systems began to plan how to read Proust speedily and still understand it. Next, your visual system raced into action, swooping quickly across the page, forwarding its gleanings about letter shapes, word forms, and common phrases to linguistic systems awaiting the information. These systems rapidly connected subtly differentiated visual symbols with essential information about the sounds contained in the words. Without a single moment of conscious awareness, you applied highly automatic rules about the sounds of letters in the English writing system, and used a great many linguistic processes to do so. . . . As you applied all these rules, you activated a battery of relevant language and comprehension processes with a rapidity that still astounds researchers. To take one example from the language domain, when you read the 233 words in Proust's passage, your word meaning, or semantic, systems contributed every possible meaning of each word you read and incorporated the exact correct meaning for each word in its context. (Wolf 2007, 7–8)

This excerpt doesn't even include what happens in cognition when the reader moves beyond Proust's words to compare the meaning of the text to the reader's experiential knowledge in order to find comparisons and reference points to understand the denotative and connotative meaning (10). And yet Wolf's account here, which is itself highly contracted and condensed, does a good job of underscoring both the extraordinary neurological or cognitive complexity of reading and the speed of it. Her account lets me return to Hayles to say that the conscious portion of what happens in reading is only the tiniest fraction of the cognitive activity taking place, and that consciousness turns out to have an extraordinarily slow running speed compared with the corporeal systems, always plural, that are always functioning even within a body.

In order to attune to how reading not only relies upon but changes thinking processes, we have to scan beyond the brain. William Connolly's *Neuropolitics* puts us on track, writing that "thinking is a complex, layered activity, with each layer contributing something to an ensemble of dissonant relays and feedback loops between numerous centers. These loops include many different bodily sites sending signals about the state of the body to the brain" (2002, 10). In the first instance, this supports Wolf's linking of the brain to a visual system—what Donna Haraway calls "our bodies endowed with primate colour and stereoscopic vision" (1991, 190)—when reading, or our similarly primate auditory capacities when hearing spoken language, and tactile fingers when reading Braille. But what's at stake is not simply the input of sensory information from eyes, ears, and fingers that is then translated into thinking in conceptual terms. We also have to consider here Elizabeth Wilson's polemical challenge to the restriction of cognition to the brain in *Gut Feminism*, which argues that mentation takes place not just in the brain or central nervous system (which processes information from a dispersed set of bodily zones) but also throughout the body: in the gut, or what she often calls "the substrata" (2015, 63).[10] Theorizing the "disseminating, multiplying, and mobilizing mind" (106), Wilson proposes that the entire body actually thinks.

As Connolly argues, our nervous systems are given to what he calls "side perceptions" that function at the level of infraconscious perception. These are things that enter our body's perceptual system, agitating or informing our consciousness without being available to conscious processing. Taking up the gap between a body's senses or gut mentations and the cognitive processing of what enters there in consciousness, Connolly argues that "perception . . . seems pure and unmediated to us. But it is not. It is a double-entry activity guided by the concerns of possible action. . . . Perception is subtractive, and the virtual memories mobilized during it help to determine what is subtracted" (2002, 26–27). That is, the most crucial task of perception is a sorting and filtering of the flood of sensation in order to let some of it into consciousness.

This gap is, as affect theorists have argued, precisely where two crucial events take place that have enormous political consequences or, maybe more accurately, enormous consequences for how we think the political.[11] Building on these theories, I would say that in the literacy situation, before any consciousness knows the body is perceiving something, let alone interpreting it, it is already responding at a neurological level, which leads to shifts in both the affective system (in the sense of affects as something like feelings) and the body's motor capacities. That is, already before we know we are sensing a thing, we are moving toward or away from it corporeally, and we are being moved by it in the sense that our emotional or affective state is being modulated. This lets me say that not only is feeling or emotion a kind of knowledge, it also seems to be the case that all knowledge in the sense of conscious cognition is belated, arriving on the scene in a certain mood that primes the body to think it. This is the scene of what Brian Massumi (2015) calls "ontopower," where state apparatuses—via their amanuenses like schools, the military, and other institutions of discipline and control—work on our bodies' perceptual systems directly. His specific examples are drawn from the way that a post-9/11 US government modulates fear and suspicion in the populace, but his account can be recalibrated for other contexts. At stake is how we become subjectivized as the kinds of creatures who are primed to respond to the unexpected in particular ways that are amenable to the imperialist state. Politics, then, is no longer simply a matter of conscious resistance or acquiescence, nor is it a matter of representation: it is about perception, attention, movement. All of this happens "below the personal stratum [where] it [is] no longer human, but precisely organic" (Protevi 2009, 135).

This gap between what affects us and what we consciously think, where the latter is miniscule compared to the flooding of the body's senses, is also precisely where most nonhuman agency touches the reader. In some way, we all know this, which is why Teresa Brennan can open *The Transmission of Affect* with the question, "Is there anyone who has not, at least once, walked into a room and 'felt the atmosphere'?" (2004, 1). The room, or whatever environment a body moves through, affects that body, moving it in the double sense I drew out above. As Brennan puts it, "The transmission of affect, if only for an instant, alters the biochemistry and neurology of the subject" (1). How can we locate these circulating affects in a scene of reading? Thinking back to Sara Ahmed's (2006) *Queer Phenomenology*, we can start by thinking about the objects and furniture that make the reading possible: a chair or couch with particular upholstery and cushioning, perhaps a coffee table or a carpet where our feet rest.[12] If it is daylight, the relative conditions of the sun passing into the room through windows creates a certain mood (we might need to reverse the directionality of the pathetic fallacy here). If that light is not sufficient for our primary ocular capacities, we light candles or turn on lamps. There might be music playing—some Ornette Coleman, or Brahms, or Brian Eno, or Sunn O)))—or the so-called "ambient noise" might recede from conscious attention or press in on consciousness. Perhaps there is the sound of birds or crickets or barking dogs, or a hum from electrical appliances. The room will have a temperature, which might make you more or less aware of the relative weight of your clothing. You might need a blanket, or to remove a sweater.

I'm imagining, of course, conditions in which we—by we, I mean academics mostly—have control of such things, and the enumeration so far has been idyllic. For our students, and for us, things can be more hectic: the blaring of the stereo, the flickering of multiple LCD screens, yelling children at home or peers in the residence halls, traffic sounds, fighting neighbors, gunshots. The room might smell like freshly baked bread, or patchouli incense, or body odor that accumulates with heat, or the noxious pollution caused by a factory down the road.

Although generating such lists has become a methodological principle in some versions of posthumanist theory, the point I want to make here is rather straightforward: a literally infinite set of agencies appears around the edges of any scene of reading, and they are part of that scene.[13] All of that—the smells, sounds, sensations, tastes, visions—enters into the perceptual system, and while a very disciplined reader can subtract out a lot of it to get caught up in or carried away by the book, all of us know what it's like to have our attention split and dispersed. The attention required for literacy events is, then, a question of a subtractive relation to the totality of what is perceived by a body as it, even if sitting still, exists in a rush of agentic movement of things that always affect that body, and in affecting it, shift its affects.

The list of affects associated with reading requires, again, a litany. While the most narrowly disciplined aesthete might try to claim some

Kantian binary of simply beautiful and sublime, there are, as again we all know, many more: bland interest, heart-racing thrills, boredom, disgust, sexual arousal, anger, frustration, anxiety, relaxation, heartbreak, depression, discomfort, bewilderment, and so on.[14] I expand on this point in chapter 13 as a way of widening the frame to attend to the politics of literacy. The point I want to make more directly here is that some of this can be referred back to the scene as imagined by humanists where a reader responds simply to the words on the page in particular formal arrangements. But not all of it, maybe even not most of it. Some of it, which is entirely inseparable from the effects and affects of reading, comes from the body's being affected by all the other agencies caught up in the contact zone I call the literacy situation.

It might happen due to memory, such as when a word or a phrase or a scene recalls for us something from our own past (which, as Wolf argues, is neurologically necessary for any act of reading). Or it might be that our affective state is due to something not, strictly speaking, part of the text: the way a book feels in our hands, or smells, or looks; the way a dying candle can diminish our energy for focused reading; the way a particular fabric rubbing our skin generates a kind of erotic pleasure that feeds into the significatory practice.

But this affective openness, this constitutive porosity of both our bodies and the contact zone of literacy, is also where the politics of reading appear (and not, as some scholars seem to think, only in matters of representation, although those clearly matter too). Drawing on affect theory as well as Wynter's extension of Fanon's notion of sociogenesis, we have to say that our somatic, corporeal responses to things—the functioning of our bodies' perceptive and affective systems—are organizationally shaped by political categories and forces. As Protevi puts it, "The differential relations of our autonomous reactions and their approving or disapproving reception by others form patterns of acculturation by which we are gendered and racialized as well as attuned to gender, race, and other politically relevant categories" (2009, 35). Because to be Man one has to identify with and be identified as having a race, a gender, a class, and a sexuality, those categories (which are part of Man's humanizing assemblages and their production of subjects) shape how we feel, perceive, and respond to the world. Given how those categories are related to restrictions upon movement and orientation in space, the particular nonhuman agencies affecting readers are likely to be analyzable in raced, classed, and gendered terms.[15] In addition to all of this, to be Man is to have disciplined one's perceptual system in such a way that one does not attend or attune to the nonhuman forces acting in and as the literacy situation. If, as Sara Ahmed (2008) says, there is a politics of attention, there is a politics of perception too.

Thus, when reading happens, there is no such thing as a single meaning generated from a text by an ideal, disinterested, unmarked subject. As reader response theory studied with great vigor, the race, gender, class, sexuality, and social positionality of the readers has everything to do with the kinds of meanings that get made, the kinds of identifications and disidentifications that are generated.[16] But those readers are not simply responding to a text via a sense of themselves as instances of identity categories: they also respond to an entire affective scene of contact among their body, a material and semiotic text, and the ensemble of human and nonhuman agencies affecting them at every moment, even if those touchings do not appear to their consciousness.[17] This scene is what I call the literacy situation. Indeed, as Sedgwick insists, "It is the insufficiency of the fit between the affective system and the cognitive system—and between either of these and the drive system—that enables learning, development, continuity, and differentiation" (2003, 107).

Let me loop back to the way that reading enables brain changes. Maryanne Wolf writes, "The generative capacity of reading parallels the fundamental plasticity in the circuit wiring of our brains: both permit us to go beyond the particulars of a given. The rich associations, inferences, and insights emerging from this capacity allow, and indeed invite, us to reach beyond the specific content of what we read to form new thoughts. In this sense reading both reflects and reenacts the brain's capacity for cognitive breakthrough" (2007, 17). Through repetition—think of the complexity of the work done with just those 233 words of Proust, and repeat it for the entirety of that three-thousand-or-so-page novel, and across a lifetime of reading—the circuitry of the brain is constantly remapped due to a biocultural plasticity.[18] There is, then, no such thing as simply a "brain." Brains are always emergent in particular bodies—ones with sensory, affective, perceptive, cognitive, sexual, motor, hormonal, and so on, systems— that are always acting and being affected by what the poet Li Young Lee calls "this room and everything in it," and everything in every room and space they ever move through. This brings us back to the politics of orientation, of movement, of circulation. For how and where a body moves or is allowed to move is inescapably written into the body, into the brain, into the subject, and into the meanings generated when that subject collides with other entities in literacy.

So, yes, reading changes us, but the agency for this change is dispersed far beyond a human consciousness, and this change includes affects and effects that are seldom part of the humanist account. What happens when I read is unpredictable, finally, because of the unanticipatable participation of a host of agentic participants in the literacy situation that are making me up as a reading thing. The following two chapters extend this argument, first by focusing more narrowly on one type of affective collision—smell—that is almost never discussed as part of literacy events. This counterintuitive inclusion of smell within literacy situations is motivated by a close reading of James Joyce's *A Portrait of the Artist as a Young Man*, and following the novel's attentions to Stephen's animality leads me to chapter 13, where I unfurl a much wider field of pleasures caught up in literacy than are usually posited. This allows me to claim both that literacy is inescapably erotic, and that it is precisely in the erotics and pleasures of literacy that literature's imbrication in social violence and dehumanization become most apparent.

12

THE SMELL OF LITERATURE

After chapter 11's proliferation of affective encounters that take place in literacy situations, I want now to focus on one: smell. This focus is animated, in part, by how Man has tended to view smell as one of the lowest, most animal of the human senses, a denigration that makes me feel like recuperating it. One consequence of this is that aside from some fascinating experiments with olfactory art brought to my attention by Hsuan Hsu, there has not been considerable attention paid to olfactory aesthetics, or the role of smell in aesthetic experience.[1] And yet, as I argue, smell is a crucial part of the politics of orienting bodies that happens in literacy situations (and, occasionally, events). Unsurprisingly, smell as an affective capacity is captured by statist regimes of discipline and control, which modulate literacies of smell in humanizing assemblages.

In *Civilization and Its Discontents*, Sigmund Freud offers what is probably the most famous statement on this matter. One of the book's central theses is that "it is impossible to overlook the extent to which civilization is built up upon a renunciation of instinct, how much it presupposes precisely the non-satisfaction (by suppression, repression or some other means?) of powerful instincts" (Freud 2005, 84). In the wake of Massumi's (2014) transvaluation of instinct as precisely the source of the (human) animal's play, and therefore semiotic capacities, it is tempting to see this not as about renunciation per se but about what Freud would call sublimation or what I think is better conceptualized as reorientation, redirection, or disciplining. Freud's footnote in chapter 4 clarifies what this has to do with smell, and the (human) animal body. Writing about how children have to learn disgust when confronted with the smell of their excrement, Freud briefly speculates on how "such a reversal of values would scarcely be possible if the substances that are expelled from the body were not doomed by their strong smells to share the fate which overtook olfactory stimuli after man adopted the erect posture" (2005, 88). That is, for Freud it is the human's uprightness that shifts its relation to smell and makes smell itself "doomed" in terms of its role in Man's civilization. After such a shift in humanimal posture, it becomes possible to downplay the importance of smell and foreground vision.[2] This shift enables Man to have contempt for nonhuman animals whose orientation in the world is still propelled by smell. Freud singles out here the dog, "an animal whose dominant sense is that of smell and one which has no horror of excrement, and that is not ashamed of its sexual functions" (88). What Freud here signals is another version of the splitting that happens in order to make the human animal into Man: the human has to doom one of its crucial sensory capacities (that is, redirect its engagements with the world), and this splitting leads to a projective contempt for the nonhuman animals whose sense of smell orients them in the world. Like a lot of the projective operations of Man, I'm interested in how this is a fantasy that belies the extent to which human animals too are oriented by smell. Indeed, I'd like to now think about smell as a crucial part of any literacy situation, and in so doing follow Roy Sellars's argument that the "sense of smell in reading should not be neglected" (1997, 185).

My point of departure is James Joyce's *A Portrait of the Artist as a Young Man*, a novel that is routinely held up as one of the pinnacles of the modernist novel. Taking a cue from Donovan Schaefer's argument that *Ulysses* "might be called a piece of animal literature" (2016, 134), I want to foreground how for Joyce language is not a site of the human's greatest divergence from other animals. Rather, for Schaefer the text insists on "the intermingling of language with bodies" (120). What emerges from this is a conception of language as extrahuman or more-than-human, as "an accident, an uneven and inconsistent material web that can stick to human experience but is only adventitiously embedded in our processes of embodied determination" (124). I suggest that Joyce moves toward not only a corporeal, fleshy account of language and literacy, but crucially links his protagonist Stephen's own literacy practices to smell, prefiguring what I call a literacy of smell, one that is operative in a wide variety of animals.[3]

The five chapters chart the *Bildung* of Stephen Dedalus, a young Irish boy growing up and being educated in a British colony. The telos of the book, as the title suggests, is Stephen's becoming an artist, a telos that is figured in two linked ways. First, Stephen spends the last pages of the book detailing a theory of aesthetics that is often taken to be Joyce's theory of aesthetics, and one that critics therefore use as a map of how to make sense of the book.[4] The reading I offer below is motivated by calling this interpretation into question. Second, the book ends with Stephen deciding to leave colonial Ireland and go into exile so that he can be free to practice his art. This double end, then, necessitates thinking about relations between aesthetics and Man's colonialist politics, and I approach that entanglement by focusing on how Joyce's presentation of Stephen's movement toward art is thoroughly bodied and corporeal: indeed, it is oriented by Stephen's sense of smell.

The novel foregrounds, repeatedly, Stephen's perception that his life is shaped by British colonial power and its intersections with the imperial functions of the Church.[5] Put differently, Stephen's becoming is inescapably entangled with Man's institutions and humanizing assemblages. I want to begin with one site of this entanglement: language. Beginning with a scene of young Stephen overhearing the adults debate politics and religion (never separable in the context of Irish colonialism), we read an adult refer to "the language with which the priests' pawns broke [Irish nationalist revolutionary] Parnell's heart and hounded him to his grave" (Joyce 1994, 21). That is, language—literacy—is first explicitly figured in the novel as force by tying it to heartbreak and death. Before he can understand, then, Stephen's attunement to language and literacy is oriented by a sense that when they are entangled with the state, they wound and kill.

This colonial restriction of language is not simply about significatory content, but about how language bodies the speaking subject.[6] Late in the book, when Stephen is speaking with the dean of his school, he famously remarks, "The language in which we are speaking is his before it is mine. How different are the words *home, Christ, ale, master*, on his lips and on mine! I cannot speak or write these words without unrest of spirit. His language, so familiar and so foreign, will always be for me an acquired speech" (137). Stephen's relation to the English language is always dis-eased. Rather than knowing Irish, Stephen has only ever learned English and Latin, languages that are imposed by colonial authorities and humanizing assemblages, and this renders even what is most familiar to him—as a young man becoming a writer—always already alien, and alienating. Stephen, as a colonized subject, is identificatorily bound to Man and distanciated from it. He is always not-quite-human, even as his education, his masculinity, and his whiteness enable a much closer proximity to Man than many caught up in humanizing assemblages were and are allowed.

The tension of being colonized orients Stephen away from Ireland toward "exile" (181). This is expressly figured in terms of movement away from Man's colonial assemblages: "I shall go away" (179). Although Stephen vows to leave Ireland in order to wander Europe (a geographical horizon that betrays the extent to which his relation to Man is not one of total bewilderment), the theory of aesthetics that he offers in the final chapter of the book resonates persistently with Man, although the dissonance is crucial. Without going into the detail this is often given in criticism of the novel, I can say that Stephen sees art as necessarily formal (154), objectified (155), and whole (155). He writes, of aesthetic beauty, that it "is apprehended luminously by the mind which has been arrested by its wholeness and fascinated by its harmony" and that this "is the luminous silent stasis of esthetic pleasure, a spiritual state very like to that cardiac condition which the Italian physiologist Luigi Galvani, using a phrase almost as beautiful as Shelley's, called the enchantment of the heart" (155). Until physiology comes up, Stephen's theory underscores art as about the mind, not the body, and about rationality and stasis.

What is so fascinating about this is how much this theory is undercut by most of the novel up to this point, which underscores the extent to which critics seize on this theory as a kind of interpretive instruction manual because it confirms their disciplined orientation toward Man. Let me sketch how the novel disconfirms this theory by sniffing out how it figures smell, the body, and a sense of aesthetic encounter disinterested in Man.

As early reviewers of the novel noted with disgust, Stephen's movement through the world is led by smell. Indeed, there are very few scenes in the book that don't turn on smell: the smell of a chapel (9), "the faint smell off the rector's breath" (31), "the smell of evening in the air, the smell of the fields in the country . . . [and] the smell there was in the little wood" (40), "the troubling odour of the long corridors of Clongowes" (115), "the fragrance falling from the wet branches" (126), the smell of "her body" (170). This extremely partial list is enough to provide a sense of Stephen's orientation in the world. Like the dogs Freud suggests humans view with contempt, and in stark contrast to his stated aesthetic philosophy at the end of the novel, Stephen's aesthetic experience of the world is precisely about his body and movement, about smell, about orientation. Due to this insistence on smell, it's not particularly surprising when Stephen declares "in polite parenthesis" to his friend, "We are all animals. I am an animal" (149). This parenthetical affirmation of his human, or more specifically Irish, animality occurs just pages before he offers up the disinterested, disembodied, and finally humanized theory of art. Part of the novel's tension, then, adheres in Stephen's shuttling back and forth between a desire to approximate Man and a desire to affirm his animality.

In the middle of the novel, after a very long narration of a scene in church where a priest discourses on the horrors of hell, many of which turn out to be about smell (85), Stephen temporarily attempts to reorient himself away from his senses and toward a priestly, holy, disembodied relation to the world. While mortifying some of his senses doesn't present too much trouble, it is smell that is the sticking point: "To mortify his smell was more difficult as he found in himself no instinctive repugnance to bad odours, whether they were the odours of the outdoor world such as those of dung or tar or the odours of his own person among which he had made many curious comparisons and experiments" (107–8). Stephen's sense of smell, then, ties him to life (it refuses to be mortified) and to a relation between his animal capacities for being affected and nonhuman agencies in particular.

Smell, in mammals at least, involves the body's capacity to be affected by the swirl of entities that constantly collide with it. It is, in a sense, a kind of touch since it is often microscopic particles that make contact with the olfactory perceptual system. These might be solid particles (emitted by smoke, or pollution, for example) or gaseous particles. Although Stephen follows Man's common sense in referring to "the odours of his own person," that formulation obscures how what we call body odor is in fact a multispecies encounter: it is the activity of microscopic bacteria on and in the (human) body that generates those smells. Smell, even if only of one's "own person," is always a zone of contact with innumerable others.

As Stephen makes very clear in his ruminations on smell, one of its most obvious affective capacities is the modulation of mood. Taking in the odor of "piss and rotted straw," Stephen declares, "It will calm my heart. My heart is quite calm now" (60). This affective capacity of smell is, of course, well known and highly commodified: we can buy myriad lotions, candles, incenses, bath bombs, and so on that are marketed as aromatherapy. While this commodification undoubtedly polices the borders of affects in the service of expropriating capital—does the Calm candle really calm everyone?—such marketing allows us to consider how, like all of the body's sensory and perceptual systems, our literally aesthetic capacities (from *aesthesis*: sense touching) are primed in particular ways by humanizing assemblages in order to regularize them, (re)direct them, police them.

As Anna Tsing declares, "Smell draws us into the entangled threads of memory and possibility" (2015, 45). It concerns, for human and nonhuman animals alike, movement and orientation, and it does this through "a particular form of chemical sensitivity" (45). This sensitivity moves us, makes us respond, and "response always takes us somewhere new; we are not quite ourselves anymore—or at least the selves that we were, but rather ourselves in encounter with another" (46). Tsing's *The Mushroom at the End of the World* is rich in details about her olfactory encounters with mushrooms and ecosystems, even though "we don't know how to put much about smell into words" (46). Smell, then, necessarily opens us to what Tsing calls "an intriguing nature-culture knot" touching on "the indeterminate experience of encounter" (52). Smell is being touched, and in that touching—even before we have the conscious awareness of what we smell—we begin to move, and not only toward and away. Smell is multidirectional.

Tsing's attunement to smell is compelling because it takes things we all know as part of our daily experience of the world and uses that bodied knowledge to reconfigure disciplined attention to a specific problem: where can we find "the possibility of life in capitalist ruins"? In my years of moving through educational institutions by following paths laid out for disciplined attention to literature and literacy, I cannot recall ever encountering the idea that literature has a smell, let alone that the smell of literature is a crucial part of its force, its effect, its affects. From within that disciplined orientation, I can at best arrive at what I did above: reading a novel for its representation of smelling. But taking Joyce's representation of smelling seriously, especially as a counterforce to the aesthetic theory offered by Stephen, means that that representational practice is geared toward orienting my attention outside of the words on the page as signifiers. When I can resist being lured by Stephen's predictable (and, actually, quite boring) focus on representation, I find myself sniffing around me, and when I do that, I find that I'm not alone with a book, but suspended in a swirl of matters and agencies.

Teresa Brennan's *The Transmission of Affect* moves in this direction, seeing a body's olfactory openness as a crucial means by which affects circulate. Asking about how "the affect in the room is a profoundly social thing," she turns to smell (Brennan 2004, 68–69). Drawing on research about the human body's emission of pheromones, which are then received by another body, thus triggering hormonal changes, she declares that "one detects pheromones by touch or smell, but smell is more common" (69). This account enables a highly specific way to think about how a mood can be shared, how it can spread, and how it can generate a collective vibration in a particular space, but it also strangely limits the circulation of affects to what happens among human bodies. I return to this aspect of affective transmission in chapter 14, but here I also want to ask about other ways smells affect reading.

Let me take up a banal example for those of us whose lives are lived with books. If I go to my shelf—or one of my shelves—and pull down a book I haven't read in years, there is some chance that its materiality—the precise texture of its cover, its heft and size, the particular fanning out of its pages due to the wear of use—will produce memory tied heavily to affect. A particular copy of Whitman's *Leaves of Grass*, for instance, reminds me of unwrapping it for Christmas (a gift from my mother) and spending long hours reading it on uncomfortable concrete benches outside the old underground bookstore at the University of Minnesota where I was a student. There is a particular smell to this book that calls me back to my dorm room as an undergraduate, to the anxieties and excitements of those days, the feeling of walking into a warm space after trudging across the frozen campus (and the shifts in smell accompanying these movements). These experiences, for me, are inseparable from my struggles, as a first-generation college student from a working-class family, to body myself into the class positions affirmed by the university. Whatever sense I make of *Leaves of Grass* is inseparable from this.

Books all have a smell. It's partly due to the materials on which the inscriptions are made (particular stocks of paper) and partly due to the inks used to make those marks. It's also a record of the book's circulation through spaces of manufacture, retail, reading, and shelving. There is a contingency here that is individuating. A book on which I've spilled water or coffee or tea, or blown cigarette smoke, has olfactory traces of those events. And those encounters, or the conditions of the book's sitting still (which is never, given the swirl of agentic matter that is the world, actually reducible to stasis), make books host to microorganisms: bacteria and fungi principally. A book's smell can evoke memories, generate excitements, and even make us sneeze. A book is a multiplicity, a host of entangled and always-becoming agencies, and as a multiplicity it affects its human reading in a multiplicity of ways.

Since, as Maryanne Wolf (2007) details, our bodies' neurological responses to literacy events involve calling up a whole history of past experiences with language and everything else when we read, there is no way to disentangle the smell of reading from an experience of cognition.[7] It is part of the affective encounter. Joyce's novel is driven by Stephen's struggle with Man's disciplining of the body's capacities as he becomes an artist. Ben Highmore calls this disciplining "the pedagogy of disgust" (2010, 130), which habituates into the body of Man a reflexive, corporeal, aconscious response to the smells of less-than-human humans encountered in one's home country (immigrants, the impoverished) or elsewhere (foreigners). That is, smell comes to function as a mechanism of border policing between self and other, familiar and alien, and is thus profoundly shaped by imperialist state power. Recalling my proposal in chapter 10 that literacy is always about territorialization, I want to suggest that there are animal literacies of smell that indexically generate territories based on writing in excrement, or musk, or other scents. Human and nonhuman animals orient themselves in these territories based on the smells of food, or other animals, or excrement, or toxins.[8] State formations, then, can be said to capture this animal or animate capacity and reorient it, discipline it.[9] Smell too has a sociogenic function; we are disciplined to know what it means to smell like a human being.[10]

Second, and more affirmatively, this lesson puts us on a trail to be sniffed out leading to a much wider accounting for pleasures of the text (always plural) than is generally considered within humanist accounts of the scene of reading. Derek Attridge has written, "Reading Joyce is an activity which extends from the small-scale pleasures of appreciating the skillful organization and complex suggestiveness of a single sentence or phrase to the large-scale project of constructing a model that will impart unity (provisionally at least) to an entire book or an entire *oeuvre*, or even the entire *oeuvre* together with the history, personal and public, of which it is part" (2004, 3). This range, which is symptomatic of the disciplinary reach of literary study as captured by the humanities, seems to me far too restricted in that it still locates literature as something that can be understood by taking into account a mind and signifying structures of (a single) human language. In order to begin to draw other pleasures forth—pleasures that are outside, alongside, and underneath such conscious pleasures—I briefly return in chapter 13 to the tension between Stephen's theory of aesthetics and Joyce's presentation of Stephen's movement toward art.

13

PLEASURES OF THE TEXT

Stacy Alaimo argues that "pleasurable practices may open up the human self to forms of kinship and interconnection with nonhuman nature" (2016, 30). This is so precisely because "pleasure, impossible to confine within dichotomies of nature and culture, body and mind, pulses through an imaginative materiality" (42–43). Pleasure is not simply human, and any pleasures taken by a human inescapably arise at points of contact between that human and other entities, affects, agencies. Pleasure, then, is a scene where the continuity between humans and other animals can be tracked in literary ethologies, and it is also one of the most crucial aspects of the literacy situation and its erotics. Indeed, I argue that it is in the unevenly distributed pleasures of literacy that some of the politics of literacy situations become most apparent. Enlarging our sense of how pleasures are modulated in and through literacy will enable me, in the final chapters of *Animate Literacies*, to theorize the politics of literacy in general, and of literacies in educational institutions more specifically, in ways that attune to both the entanglement between human animals and a host of nonhuman agencies animating them, and to the ways literacies are modulated by humanizing assemblages.

Let me return to where I left off in chapter 12. While Stephen presents aesthetics at the end of *A Portrait* as a matter of a mind contemplating stasis, wholeness, and harmony among parts, the novel's narration of his coming to the practice of writing figures his attachment to aesthetics very differently. Stephen's early experiments with writing often hinge on trying to describe a particular encounter in the world where affects, memory, aesthetics, and corporeal pleasures mingle: he sees a girl at a train station. The affects generated as a result of this encounter course through Stephen and exert a powerful force on his attunement to the world. Joyce writes, "All day he had thought of nothing but their leavetaking on the steps of the tram at Harold's Cross, the stream of moody emotions it had made to course through him, and the poem he had written about it" (1994, 53). Poetry emerges then as a response to an affective state inseparable from the body's erotic response to the world. Indeed, it comes to be a kind of masturbatory release: "The old restless moodiness had again filled his breast as it had done the night of the party but had not found an outlet in verse" (53). Far from a question of stasis and wholeness, writing for Stephen is about corporeal pleasures and erotic affects.

This puts me on track to gather a wider range of pleasures of the text than are usually posited in humanist conceptualizations of literature. For a sense of how wide a scope has often been allowed, I want to consider Roland Barthes's *The Pleasure of the Text*, where he differentiates two kinds of pleasure signified by two French words: *plaisir* and *jouissance*, translated into English as pleasure and bliss respectively. Barthes writes, "Text of pleasure: the text that contents, fills, grants euphoria; the text that comes from culture and does not break with it, is linked to a *comfortable* practice of reading. Text of bliss: the text that imposes a state of loss, the text that discomforts (perhaps to the point of a certain boredom), unsettles the reader's historical, cultural, psychological assumptions, the consistency of his tastes, values, memories, brings to crisis his relation with language" (1975, 14). The bifurcated pleasures here—where plaisir shores up a sense of self and jouissance undoes it—delimit something of the scope of reading's force when it is taken to be reducible to an encultured mind encountering a signifying text. But, as I have tried to argue in chapters 11 and 12, the affective force of literacy events is not thus reducible. Taking into account the corporeal, affective collisions of literacy necessitates speaking of a dispersion of pleasures of the text, always plural.

Stephen's erotic pleasure in literary practice should trouble disciplinary regimes of cordoning off those texts that stimulate aesthetic affects from erotic ones.[1] The history of pornography reveals the extent to which the state directly polices literacy events, cleaving off certain affects and pleasures in order to tidy up a chaste sense of what "literature" means.[2] Theories of the novel—which emerges more or less in tandem with the invention of pornography as a category of text—tend to situate its formal properties in relation to the politics of nation-states.[3] In one sense, this is because in their formal focus on individuals, novels were part of a larger stream of discourses in early modernity articulating the liberal subject that concretizes capitalism as an economic system, and the democratic nation-state as a political one. But it is also because the novel's emergence and continued practice is entangled with state apparatuses (and for all the reasons Watt [1957] enumerates in his materialist account of the novel's emergence). This is, in a way, obvious given Benedict Anderson's (1983) thesis that print capitalism (chiefly, in the eighteenth century this means novels and periodicals) was the material condition of possibility for the emergence of the kind of nationalism (imagined community) that made the nation-state sustainable (even if it had formally emerged in the seventeenth century with the Treaty of Westphalia).[4]

While the (often imperialist) Western nation-state is virtually omnipresent in histories of the novel, it has seldom been forwarded that the novel is perhaps best thought of as an attribute of state power.[5] In excluding pornographic novels from taxonomies of the novel, researchers thus, in effect, side with state power, cordoning off texts that, were they to be included, would fairly significantly affect conceptual definitions of the novel, if not precisely in formal ways (pornography also regularly took the form of realist narratives focusing on individuals) then in terms of how we assess the effects, and affects, of literary encounters. The result of this is a sanitized sense of what novels are and what they do. It foregrounds what I have called its humanizing function while downplaying its dehumanizing and its erotic functions. Novels do not just edify and entertain: they also turn us on, and fuck us up, or prime us to fuck others up (even without noticing).

While that literary historical problem is an interesting one, I want to focus here on a text that is eccentrically entangled with pornography: Paul Preciado's (2013) *Testo Junkie*. This text refers to itself as a "somatopolitical fiction" (11), one that combines a detailed history of hormone pharmacology, a queer and antistatist reconceptualization of biopolitical theory, and pornographic writing. While academics are quite used to encountering theoretical speculation and provocation in books containing extensive presentations of archival research, it is the inclusion of pornography that sets this book apart.[6] What I want to consider here is the possibility that these forms are not really separable, nor are the affects and effects they produce: Preciado renders pharmacological history and biopolitical speculation erotic acts, and makes pornographic production and consumption a directly historical and political event.

Preciado's text has an argument, of course. He tracks how pharmacology and the imperialist state have become entangled in a way that exceeds the now canonical framing of contemporary politics as biopolitics. He writes, "Follow me: the changes in capitalism that we are witnessing are characterized not only by the transformation of 'gender,' 'sex,' 'sexuality,' 'sexual identity,' and 'pleasure' into objects of the political management of living (just as Foucault had suspected in his biopolitical description of new systems of social control), but also by the fact that this management itself is carried out through the new dynamics of advanced technocapitalism, global media, and biotechnologies" (2013, 25). Hormone therapies and modulations, new possibilities for mediating the corporeal literacies generally subsumed under the heading of "pornography," and shifts in the global flows of capital are, according to Preciado, rewriting what it means to be a person. The present, then, is marked by struggles over how to contain and direct this shifting. The humanizing assemblages that articulate Man seek to capture this in certain ways, and Preciado's text focuses on experiments that would move away from such capture. Punctuating the text are long, detailed descriptions of Preciado's experiments with taking testosterone illegally and tracking his body's becoming otherwise, especially as it concerns a range of bodily pleasures and encounters.

Before we get to Preciado's argument, we read about him applying testo gel to his left shoulder before picking up two dildos while a digital camera runs:

> Next I slide the dildos into the openings at the lower part of my body. First, the realistic-looking one, then the ergonomic one, which goes into my anus, which is a multidirectional space without any bony edges. This time, it's the same. On my knees, I turn my back to the camera, the tips of my feet and my head pressing against the floor, and hold my arms behind me so that they can manage the two dildos in my orifices. (19)

The body/illegal hormone/dildo/camera assemblage is for Preciado precisely the site of the play over state control of subjectivization and population (the object of biopolitics, according to Foucault). That is, Preciado's account of the biopolitical would see in moments like this—where a human body is in a literally slippery set of relations with nonhuman agencies of various kinds—the place where politics is most operative. This is an encounter where what Massumi (2015) calls "ontopower" operates in order to prime the body to respond in ways that are in line with state objectives, while the body's animal politics seeks out margins of maneuver, room for creative experimentation. What we see here is a Spinozist politics of seeing what the body can do, and Preciado's experimentation is always in relation to a host of pressures to direct the body, its affects, its relations to other bodies, and its pleasures toward Man. Preciado's experiments seek out alternatives that capitalize on pleasure as the more-than-human and (mostly) other-than-conscious scene of modulating the body's capacities in milieux that cannot be disentangled from humanizing assemblages and apparatuses of capture.

I'm interested in Preciado's text here because there is no way to parse my thinking about his arguments—which take up medical history, political theory, and a range of feminist and queer critiques—from how I feel while reading. Preciado's book turns me on, in the sense that my body's encounter with it (especially in tandem with the swirl of agencies surrounding my body as I read) opens my body to a different, more open, more corporeal attunement to what is happening than some other texts do. This is a text that unfurls the very possibility of a distinction between mind and body, thinking and what I want to call *erotics*. Even if one isn't sexually aroused by Preciado's descriptions of sex acts (which are actually much hotter than most of the literary pornography one can find online), the text ceaselessly affects the reader's body. And this affective state opens onto directly political questions: "How could we have entrusted the state with the management of desire, sexual fantasy, the material sense of embodiment? Am I a body? Or should one say, Am I the body-of-the-state?" (Preciado 2013, 257).

These questions take us to the site at which corporeal pleasures cannot be thought or felt outside of statist apparatuses of capture. Preciado argues that capitalism increasingly operates according to a mobilization of a kind of "somatic and affective capital" he calls "potentia gaudendi": the potential to cum (285–86). As Annamarie Jagose (2013) has traced in detail, a lot of queer theory has been attentive to how state apparatuses of capture and control have been able to work through orgasm, thus proving Foucault's basic point that sexuality names not a force but a site of relay for the forces of power-knowledge. But things are more interesting when one undoes the empirical solidity of the orgasmic, freeing it up from the kind of definitional policing undertaken by sexology, sex manuals, and the popular advice linked to gendered magazines like *Cosmopolitan* and *Men's Health*. Do we know what an orgasm is, what it involves, what it draws into its movements? What Preciado makes explicit is something already implicit in Stephen's experiments with poetry: there is not one orgasm, but many, and a political redirecting of the body's pleasures might take the form of experiments to not recognize pleasures in the ways we are told by common sense are at play. Preciado writes, "It is fundamental not to recognize oneself. Derecognition, disidentification is a condition for the emergence of the political as the possibility of transforming reality" (2013, 397). States require recognition, as indigenous scholar Glen Sean Coulthard (2014) has underscored, but bodies and pleasures may be operative in corporeal, experimental, affective, and directly political ways without cohering into anything recognizable to a state.

My account of pleasure has, so far, hovered too close to sexual pleasure for my taste, and while I want to insist that the pleasures of literacy can be sexual in that sense, I want to scan outward from these toward a wider field of what I call the *erotics of literacy*. My shift in focus here is motivated by Audre Lorde's famous essay "Uses of the Erotic," which is interested in precisely the play between a body's capacities—which she calls "the erotic" and specifically ties to "a deeply female and spiritual plan . . . within each of us"—and the movement of "oppression [that] must corrupt or distort those various sources of power within the culture of the oppressed" (2007, 53). Tracking how this female erotics has been captured and "misnamed" by what she calls "male power," Lorde insists that "pornography is the direct denial of the power of the erotic" because, to her mind, it "emphasizes sensation without feeling" (54). One could say that for her, pornography splits the two dominant uses of the concept of affect and valorizes one. While I am more interested in pornography's possibilities than Lorde, this formulation provides a caution against reducing the erotics of literacy to the merely sexual, at least as that has been restricted by sexology and its vocabularies.

The erotic for Lorde is about "sharing" (56), it is about the "capacity for joy" (56), and it is about affirming "the *yes* within ourselves" (57). Her list of "erotically satisfying experiences" is instructive in this context: "dancing, building a bookcase, writing a poem, examining an idea" (56–57).

Writing, reading, and even handling books are erotic, and this is both the source of their particular power and the precise point at which state power can seize on the capacities of literacy to capture and redirect them.

There is, as any person who has moved through statist educational systems will know, a profound and disturbing pleasure that adheres in having read more, in having thought more about bigger ideas, bigger books, harder theories. According to Sara Ahmed (2014), this type of pleasure might be thought of as the pleasure of "white manning." When linked to the severe restriction on what might be read to what should be read that constitutes the mechanism of canon formation, this type of pleasure easily interfaces with the work of maintaining male supremacist, white supremacist, Eurocentrist capture of educational potential. There is an almost ubiquitous pleasure here in domination tied up with the project of humanizing education, which can produce profound distress for those of us who explicitly frame our politics against this kind of domination but whose corporeal and pedagogical practices continue to be oriented toward it.[7] No account of the pleasures of the text can ignore this form of pleasure, for it is one that structures much of how Man has captured literacy and its affects/effects.

But there are other pleasures. As the two previous chapters have already begun to track, literacy is irreducibly corporeal, and while Barthes gives us a good sense of the range of pleasure that adheres in an entanglement between mind and script in literacy events, the literacy situation is precisely that "relational milieu that exceeds the human or wherein the human is more ecological than individual" (Manning 2013, 76). Reading is, as I proposed in my ethological account, about animals spending time with marks, and this duration of literacy is corporeally lived. My love for some books is less about their intellectual, narrative, and formal contents than about the way touching them and being touched by them affects me. We have to consider the way that books feel as objects, the ways that texts touch our hands, our laps. There is a heft to a book, a shape, a precise texture to its pages and cover.

Pleasure and repetition are intimately linked, and, to an important degree, what I love about literature is not any particular book but a particular corporeal practice. I love the event of sitting with a book, and the way that the nonhuman agencies swirling in and around that event affect my body as much as my cognition. Reading is, as much as it is about learning or narrative pleasure, about sitting in cafés, in my favorite chairs, in front of a classroom. It is caught up with pleasures of drinking coffee, or tea, or wine, smoking cigarettes or pipes. There is a posture and a bodied practice to reading that becomes part of what any singular event of reading means: even when I don't enjoy whatever text I'm reading, I may still spend my time with the marks because of this corporeal pleasure. And then there is the erotics of rereading, where repetition reveals modulations of pleasures distributed differently each time. This can be heightened when I take notes and can enjoy discovering marks made by a past version of my self (or someone else) in the margins.[8] All of us who teach literature know this well, if only negatively, since many of our students have not been habituated to these pleasures of the text and so their experience of the narrative, rhetorical, and formal dimensions of a novel, let's say, don't necessarily emerge against this background pleasure.[9]

I'm also struck by the pleasures of simply being in the presence of books. That is, I am always affected by books even when I am not reading them. As someone who grew up in a working-class home, it's hard to separate the pleasures I experience with books from a decades-long attempt to rework my habitus, bodying myself into the forms of class privilege that enable flourishing in universities. I cover my walls with them, at home no less than in my office. I actively seek out, as much I can, the spaces of the library and the bookstore because "the library is an erotically charged space" (Adler 2017, 14). There is, of course, a pleasure in searching through the collections in those archives: the joys of an unexpected find, or a rare one (Benjamin 1999, 489). Part of this, no doubt, can be referred back to a kind of possessive investment in accumulation, as Benjamin makes clear, but I think at another level it's about a sense, however undeveloped in most of us, that the materiality of books affects us in ways that aren't conscious, but aren't for that any less real (this is, no doubt, part of why interior designers love books). Books, even unopened ones on shelves, signal a certain lifestyle, tied to class, and so my pleasure of them is inextricable from the pleasure of learning to inhabit a class habitus that is always in a sense aspirational for me. Literacy events make, unmake, and remake us, and there is, or can be, enormous pleasure in this movement of becoming. (Becoming can also be, as Douglass's *Narrative* reminds us, agonizing.) My shelves of books promise me a fantasy of class privilege that I've had to work to inhabit, and for this very reason they may strike others as alienating and unwelcoming. Benjamin writes, of "a collector" of books, "Not that they come alive in him; it is he who lives in them" (492): books, then, contribute to environments in which some kinds of life can flourish, and this must be understood materially, especially if we are to be simultaneously attuned to how these lives flourish on condition that other lives be restricted, destroyed, stunted.

I would like to propose that all of these pleasures constitute something like an erotics of literature, where the contact zone of literacy situations produces corporeal (if not always conscious) pleasures. I do not wish to focus on these instead of the pleasures of a good narrative, or coming to understand a theory, or any of the other pleasures that figure into most humanist salvos on behalf of reading. They are, as agentic participants in the literacy situation, contributors to the material and corporeal conditions of possibility for those other pleasures. They are also, although humanists tend to ignore this, the ones that may be the most out of reach to many people. I want to recall here Ahmed's statement that "attention involves a political economy, or an uneven distribution of attention between those who arrive at the writing table, which affects what they do once they arrive (and, of course, many do not even make it)" (2006, 32). Pleasures, like attention, are unevenly distributed, and this has everything to do with what she calls the "conditions of arrival." Many pleasures of the text, perhaps especially those that come to stand in as the only pleasures of the text in humanist accounts, are difficult to access for many (this is one of the main lessons of Douglass's *Narrative* and Morrison's *Beloved*). Benjamin signals this indirectly in his "Writer's Technique in Thirteen Theses," insisting that "anyone intending to embark on a major work should be lenient with himself and, having completed a stint, deny himself nothing that will not prejudice the text" (1996b, 458). The pleasures in "deny[ing] himself nothing" may make for good writing, but while some of the bodies that find their way to tables to write can no doubt heed this advice, there are pleasures unfolding in vastly different conditions: scrawling on walls (like young Douglass and his chalk; or prisoners carving into their cell walls), spray painting graffiti on trains, composing poems aloud that will never be in print, weaving and unweaving nests.[10] Indeed, we should remember that before he could even read, Douglass took pleasure in carrying his book with him everywhere he went.

The pleasures of the text that are affirmed in humanism, then, are never innocent, never removed from a complicity with forms of social segregation and manufactured inequalities in literacy and access to leisure time, from the deforestation and toxic production of paper, from the networks of distribution and labor that make every book possible, from the entire history of literature as a humanizing and dehumanizing assemblage. Let me return to Preciado, who foregrounds something similar in the way he writes his experiments with testo gel:

> These new scientific and commercial practices established the first regular trafficking networks of biological materials among gynecologists, laboratory researchers, pharmaceutical industries, prisons, and slaughterhouses. Sex hormones are the result of such traffic. Each time I give myself a dose of testosterone, I agree to this pact. I kill the blue whale; I cut the throat of the bull at the slaughterhouse; I take the testicles of the prisoner condemned to death. I become the blue whale, the bull, the prisoner. I draft a contract whereby my desire is fed by—and retroactively feeds—global channels that transform living cells into capital. (2013, 163)

These pleasures cost a lot, and those costs are often distributed far beyond what most of us consciously take into account (thanks to what Marx calls "commodity fetishism"), and I think any account of literature, today, has to attune to this. Indeed, I want to propose that the imperialist state's capture of literacy requires this inattentiveness, and that a political redirection of the energies dispersed in literacy away from the state begins with the literacy situation: with everything that happens to bodies before, during, and after reading events that gets lost when literature is captured as one of the humanities and reduced to simply a transaction of meaning. Literacy is inescapably erotic, and language, once no longer understood as simply a human activity, cannot be thought without thinking touch, contact, materiality, and corporeality. Which means we also have to think of pleasures appearing around and underneath the pleasures of conscious meaning making, but also the pleasures of fugitive, furtive, ephemeral acts of literacy: pleasures that animals, including human animals, take in weaving their nests and webs, creating ephemeral territories within which they orient themselves. These too are pleasures of the text, and foregrounding them ushers us toward a different sense of what literacy and literature are by recalibrating our sense of what they can do.

14

THOSE CHANGEFUL SITES

Writing from within a discipline that is said to be dead or dying due to the ongoing crisis of the humanities, Gayatri Spivak calls for "expanding the scope of Comparative Literature." Although I want to expand the scope of the study of literature considerably beyond what she proposes, her account of how the reading of literature matters is indispensable for my thinking about what literacy events do. She writes that entering the study of literature, "we stand . . . as reader[s] with imagination ready for the effort of othering, however imperfectly, as an end in itself" (Spivak 2003, 13). Reading literature, then, makes us other than we are. Literacy events change us.[1]

Although Spivak's account is rather complex, and offered in a series of lectures that is far from formulaic and systematic, I want to highlight three of the ways that, for her, literacy changes us. First, the close attention to the language of literary texts can dislodge us from a particular affective conditioning that results from our emergence from assemblages of humanization: we are taught to fear the unknown, the unanticipatable, the aleatory. Man loves planning, regularity, the smooth and orderly flow of what Benjamin calls "homogeneous empty time."[2] Spivak writes that "we must learn to let go, [and] remember that it is the singular unverifiability of the literary from which we are attempting to discern collectivities" (2003, 34). Unsurprisingly given her affiliation with deconstruction, Spivak insists on undecidability, and argues that "the fear of undecidability is the planner's fear" (47). This fear—of what is not subject to the decision-making arbitrariness of sovereignty—is what literature can "displace" (23).

Second, and perhaps in a move that is simply a more generalized version of the first change, literature "can perhaps rearrange our desires" (23), or even more pointedly, it involves "the uncoercive rearrangement of desire" (101). It can lead us to affective states of bewilderment in which we lose the ability to plan, and our desire for planning, such that our desires themselves are redirected. If Man's humanizing assemblages involve, as I argued in my reading of Douglass's *Narrative*, the education of our desires, then a pedagogy making tracks away from man must necessarily intervene in that same field. If we take up Erin Manning's conception of desire as "the body in movement" (2006, 36), we can see how pedagogy becomes about precisely a kind of priming of our bodies' capacities either toward Man or in the direction of other, plural forms of performing the human. We might then link this with Donna Haraway's famous subjunctive suggestion in "A Cyborg Manifesto" that "perhaps, ironically, we can learn from our fusions with animals and machines how not to be Man, the embodiment of Western logos" (1991, 173). If we have to learn to be Man through humanizing education, we can learn to be otherwise, and this necessitates thinking about our movements, our desires.

Third, reading is an activity that allows for discerning collectivities. Spivak writes, "The question 'Who are we?' is part of the pedagogic exercise" (2003, 26). Rather than asking "Am I right?" or "How much do you know?" or whatever other questions anchor what Jane Tompkins (1994) calls the "pedagogy of the distressed," the force of education adheres in the question "Who are we?" Spivak rightfully has no patience with an answer that would transform education into induction by asserting some common culture or nationalist unity, nor even one that is predetermined in terms of political affiliation or identity. In fact, it is a question that cannot even be asked well within the terms of identity and identity politics. It cannot even, except by an extreme violence that has come to seem unavoidable, be circumscribed around "the human family itself" (Spivak 2003, 27). Rather, "real answers come in the classroom and are specific to that changeful site" (26). In the classroom, Spivak sees the force of literature as issuing from asking questions without knowing in advance that answers will ever be forthcoming, and in asking those questions finding ourselves exposed to collectivities that are not durable, but which have the political, ontogenic effect of rearranging our desires.

A crucial aspect of Spivak's project of expanding the scope of literary study involves a call to move the field away from its historical focus on the literatures and languages of Western European countries. It thus has a certain relation to the canon wars of the 1980s and '90s, when educational institutions in the West were pressured to expand curricular offerings to include literatures by women, queer folks, racialized minorities, and non-Western authors. It is entirely possible to read these debates and shifts as a curricular response to what were, in effect, much more radical calls for an opening up of educational institutions to historically excluded populations and for a radical redistribution of social and economic resources. Instead of addressing those demands, as Roderick Ferguson has argued, the university "evolv[ed] ways in which institutions could use rather than absolutely dismiss the demands of minority activists" (2012, 58). This involved, as part of what is often called the project of multiculturalism and the attendant formation of interdisciplinary fields of minority study—indigenous, women's, gender, Chicano/a, black, and so on—a reconfiguration of the university's operationalization of Man. Man, as the only telos of humanizing education, becomes differentiated, and the study of Man now accounts, as part of curricular design, for what has long in fact been true: that to be recognizably human in modernity required one to have a gender, a race, a nationality, and (by the end of the nineteenth century) a sexuality.[3]

Such a shift is precisely the kind of emergency repair to humanism that Paul Gilroy (1993, 55) rejects since it simply begins to include with the orbit of the human some of those who have historically been rendered ahuman, inhuman, and less-than-human. It shifts the valence, but not the humanizing mechanism itself and its inescapable dehumanizing exhaust. This recalibration—without disruption—of humanization involves what Ferguson calls "calculation" (2012, 34). The university can now account for a diversity of experiences within the human, but it does in a way that "does not jettison a concern for the positivities long associated with man" (34). To use terminology from Deleuze and Guattari, if the radical student movements of the 1960s and '70s sought to deterritorialize learning away from Man and disperse capital—educational, cultural, and financial—throughout the social body, then the university powerfully reterritorialized on Man, now diffracted by minority difference.

I would like to think about two ways in which the arguments I have forwarded in *Animate Literacies* can reconfigure how literature is engaged in the university (or other school) classroom, opening up opportunities for bewilderment. I take as my example a class reading *Frankenstein*.[4] As I hinted at in chapter 11, the monster, after fleeing the scene of his creation, finds himself in the woods where he is able to hide in a hovel while looking through "innumerable chinks" toward a father and two children living in a hut (Shelley 2012, 72). After spending days observing the "lovely creatures" (74), the monster makes a "discovery": "I found that these people possessed a method of communicating their experiences and feelings to one another by articulate sounds. I perceived that the words they spoke sometimes produced pleasure or pain, smiles or sadness, in the minds and countenance of their hearers" (75). This account, which I would argue constitutes a furtive ethology of literacy practice, foregrounds that sounds—which the monster, like Saussure, gleans are broken into discrete units through difference—produce affects. Here, the two senses of affect—as touching and as emotion—are inseparable: in having their aural organs touched by sonorous waves, their bodies' affective systems are modulated. The evidence for this is largely corporeal—their "countenance" displays the changes—but the monster already moves from the empirical to a more speculative reference to "mind."

Having begun his autodidactic literacy education, the monster notices that the humans spend time with books. I quote: "This reading had puzzled me extremely at first; but, by degrees, I discovered that he uttered many of the same sounds when he read as when he talked. I conjectured, therefore, that he found on the paper signs for speech, which he understood, and I ardently longed to comprehend these also; but how was that possible when I did not even understand the sounds for which they stood as signs?" (78). The monster, here again, entangles a nascent understanding of the materiality of literacy practice with affects: conjecture produces ardent longing. The monster's approach to literacy enables a class to discuss literacy in terms of events that emerge from the material and relational milieu I call the *literacy situation*. More specifically, it lays out a preliminary form of attention that can be generalized into the ethological and ecological attention to literacy I sketched in chapter 10.

In order draw this out, when I assign *Frankenstein*, I ask students to keep a reading journal. While they may use this to keep track of passages or ask questions about the meaning or form of the novel, I insist that they keep track of where, when, and in what circumstances they read. While many teachers assign a set number of pages, usually listed on syllabi, they seldom give any attention to the situation in which that reading will happen. Although many of us who teach literature have developed very specific habits and environments for reading—a favorite chair with good light, a preferred beverage, a room in which one can control the ambient sound—students seldom have access to these rituals. When they report back, we find that many of them read for very brief durations—five to thirty minutes at a time—in situations that appear somewhat haphazard as they go about their days: standing in line at the dining hall, in an unoccupied classroom, on the bus as their team travels to a game.[5] Most of them report distracting noises—talking, music, the sounds of television or video games. When they read in classrooms, most note that the ecological motion detectors turn off the lights after a few minutes without sensing their movement, causing them to have to move in ways that the device can register.

By generating a list on the board of the presence of these externalities to what teachers largely presume will capture their attention, we realize that many students who have not been be absorbed in their reading can account for this largely in terms of the literacy situation. In other words, differences in student interpretations of the novel—and differentiated levels of engagement—are often far less about the cognitive or conceptual aspects of literacy events than about the materiality of the situation and the agentic participation—one may want to say disruption—of a range of human and more-than-human participants. Tracking these situations can enable complex accounts of the politics of temporality, campus spaces, and the technologies of lighting, air conditioning, and inhabitancy that structure life in universities.

The monster's affects also gesture toward a reconceptualization of learning as not primarily a matter of cognition or conceptual mentation but rather of feelings. Megan Watkins's account of pedagogical affects both clarifies the monster's experience and engenders a way into discussing the politics of emotion in the classroom. Watkins writes that "the techniques teachers utilize in classrooms can act as a force promoting interest, which over time may accumulate as cognitive capacity providing its own stimulus for learning" (2010, 278). These accumulating affects shape engagement and the desire to learn. What this means is that not only are classrooms sites where affects circulate (for instance, in pheromones that modulate hormones as part of the generation of collectivities[6]), student responses to readings and discussions are often driven more by emotion than by rational or conceptual cognition. Boler has offered the most thorough account of how "affect occurs in the specific site of the classroom," and her argument crucially foregrounds how affect is "mediated by ideologies and capitalist values and its entailed gendered forms" (1999, 5). That is, the way a classroom feels to a student is powerfully informed by accumulated affects referable to students' histories of movement through social spaces shaped by (settler) coloniality, class, race, gender, sexuality, ability, size, and other vectors of intrahuman social stratification.[7]

This approach helps to clarify why one of the most visible sites of conflict on campuses in the United States (but not only) today is the question of safety and safe spaces.[8] Although the public debate can be messy and contradictory, the simplified framing in much of the US national press sees this as a standoff between students, assumed to have progressive politics, that fear being triggered by racist, sexist, homophobic, or other politically incorrect speech, and faculty and administrators (plus more conservative students) who see these feelings getting in the way of open and rational debate.[9] Jack Halberstam (2014) has theorized this in terms of a generational shift, one that touches on the enormously different material conditions of political life for a younger generation of LGBTQ and progressive students, conditions that give rise to a call-out culture: "I rarely go to a conference, festival or gathering anymore without a protest erupting about a mode of representation that triggered someone somewhere. And as people 'call each other out' to a chorus of finger snapping, we seem to be rapidly losing all sense of perspective and instead of building alliances, we are dismantling hard fought for coalitions." And interestingly, the terms of the debate about safe spaces have undergone something of a reversal in the last thirty years. Writing in 1989, bell hooks challenged the fetishization of safe spaces by white liberal women: "Unlike the stereotypical feminist model that suggests women best come to voice in an atmosphere of safety (one in which we are all going to be kind and nurturing), I encourage my students to work at coming to voice in an atmosphere where they may be afraid or see themselves at risk" (1989, 53). While the recent campus activism in the United States linked to the Black Lives Matter movement and its challenges to racialized state violence have redistributed the ways this debate positions students based on racialized, gendered, and sexualized identities, hooks is already attuned to what Rebecca Wanzo (2015) more recently called "the deadly fight over feelings."[10]

If we acknowledge that "safety is not something one does or achieves, nor is it an a priori state of being; rather, it is something one feels" (Gilbert 2014, 38), we have to say that the debates about safe spaces on college campuses have the virtue of attuning us to the complexities of education as an inescapably affective experience. More importantly, because affects are both individual and collective, internal and external, thinking about the affects of education requires us to give up on fantasies that classrooms can simply be safe or not.[11] Rather, what we need are classroom practices that attune to the complex affective accumulations students bring to the room, as well as the more-than-human circulation of affects within the classroom in such a way that the possibilities for movement and disorientation that are always materially (if virtually) present in the situation can lead to events of bewilderment. Bewilderment happens neither in some imagined pure scene of safety nor in conditions of risk associated with a lack of concern for the feelings of others. Rather, it occurs when a classroom collectivity (always more-than-human) achieves a particular intensity of affective attunement that I would like to call *love*. This is love not as banal affirmation or empty romanticism but precisely as the kind of attention to the situation "as it is" (Casarino 2002). This is love as the "infinite openness toward those with whom we are directly engaged but also ways of being accountable to those absent beings whose lives, labors, and agencies have always made up the conditions of hospitality itself" (Singh 2017a).[12] Hospitality, when calibrated beyond the human and attuned to the hauntings of Man's violence, opens the classroom to those unanticipatable affects I call *bewilderment*.

And yet, while shifting pedagogical practice in classrooms at the university and in primary and secondary schools is an important site of political struggle, it is, at best, a limited one. I mean this in two senses. First, it continues to play a game of seeking recognition from the state of cultural differences, a game that, as Glen Sean Coulthard has painstakingly demonstrated, ultimately props up the (settler) colonialist state as a legitimate framework for social organization. But second, it ignores the extent to which a more primary site of struggle—access to schools—has already been dramatically restricted according to logics of highly racialized inequality. This is why it is politically crucial to expand a focus from a narrowly defined literary study toward a wider field of literacy. Even bracketing for a moment how literacy is a constitutive feature of animate life beyond the merely human, this expansion allows for crucial questions.

John Guillory asks, "Who reads? What do they read? How do they read? In what social and institutional circumstances? Who writes? In what social and institutional contexts? For whom?" (1993, 18).

Given the staggering numbers of students, even in extremely wealthy countries like the United States, who do not graduate from high school and who experience what I can only think to call the corporate and statist manufacturing of illiteracy, it is dangerously naive to think that the struggle to shift curricula within higher educational institutions, or even secondary schools, is going to make much of a difference.[13] While I have tried to attend in this book to the ways in which my love of literature is shaped, in part, by the pleasures I experience when closely reading difficult literary narratives, I have also tried to call attention to how those pleasures—and the possibilities they afford for undoing my self—are out of reach for many people, and that having access to them requires forms of discipline that are always violent and are, for many, explicitly pitched in assimilationist terms (even as this discipline is a condition of possibility for many of the pleasures of the text I drew forth in the last chapter). That is, getting into the college classroom to closely read literature—and even doing that with an openness toward othering as an end in itself— often requires epistemicide: schooling out of people any non-Man ways of performing the human, thinking about the human's entanglements with nature, and participating in collectivities not recognized by the state.[14]

We have to think, then, about literacy events occurring outside of classrooms, since access to classrooms (where the reading Spivak calls for can take place) is socially and politically limited. Indeed, access to those sites is controlled precisely by a statist capture of literacy, narrowly defined by the imperialist state as specific basic reading and writing skills. The narrowness of the state's conception of literacy is carefully constructed in order render illiterate many people whose daily lives would be impossible, in fact, without the literacy capacities they supposedly lack. At issue, increasingly, is the function of standardized testing apparatuses, many of them designed by state-corporate committees, which are premised on epistemologies and technologies originating in state-military sorting operations and in racist pseudoscience. In other words, despite what school administrators will tell you, by becoming haunted by the directly imperialist, racist, and violent conditions of their emergence, we can easily say that such tests are designed to legitimate the social sorting of people into the mostly white classes who will take on managerial roles and the racially minoritized people who will have to accept following directives. These differentiated roles come with vastly different kinds of access to wealth, physical mobility, and exposure to violence (often state authorized).

Rather than simply calling for a recalibration of the system to allow for more people to be let into the classrooms and humanized into Man, it's imperative to recognize that the system itself is, and always has been, a mechanism of social sorting where the humanization of some is paid for by rendering most inhuman or less-than-human. In other words, however nice it sounds to say, with Horace Mann, that education is the "great equalizer," it has functioned, at a systemic level, to massively restrict the movements of most people, orienting them toward the kind of low-wage labor that is the condition of possibility for Man's comfort. It is for this reason that my attention to literacy in *Animate Literacies* has focused so much on the literacy practices of Man's others: to do otherwise, as is almost always done, inevitably props up a universal humanization as political teleology. Queer, feminist, postcolonial, black, and indigenous scholarship has demonstrated, loudly and in the most creative ways, the violences that proliferate when one takes Man—the white, Western, masculine, heterosexual, able-bodied, rational subject—to be the human. This same thing is true when one takes a highly restricted conception of literary study as the whole of literacy.

Rather than imagining a world in which everyone would be admitted into the elite classroom to become fully human through discussion of literary fiction and the great books of the various canons, I want to reverse the directionality and track how other literacies are entangled with alternative ways of being human. Instead of a unifying rush toward assimilationist inclusion, I want to call for a mass exodus from Man's classrooms, seeking out other changeful sites.

I am inspired in this imagination by Stefano Harney and Fred Moten's concept of study. In *The Undercommons*, they write, "To abuse its hospitality, to spite its mission, to join its refugee colony, its gypsy encampment, to be in but not of—this is the path of the subversive intellectual in the modern university" (2013, 26).[15] In but not of: the exodus that I am calling for here might still happen in the classroom built on occupied territory.[16] But even when it happens on the grounds—public or private—of the statist university, it takes place elsewhere: in the undercommons. Moten says,

"When I think about the way we use the term 'study,' I think we are committed to the idea that study is what you do with other people. It's talking and walking around with other people, working, dancing, suffering, some irreducible convergence of all three, held under the name of speculative practice" (110). Study happens, then, anywhere people come together or, better, move together. Moten pitches this explicitly as a question of the generation and circulation of affects: "How come we can't be together and think together in a way that feels good, the way it should feel good?" (117). Our collective movements with other bodies, which necessarily involve collision and improvisation, move us, affect us. They underscore that this is not a matter of being against the university, since that involves recognizing it and being recognized by it, which is to say that critiques of the university, especially in academic writing, are formally part of the university, whatever the content of the critique. Instead, it's about redirecting our movements. It harmonizes with what I earlier called bewildering education: educational encounters that set us moving away from Man without knowing where the movement will take us.

"The undercommons in some ways tries to escape from critique" (Harney and Moten 2013, 38). It is not about measured, reasoned, evidence-based analysis. It is not about simply calling attention to what's wrong with the present state of affairs. Instead of critique, Harney and Moten call on us to flee professionalization in study. The goal of study is not against any specific state or country "but a movement against the possibility of a country" (2013, 41). They write:

> Ruth Wilson Gilmore: "Racism is the state-sanctioned and/or extra-legal production and exploitation of group differentiated vulnerabilities to premature (social, civil, and/or corporeal) death." What is the difference between this and slavery? What is, so to speak, the object of abolition? Not so much the abolition of prisons but the abolition of a society that could have prisons, that could have slavery, that could have the wage, and therefore not abolition as the elimination of anything but abolition as the founding of a new society. (42)

Inspired by this abolitionist movement, I want to shift the scale at which we consider literacy to see that outside of its statist restriction, literacy—like study—always takes place. Taking up Harney and Moten's call to "destroy and disintegrate the ground on which the settler stands the standpoint from which the violence of coloniality and racism emanates" (132) requires us to decolonize literacy, as it were, practicing it in ways that resist statist capture of its potentialities.

To recall claims from throughout the book, literacy events happen whenever entities collide and signification takes place, where this touching has the effect of reorienting the movement of the bodies. These events are, as *Beloved* teaches us, dispersed in time and in space.[17] By thinking about touching as a capacity of all bodies—which can affect and be affected—it is possible to see these events as always (even when the event might look to a humanist like two humans talking to each other) involving the agency and participation of nonhuman actants: air, paper, ink, electricity, computer screens, papyri, clay, wax, chalk, string, trees, urine, whips, spray paint, sound waves. But, as Kyla Schuller (2018) reminds us, we cannot let this lead to a flattening of agency, especially since the intrahuman politics of race and gender often adhere precisely in how (according to different sociogenic scripts authorizing Man) different bodies are written into different animacies, often via the logics of what she calls "impressibility." Attuning to this complex relation of differential agencies and animacies (Chen 2012) requires not only that we see literacy as happening everywhere all the time, but that literacy is a constitutive feature of the social as such. And the social here cannot be limited to humans. These literacy events connect participants of different species, and they always include participants that aren't animal even if they are animate.[18] Literacy events allow for the discernment of collectivities, and they inescapably change us, but these collectivities are never just human, and the force for change issues in part from the nonhumans involved in the literacy situation.[19] Literacies are a condition for the emergence of a human, which means that they are in fact operative outside of and around this human. The human is social precisely because it is part of a wider sociality. My insistence on nonhuman agency is not then, as it may well be for some thinkers of nonhuman objects, a retreat from the social or the political.[20] It is, instead, an insistence that there is no thing outside the social.[21] Thinking literacy as irreducibly social—where the social is a natureculture phenomenon—necessitates an entirely different conception of the political than the restricted one proffered by Man as part of its humanizing assemblages.[22]

15

LITERACIES AGAINST THE STATE

The history of modernity is often told triumphantly, or in a melancholic key, by reciting the emergence of a particular form of state apparatus (the nation-state) and a particular form of economic circulation (free-market capitalism). The emergence of this political-economic structure cannot be thought without underscoring the constitutive relationship it has to the violences of colonialism, racial slavery, a recoding of patriarchal gender-ings, and the increasingly industrialized havoc visited upon the earth's ecosystems. Drawing on Wynter, I have been using the word "Man" as shorthand for the subject that is this composite system's hegemonic form, one that cannot in fact come into being without the disavowed processes of dehumanization and reification that justify such widespread violence.

Although Man, as the overrepresented form of the human, begins to emerge in early modernity through a recalibration and reconfiguration of older ideas about humanness, at a global level of political forms, it achieves a particular consistency or intensity when it is installed as the subject of human rights discourse. If the human of human rights is a fic-tion, as I argue in chapter 4, this fiction is part of the ongoing writing of bodies—or, more specifically, the bodying and writing of Man become inseparable—and this writing ties the always-being-written subject to international law.

After World War II, the United Nations ratified the Universal Declara-tion of Human Rights, and it was at almost precisely this moment that Hannah Arendt (1968), surveying the movement of refugees and bodies consigned to camps, declared the "end of the rights of man." The most obvious cause of this end was, for her, "the decline of the nation-state." What Arendt realized, and Giorgio Agamben constructed an entire theory of biopolitics around, is that the political facts of the war revealed how the human as such, removed from its protection by a nation-state, cannot be protected within the logics of human rights. At the moment when human rights became universal, their absolute insufficiency was made most apparent. At the same moment, the human was recoded as less an organism or entity than a problem of data. This is, in part, about the shift from disciplinary to control societies that Deleuze (1992) diagnoses, and it helps to see how the human is calculated as part of what Michelle Murphy (2017) calls "the economization of life." Management of the population aims no longer at bodies per se, but at capacities, attention, perception, and affect.

The study of literature as it is most often practiced today, as one of the humanities, is unthinkable without this political horizon. Its political justification, when one is offered, is that it is a crucial part of subjectification processes that produce subjects tethered to Man who can be the fully human citizens, workers, and consumers who participate, rationally, in the global networks of state and corporate circulation and accumulation. Indeed, after the tethering of population to the macroeconomic field of intervention called the economy, a population's literacy rate has become a crucial factor in a state's Human Development Index number, which is used to administer aid, investment, and intervention on a global scale.[1] Literacy, and the study of literature, are always coded as good or useful, and this use is directly implicated in a politics oriented toward Man. *Animate Literacies* offers an alternative way of thinking about literature and literacy, and this requires an alternative horizon for politics, one not oriented around Man and its humanizing assemblages.

Conceptually, I want to take up Deleuze and Guattari's notion of the "apparatus of capture" (2002, 424). While there is, ontogenically, the ongoing and multiform movements and becoming of bodies—of all types— and their collision in events that ephemerally collectivize them, "the state apparatuses effect a capture of the phylum, put the traits of expression into a form or a code, make the holes resonate together, plug the lines of flight, subordinate the technological operation to the work model, impose upon the connections a whole regime of arborescent conjunctions" (415). That is, the state imposes upon the desiring-production that ontogenically constitutes the social a set of forms to harness it, direct it, rein it in. The concept of apparatuses of capture is crucial, for it sees the state as a kind of parasite, functioning only by siphoning and redirecting the energies that are always in circulation. The social does not need the state, but the state cannot exist without the social.

Deleuze and Guattari write that "warding off the formation of a State apparatus, making a state formation impossible, would be the objective of a certain number of primitive social mechanisms, even if they are not consciously understood as such" (2002, 357). That is, the movements that constitute social collectivities do not and need not be consciously opposed to the state.[2] Conscious opposition and the politics of recognition and representation are easily captured by the state, indeed they prop it up. This is so, in large measure, because of how states require identities for legibility, which means that political claims made on the basis of identities are always already caught up in the state's assemblages of humanization.[3] Against the state, what Deleuze and Guattari call "the nomadic trajectory" "*distributes people (or animals) in an open space. . . .* It is a very special kind of distribution, one without division into shares, in a space without borders or enclosure" (380). That is, it effects the deterritorialization of all state-regulated spaces. It sees politics as movement, as touching, as collision, as the social scene of encounter.

For this reason, I want to suggest that literacy events and the situations from which they emerge—as the collective touching of agencies and entities involving semiosis—are always political. Their politics lie not in representational practices—for those constitute only the most miniscule portion of the affects and effects of literacy—but in their role in distributing and regulating movement. As captured by the state, literacy becomes a way to segregate bodies, restricting most movement in order to channel energies along paths amenable to the functioning of Man (and state/corporate investment strategies that seize on attention and perception). *Animate Literacies* would pursue other directions, valorizing literacies against the state. I want to sketch some of the contours of these literacies now, but I want to insist that they are always and of necessity proliferating, mobile, excessive, and ephemeral. There is no plan for a literacy against the state, for that would already fall back into the state's logic.

These literacies, at least among humans, would make legible the violence of humanization. We have to learn to read the forms of inscription on bodies, including our own bodies, that write us into being in relation to Man. This involves conceptualizing race, gender, sexuality, ability, nationality, class, and species as forms of writing that demarcate and distribute bodies in relation to social spatialities, and it means experimenting with new forms of writing that would scramble statist codes, freeing up movement in unpredictable and unexpected directions.[4] But we have to remember that a shift from the level of identity to a politics of affects, movements, and ephemeral connection is not, in itself, enough to disrupt humanizing assemblages. Dana Luciano and Mel Chen, riffing on Jasbir Puar, write that "the unhuman takes its place as one exemplar of the biopolitical shift from disciplinary to control society, as power works increasingly through the permeation of material bodies, instead of through discrete, identity-marked subjects legible against a standard of humanity" (2015, 188). Man is already diagrammatically imbricated in assemblages of humanization that operate on molecular, perceptual, and affective levels. Much of this work takes place through literacies of data extraction and data management.[5]

There are, instead, affective, felt literacies, literacies operating beyond a statist capture of literacy and its fetishization of "written monuments to [Man's] history" (Wynter 1984, 35). While a fiction of "lacking Letters" (35) has been the state's alibi for seeing whole populations as having no history and thus needing to be written into existence through humanizing assemblages, literacies against the state affirm nonwritten, nonpermanent forms of literacy.[6] There are literacies of smell and of touch, affective literacies, literacies that take place far outside of human language. This emphasis on affect, on touch, suggests that we need to cultivate practices of what José Esteban Muñoz calls "touching inhumanity" (2015, 209).

These literacies do not (necessarily) congeal into the formation of persons with identities organized into communities of common being.[7] Instead, they enable us "to invent improbable manners of being, new modes and styles of living, polymorphous affective intensities, and new relational virtualities and friendships" (Joy 2015, 222). These new modes, as Eileen Joy calls them, exist not in conscious opposition to the state and its institutions, but involve "creating new para- and out-stitutional spaces in which anything at all might unfold that otherwise could not find a means, mode, or space for expression" (223).

Literacies create such new spaces—literacy is an assemblage of territorialization, or rather of deterritorialization—for bodies to mingle and collide. This is politics. Erin Manning writes that "politics is that which orients me toward an other in a movement, in a directionality" (2006, 14), and she ties this directly to touch and to literacy: "Language in circulation, gestures in movement: this is a politics of touch" (14).[8] This politics of touch requires thinking about the human itself as already a multiplicity, a network of systems, a confluence of entities, agencies, and bodies.[9] Elizabeth Grosz writes, "We need to understand the body, not as an organism or entity, but as a system, or series of open-ended systems, functioning within other huge systems it cannot control, through which it can access and acquire its abilities and capacities" (2004, 3). The prepersonal realm where the body's abilities and capacities are modulated and oriented is precisely where the politics of touch are most operative, and it is this scene that I have been trying to call attention to through my use of the concept of the literacy situation. This scene is necessarily open ended, and while it is often captured by statist modes of politics, thinking the state as an apparatus of capture enables me to clarify one of the reasons that thinking literacy as primarily affective is so important: while state politics can mobilize conscious thought and opposition, literacy encounters—in the situation and in the event—reconfigure the body's affects. It seems to me, then, that the task is less to conceptualize a politics that would withdraw from and wander away from the state than to attune to how we are constantly feeling the affective pull in other directions anyway.

The human, as a system made up of open-ended systems, is less an entity than a temporal consistency; any organism is.[10] Through evolutionary drifts—biological, cultural, historical, political, environmental—the human system is slightly out of sync with the flows of matter and other forms of life that move around it, in it, and through it. This temporality, which is also a question of scale, requires us to scope and scale our attentions to the human and literacy in order to feel out its contours. Depending on how one frames or focuses, the object in question can appear—or feel, or smell—quite different. Elizabeth Grosz writes, "As isolatable systems, fixed entities, objects with extrinsic relations to each other, the material universe is the very source of regularity, predictability, and determination that enables a perceiving being to perform habitual actions with a measure of some guarantee of efficacy. Yet as an interconnected whole, the universe itself exhibits hesitation, uncertainty, and openness to evolutionary emergence, that is, the very indetermination that characterizes life" (2010, 151). There is, then a question of scale and speed when thinking the politics of touch in literacy. What Grosz calls "regularity, predictability, and determination" corresponds to a molar view of time that is easily captured by the state.[11]

Glen Sean Coulthard underscores how this statist temporality operates with regard to a pedagogy that would restrict the most violent forms of "primitive" accumulation to "the past." Taking up Canada's desire to capture indigenous communities in a logic of recognition that would allow "reconciliation," he writes, "In such conditions, reconciliation takes on a temporal character as the individual and collective process of overcoming the subsequent *legacy* of past abuse, not the abusive colonial structure itself" (2014, 109). That is, the (settler) colonial state would like to posit the forms of colonization, slavery, and attempted genocides that marked modernity as somehow over and done and in the past, thus fostering "inscribed habits of inattention" (Boler 1999) to the ongoing nature of statist accumulation. Against this Coulthard turns to Fanon, who "challenges colonized peoples to transcend the fantasy that the settler-state apparatus— as a structure of domination *predicated* on our ongoing dispossession—is somehow capable of producing liberatory effects" (2014, 23). This is why, to recall chapter 3, the notion of haunting in literatures of the Black Atlantic is so crucial: we need literacies that would reject the state's temporal fictions, attuning to how slavery, genocide, and colonization are ongoing events, and that the state is always capturing our energies and dispossessing land.

I want to insist that the collectivities taking shape and shifting outside of statist capture are always more-than-human, and that, as Jean-Luc Nancy has argued, Man is in fact a "stumbling block" for any thinking of community.[12] But unlike some of the thinkers who want to imagine bringing nonhumans into humanist forms of political consideration or deliberation, or who want to imagine constructing assemblies to gather what are supposedly banal "associations of humans and nonhumans waiting for their unity to be provided by work" (Latour 2004, 46), I want to pitch those purportedly prepolitical collisions and encounters as the very scene of politics. Politics does not need assemblies, voting blocs, identifiable coalitions, and large aggregate groups. To assume that politics requires this is to prop up statist politics of recognition.[13]

Instead, I want to affirm a different temporality for politics, one that Coulthard associates with indigenous conceptions of land as a network of relations, and that Jack Halberstam articulates as queer temporality: "queerness as an outcome of strange temporalities, imaginative life schedules, and eccentric economic practices" (2005, 1). This is a temporality that is about encounter, aleatory movement, collision, unmaking, becoming undone, and unworking. While this political temporality does not add up to the work of identitarian community building (or nation building), it nevertheless creates society itself: society is self-organizing ontogenesis. This reconceptualizing of temporality and scale leads to a politics of affirming the virtual set of possibilities that always accompanies present action precisely in creating a set of conditions in which entities swirl and collide. While there is haunting here—full of Man's violence and statist capture—there is also room for maneuver, for improvisation, for becoming otherwise. The "past is not something that imposes itself but is a virtuality that [entities] will actualize differently on each occasion, depending on changes in the environment" (Debaise 2017, 74).[14]

This formulation, especially when we dislodge society from a way of thinking that would pretend that it is merely human, opens us toward what Massumi calls "animal politics" emerging in play. If "ontopower" names contemporary apparatuses of capture that prime bodies' affective and perceptual systems in ways that allow state-stratified identities, forms of living, and restricted movements, then play marks the site of creative excess that sends us moving in other directions. For Massumi, "play is the arena of activity dedicated to the improvisation of gestural forms, a veritable laboratory of forms of live action. What is played at is invention" (2014, 12). Play is instinctual, nonhuman or prehuman, aleatory, and always already semiotic in its appearance in the subjunctive register of the "as if." This subjunctive capacity, which is the milieu of animate politics, opens the present toward unknown and unknowable futurity: "In this ludic mode of reflexivity, it is essentially the future that is played" (23). This play emerges not from a distinct being, especially not one with an identity, but from the whole relational field of contact and touch I call the *literacy situation*. While statist politics capture this scene by setting conditions that prime participants for some movements rather than others, attuning to the affective scene of the situation can help us to feel out the other possibilities.

The politics of literacy that *Animate Literacies* proposes is thus of the future, but it does not involve anything new. It moves not toward the state and its humanizing assemblages that homogenize all time as the time of developing fully human persons who can inflict violence on ahumans, inhumans, less-than-humans, and nonhumans. Instead, it moves away from Man, or rather it gets carried away from Man in literacy situations that are always already setting us all—human and not—in motion together.

16

FUTURES OF ANIMA-LITERATURE

Although it has come up many times in *Animate Literacies*, I have not yet focused directly on the ecological stakes of the present moment, one in which Man (as the overrepresentation of the human) has become a geological agent. The petroleumization of (some) human cultures, which Stephanie LeMenager (2014) calls "petromodernity," has, as scientists now almost universally agree, changed the geological makeup of the planet Earth.[1] Most of the time conceptualized under the heading of climate change, what many are predicting from our precarious present is a future that, barring virtually unthinkable shifts in Man's extractive and consumptive habits, will make Man's civilization impossible. The Anthropocene, as it has come to be called, may very well spell Man's ruin.

It is not difficult to see how within this moment the kinds of literacies that make literature in the narrow sense possible are unsustainable. The kinds of logging, processing, printing, and transportation that are required to produce books on a large scale are almost universally seen as ecologically destructive at this point.[2] When one takes into account the energy needs of computers and the long-term endurance of "deadmedia" in landfills, the shift toward screen-based literacies and digital humanities looks equally destructive.[3] Indeed, I am not convinced that there will be any way to continue to practice print-based literacies in the ways that have been dominant in the last two hundred years that does not contribute to and speed up the kinds of devastation associated with the Anthropocene.

Rather than either a Pollyannaish refusal to engage these questions, or doomsday-inspired gestures of hopelessness, I want to suggest now, as the conclusion to this book, a third option for thinking about the future, or, more pointedly, different futures. My point of departure here is going to be the account of the Anthropocene's reconfiguration of our notions of historical time offered by postcolonial historian Dipesh Chakrabarty. In "The Climate of History," Chakrabarty takes up how the Anthropocene calls for a rethinking of the very difference between natural history and human history (or, rather, as he points out, the difference between human history and a nature that supposedly has no history). It does this in an interesting way: the Anthropocene forces "a sense of the present that disconnects the future from the past by putting such a future beyond the grasp of historical sensibility" (Chakrabarty 2009 197). That is, history— in the sense of historiography—has always taken for granted that there is a neutral, natural backdrop for human history that is more or less unchanging. This allows us to look toward the past to imagine the future, and it makes it fairly easy for Man to engage in planning. But anthropogenic climate change makes this assumption untenable: we have no idea what kinds of climatological conditions will obtain in the near future (even, say, fifty years out). What we are facing is thus a future that probably will not take place in climatological conditions of the Holocene, which is the geological era in which all of recorded human history has taken place.

As I have argued in more detail elsewhere, this leads me to two axioms for thinking about futurity.[4] The first is that instead of a politics of unification that would gather all of humanity into one collective that is capable of exerting its geological agency in more responsible ways (a version of which undergirds almost all mainstream ecological thought), we might do better to learn from the new materialist, feminist, queer, indigenous, antiracist, and postcolonial thinkers who have long challenged the violences of humanist unity under a purportedly neutral banner of humanity. The Anthropocene, to put this differently, is often used to further the politics of humanization authorizing Man as the only possible subject of modernity, and I think our political response should be to scatter. Instead of unification, we need experiments, always plural, with as many ways of performing the human as possible. These will be necessarily differentiated, uneven, incommensurate, ephemeral, even failed. There are so many ways to not be Man, and the futures of anima-literature are bound up with these experiments.

Second, it's important to register how Man's geological agency isn't really what scientists pretend it is, since the human is not an isolated, iso-latable entity. The human is always already transcorporeal, to use Stacy Alaimo's term—a being that exists as a kind of relay point in a swirl of chemicals, energies, processes, systems, and interspecies encounters that isn't human in any recognizable sense.[5] Human agency, then, is a kind of aftereffect of nonhuman agencies, and while Man directs and orients these energies in particular (destructive and violent) ways, the ecological politics that would enable humans to fail at being Man, to fail at being geological agents, will require us to reconceive of our selves as no more ours than the Earth is. Against fantasies of enlightened human mastery over the earth, we have to remember that we are land: "We are as much a part of the land as any other element" (Coulthard 2014, 61), and this land is always a matter of "reciprocal *relationship* . . . [that] ought to teach us about living our lives in relation to one another and our surroundings in a respectful, nondominating and nonexploitative way" (60).[6] This requires, as I argued in chapter 15, ways of conceptualizing the lived entanglement of entities and agencies as directly political.

These axioms enable me to directly address two ways of thinking about the futures of what I call *anima-literature*: the study of literature as a subset of more-than-human literacy practices, where humans are entangled with a whole host of other agencies that animate literacy situations. The first concerns the futurity of literature and literacy in schools, especially in the university. I began this book by thinking about the so-called "crisis of the humanities," one that is often pitched in a narrow way that doesn't ade-quately account for either the profound shifts taking place in and around the question of what a human is, nor the ecological horizon of the An-thropocene's fracturing of historical time. Moving away from a restricted sense of literature as something like Matthew Arnold's "sweetness and light" toward a furtive, speculative concept of literacy as any significatory act taking place as bodies—human and non—collide, I have tried to offer up the possibility that we do not know what literature or literacy or even language means. Taking up Kohn's productive attempts to "decolonize language," we might agree that "signs are not exclusively human affairs. All living beings sign. We humans are therefore at home with the multi-tude of semiotic life" (2013, 42).

If many of the responses to the crisis of the humanities are animated by a desire to insist upon the ongoing relevance of disciplinary practices that have, ultimately, a very recent origin in Western, imperialist history, I want to call instead for us to wander off track.[7] If we do not know what language, literacy, and literature are, then instead of ensuring that we dwell within disciplinary regimes and institutions that pretend we have answers and construct curricula and programs of study in order to pass on those traditional answers, we might instead hitch our collective thinking, study, and speculation to a boundless unknowing.

We might pursue what William Spanos (2015, 36) calls "non-humanist humanity" and an attendant "non-humanist humanities," which involves "breaking the insidious hold that the disciplinary structure (as ideology) continues to exert" on us. Rather than sticking to our disciplinary projects and practices, thinking about and in anima-literature necessitates that we do everything possible to dismantle the disciplinary divisions that collude with the statist capture and restriction of literacy in order to differentially organize the movements of bodies in social and physical space. As Jack Halberstam puts it, "In some sense we have to untrain ourselves so that we can read struggles and debates back into questions that seem settled and resolved" (2011, 11). Thus, challenges to disciplinary structures can be linked to decolonization by deterritorializing existing conditions.[8]

There is no way to do this without moving from humanist anthropocentrism toward a wider account of not only the roles that nonhumans play in literature as we have been disciplined to think it, but also the ways that language, literacy, and even literature are practices that nonhumans share.[9] This might mean that we follow Julietta Singh in recasting the humanities as the "future humanimalities," opening disciplinary borders to see what kinds of multispecies and more-than-human entanglements lend themselves to a renewed asking of what "literature" means.[10] Or we might use this to question the provincialness of even world literature, however much that formulation can be stretched against more narrowly nationalist ways of restricting literature. Recalling David Damrosch's formulation of world literature puts us on track to do this: "World literature is not an infinite, ungraspable canon of works but rather a mode of circulation and of reading, a mode that is applicable to individual works as to bodies of material, available for reading established classics and new discoveries alike" (2003, 5). Although Damrosch does not entertain this possibility, this formulation can easily be extended beyond the human. But, if we recall the etymology of "world" that links it to the human, we might do better to recast this, following Gayatri Spivak, as "planetary literature." Spivak writes, "If we imagine ourselves as planetary subjects rather than global agents, planetary creatures rather than global entities, alterity remains underived from us; it is not our dialectical negation, it contains us as much as it flings us away" (2003, 73). We must remember, though, that humans are not the only such planetary subjects, and that any collective emerging from literacy events will never be simply human.

For all the reasons I laid out in chapter 14, anima-literature cannot simply be a question of university education, and so I want to summon once again Harney and Moten's (2013, 26) call for subversive intellectuals "to be in but not of" the university. Against professionalization, against standards, against the transmission of canons of content, against productivity in neoliberal terms, we have to remember that "we already are [more than what we are]. We're already here, moving" (19). Study, as the collective being together in thinking and moving that has no interest in state recognition, happens. It can happen in the university, but it happens everywhere. Indeed, I want to suggest that study is a way of naming any literacy event that allows for the discernment of a collectivity such that new possibilities for moving are invented and generated.

This means at least two things for those of us whose lives are committed to the study of literature, literacy, and language. First, even as we dwell with others (human and not) in the spaces of our campuses in ways that experiment with non-Man habits of being and belonging, we need to work collaboratively with those in other institutionalized spaces of education. Among other things, this is going to require people at universities, and not just those housed in programs and colleges of education, to experiment with new ways of enacting early, primary, and secondary education. The segregation of P–12 from university education, and the disciplinary authorization of the dismissal of educational praxis as merely a preprofessional concern, is politically disastrous. As the adjunctification of university faculty continues, some in the enclaves of university systems are finally recognizing that the neoliberal and corporatist takeover of P–12 schooling is trickling up, reconfiguring education into a hypernarrow indoctrination into Man as homo oeconomicus with its attendant social function of generating subjects consigned to their placement in increasingly rigid social stratifications. Thinking that we in the university can afford to pitch our politics in classrooms where students appear only on condition of surviving at least thirteen years of previous humanization (and dehumanization) in schools is absurd.

But given how dehumanizing P–12 schools are, and how tightly they are screwed into assemblages of humanization and social segregation, we have to engage political struggles around literacy wherever that occurs, especially outside of schools. If literacy is the very stuff of politics, since it involves significatory events involving the collision of moving bodies, then it happens everywhere all the time. Following from this, the scope of anima-literature as a praxis of study is quite literally unlimited, and however we come together—human and non—in the dance of anti-disciplinary agency to think and practice such literacies, there can be no a priori or even programmatic statements about what can or cannot be included, who can or cannot be included. Anima-literature is a field of attention that cannot and will not be foreclosed. And yet, I do want to suggest that anima-literature, as the study of what animates literacy and how literacy animates us, has a particular orientation, although it might be more accurate to say that it has a particular disorientation. Anima-literature moves away from Man and the imperialist state.

Let me conclude, then, with three examples that may allow us to glimpse anima-literature in practice. The first, which sometimes retains a slightly anthropocentric focus, is the recent emergence of syllabus projects that function as critical public pedagogies. In response to the state-sponsored racist violence against black, brown, and indigenous people in the United States (or on Turtle Island), experimental, nonhierarchized activist movements such as Idle No More and Black Lives Matter emerged. These movements began as entanglements between the dehumanized persons subjected to statist violence and technological media literacies, and quickly grew into flourishing, experimental networks of activists that both reimagined traditional forms of demonstration and public pedagogy, but also began to generate open-access, collective, nonpermanent syllabi for study that were linked to social media hashtags like #FergusonSyllabus, #CharlestonSyllabus, #StandingRockSyllabus, and #IdleNoMore. While some of the study groups taking up these syllabi had ties to universities and other schools, many formed in other social and institutional spaces. These syllabi and the study they connect and subtend are explicitly pitched against the state and its apparatuses of capture. Equally importantly, much of this study constelled specific instances of racialized state violence in the United States and Canada with other forms of state violence across the globe.[11] Study groups reject official curricula, instead collectively generating lists of texts that don't respect disciplinary traditions, regimes, and canons. They gear education not in the service of a humanization oriented toward Man, but toward ways of seeing the (colonialist, settler) state as violent, extractive, and unnecessary. And all this happens in ways that require, even if not always explicitly, engagements with nonhuman materialities and their affects. Texts are made to circulate, sometimes illegally, through digital and corporeal (print-based) networks. Spaces that are not classrooms become changeful sites. And crucially, these groups do not aim for credentialing, or publishing, or even recognition of their knowledge production. Instead, study becomes a collective activity of collective reorientation: toward each other (not reducible to the human), away from the state. The indigenous activism around #StandingRockSyllabus and #IdleNoMore explicitly links such study to the politics of land, thus foregrounding forms of political relation that are more-than-human and keenly attentive to both how humans are not separable from land (that is, humans are an effect of nonhuman agencies) and to how the struggle for less ecologically devastating futures cannot be decoupled from a radically decolonizing project.[12] This study generates effects and affects, but none that are easily capturable by the state.

My next two examples are more literary, and help me to return to the importance of ephemeral, nonpermanent literacies and forms of attunement to the more-than-human swirl of the literacy situation. What's at stake here is, to return to Frederick Douglass and his chalk/brick/boards assemblages, a way of valorizing the disorienting and reorienting effects and affects of literacy that do not legibly endure. While some have turned, compellingly, toward Herman Melville's "Bartleby, the Scrivener" as a model of potentiality that enables us to theorize refusal precisely through a relation to literacy—"I would prefer not to" write—I think a more useful case is found in José Saramago's Seeing.[13] As a sequel to Blindness, in which the population of an entire country is suddenly afflicted with what turns out to be a temporary epidemic of blindness, one that plunges sociality into a state of chaos that borders on the so-called "state of nature" so often imagined by modernist thinkers, Seeing begins with what I want to suggest is the most dramatic staging I've encountered of a collective literacy against the state. After the population has regained its sight, a regular election is held, one that, as elections do, serves to reauthorize the state and its violences. Although voter turnout is extremely high, "more than seventy percent of the total votes cast . . . were blank" (Saramago 2006, 16).

This is not the same as Bartleby's refusal. The voters do vote. They go to the polls. They engage in the literacy event, but they engage it by not leaving a mark. They refuse the legibility of the state, even as they do their civic duty. Obviously, the state has no frame of reference for this illegible literacy event. Calling up laws governing what happens if "natural disaster" (Saramago 2006, 18) thwarts an election, they hold an emergency special election eight days later. After "a quiet, controlled whisper" circulates through the population, one that involves very little talking and a great deal of state surveillance (18–20), the second vote offers "a confirmation and an exacerbation of the trend established" in the first election. Eighty-three percent of the ballots are blank. The state enters crisis. Again, there is no question that people voted. They voted serenely and in large numbers. But this literacy event, which writes and signifies so much, does not leave marks and is not legible to the state.

Importantly, Saramago ties this literacy to the human in a way that might summon Wynter's distinction between Man and the human, as well as this book's tracking of literacies beyond statist restriction. He writes:

> The genetic code of what, somewhat unthinkingly, we have been content to call human nature, cannot be reduced to the organic double helix of deoxyribonucleic acid, or DNA, there is much more to be said about it and it has much more to tell us, but human nature is, figuratively speaking, the complementary spiral that we have not yet managed to prise out of kindergarten, despite the multitude of psychologists and analysts from the most diverse schools and with the most diverse abilities who have broken their nails trying to draw its bolts. (2006, 21)

What we have been "content to call human nature," a phrase that suggests this is a poor way of putting things, is, for Saramago, what cannot be restricted by discipline, bolted into place, or driven out of human animals. It is not anchored in some project of humanization (which is, in fact, precisely what is resisted by the blank votes), but it is already there in children before any schooling. It is, to use Massumi's terms, what is most animal in the human. What Saramago's novel thus stages is an animal capacity to redirect literacy against the state, and to draw on literacy practices that emerge before the kinds of literacy that are legible to the state (many of us develop print literacy in kindergarten). These practices cannot be considered human: they emerge from the human's animal capacities. Saramago suggests that we can achieve large-scale political effects by refusing to be legible to the state, by doing literacy differently.

If the syllabus projects enable forms of becoming attentive to state violence that might foster experiences of bewilderment—where the affective swirl of the literacy situation sends us moving away from Man—*Seeing* highlights how such bewilderment can become contagious in ways that throw the state into crisis. While crisis is not automatically a good thing, politically speaking (indeed, capitalism thrives on crisis as even Marx noted), shifting the scale of our analysis from the molar to the molecular might make all the difference. I'm thinking about Ilya Prigogine and Isabelle Stengers's (1979) account of how dissipative structures—such as the state—that require enormous amounts of energy for maintenance can slip into far from equilibrium states. Here, chaos is not the opposite of order but a set of conditions for the emergence of new, and unanticipatable, orders. That is, all matter exists in entangled relations that carry virtual possibilities for novelty and the becoming otherwise of entities and relations. Politics here is less about control or mastery over this scene than about a kind of attunement to this more-than-human relationality that we could call land, and the cultivation of an aesthetic ethics of living with.

Julietta Singh, riffing on Frantz Fanon, calls such a cultivation "becoming sensitive": "The decolonizing politics of our present moment might reach for sensitivities we ourselves cannot yet anticipate through experimental practices that can lead us into radically other forms of feeling and acting" (2017b, 63). Shani Mootoo's novel *Cereus Blooms at Night* stages this becoming sensitive through the main character of Mala Ramchandin. Following a trauma involving abandonment and incestuous sexual assault, Mala becomes something other than human. For many in her town—a fictitious Caribbean village called Paradise—Mala appears to have become illiterate: "To everyone else, Miss Ramchandin appeared to have a limited vocabulary or at least to have become too simple-minded to do more than imitate" (Mootoo 1996, 99). But this is less a diminishment in her literacy capacity than a profound reorientation in her attunements and sensitivities.

In nighttime excursions, Mala experiments with navigating her movement through the city without her eyes: she "had to experience her surroundings, become one with the trees, shrubs, weeds, fences, thorns, water and mossy ground" (151). This becoming sensitive enables new forms of orientation and movement, movement that is in no way oriented around Man's division and policing of space. Mala refers to these relations with the nonhuman as "an uncanny communion" (152), signaling precisely how it is not the relation that is new, but the attunement. We are, as I have argued throughout this book, always entangled in myriad political relations with countless entities, most of them not human, distributed across scales of space and time.

One day, when Mala "saw something crawling on her verandah" (126), the novel stages a sustained account of the transformation in her literacy capacities: "In this phase just before Mala stopped using words, lexically shaped thoughts would sprawl across her mind, fractured here and there. The cracks would soon be filled with images. Soon the inverse happened. A sentence would be constructed primarily of images punctuated by only one or two verbalizations: a noun tentatively uttered in recognition, a descriptive word confirming a feeling or observation" (126). Here, literacy is primarily affective, and the verbal appears as a belated back-formation.[14] In this transformation, Mala's literacy practices become indistinguishable from her corporeal life: "Many of her sounds were natural expansions and contractions of her body" (127). In such a state, "every muscle of her body swelled, tinged, cringed or went numb in response to her surroundings— every fibre was sensitized in a way that words were unable to match or enhance" (127).

This sensitivity dramatically alters Mala's relations to the nonhumans with whom she is entangled, and the humans of the city whose lives are more oriented toward Man. One of the novel's other characters, Elsie, refers to Mala as "The Bird" (109), a locution that recalls Edna Pontellier in The Awakening. While Elsie uses this verbal utterance to signal Mala's vulnerability—after her becoming sensitive, she never leaves her yard, and Elsie's husband sends her monthly provisions—the novel's narrator suggests something very different.[15] Mala develops an ability to enter into intimate proximity to birds, trees, insects, and other creatures (see, for example, 114). At a crucial moment in the novel, when police come looking for Mala, she is sitting underneath a mudra tree in her yard that is home to dozens of peekoplat birds: "The peekoplats in the mudra were silent, hopping nervously, afraid to call attention to themselves and their ward beneath. The chickens in the pomerac tree had become restless and clucked with worry. Call-and-answer cook-a-doodle-doos across the village were fast paced and urgent, like warnings" (177). Mala is here one of the birds, a member of a community that is structured by the entanglement of literacy and care that I would call politics. Once we find ways to turn our backs on the state and its humanizing assemblages—actualizing the other, virtual possibilities for relation that always haunt literacy situations—we have to reject the idea that such relations are prepolitical and instead affirm the irreducibly political nature of all aesthetic/ethical touching.

What might it mean to see the dramatic, antistatist literacy event staged in *Seeing* in constellation with Douglass's fugitive literacies of chalk and wall, Watana the orangutan's weaving and unweaving of her nest, Mala's becoming sensitive, and the nonofficial practices of study happening throughout (more-than-human) societies? This is the question of the futures of anima-literature. Elizabeth Grosz writes, "Political activism has addressed itself primarily to a reconfiguring of the past and a form of justice in the present that redresses or rectifies the harms of the past. It needs to be augmented with those dreams of the future that make its projects endless, unattainable, ongoing experiments rather than solutions" (2004, 14). This strikes me as exactly what anima-literature is: an experiment, not a solution, or, better, a set of experiments. Indeed, it is an experiment in attunement driven by love—and not a love driven by fantasies structured by humanism, but a love of literacy "as it is" (Casarino 2002, xiv). Throughout *Animate Literacies* I have not aimed to construct a coherent theory of literature or to offer specific prescriptions for the future of anima-literature, but I think we can and must become bewildered from where we are. We can begin to redirect our attentions, perceptions, energies, and movements if we ask again, without pretending to know in advance what we'll find or where it will lead us: What is literature? What is literacy? What animates it? How has it animated us? How might it animate us otherwise?

Notes

1. The Human(ities) in Crisis

1. Bérubé (2013), in making that claim, is paraphrasing remarks by Richard Broadhead, president of Duke University.

2. I'm following William Spanos's (2015) call for a "non-humanist humanities."

3. See Eagleton's (1987) foreword to Daniel Cottom's *Social Figures*.

4. The insufficiency of human rights law is clearly legible in Hannah Arendt's (1968) *The Origin of Totalitarianism*, and her analysis has been extended in various theories of biopolitics such as Giorgio Agamben's (1998) *Homo Sacer* and Cary Wolfe's (2013) *Before the Law*.

5. I sketch Wynter's account of Man's relation to the human in chapter 4.

6. William Spanos argues that "however decisive their demythification of the binary logic of logocentric thinking, the various practitioners of postmodern theory have failed to break out of the established disciplinary parameters" (1993, 191). The phrase "university of excellence" is borrowed from Bill Readings's (1997) *The University in Ruins*.

7. This move owes much to animal studies, especially the work of Donna Haraway (1991, 2008, 2016) and Cary Wolfe (2009a, 2013), but it is also indebted to Charles Darwin, Friedrich Nietzsche, and those writers forming what Margot Norris (1985) calls "the biocentric" tradition in literature.

8. This phrase, again, comes from Donna Haraway (2016), but I also hear in it what Judith Butler (1990) calls "gender trouble."

9. My use of "gut" here signals Elizabeth O. Wilson's (2015) claim that mentation is dispersed throughout the body, not restricted to the mind.

10. Kyla Schuller (2018, 79) cites Constance Classen in order to draw out how the privileging of vision over and above other senses was tied to gender and race: "'The supposedly lower, feminine senses of touch, taste, and smell' were associated with domestic work, whereas 'men used their eyes and ears outside in the world.' Touch could represent the immediate grasping characteristic of the primitive, whereas sight enabled reflective consideration that strengthens, rather than compromises, the perceiver."

11. See Ian Bogost's (2012) *Alien Phenomenology*, Graham Harman's (2002) *Tool Being*, and Steven Shaviro's (2014) *The Universe of Things*.

12. This attention is one I have learned from feminist, postcolonial science studies. See Sandra Harding's (2008) *Sciences from Below*.

13. "Dehumanism," Singh writes, "aims to bring the posthuman into critical conversation with the decolonial" (2017b, 4).

14. I borrow this exhortation from Chance the Rapper's (2013) song "Lost" (featuring Noname Gypsy).

2. Beloved's Dispersed Pedagogy

1. Subsequent references to *Beloved* are given parenthetically as page numbers in the text.

2. My use of "assemblage" throughout signals Deleuze and Guattari's (2002) concept from *A Thousand Plateaus*. It refers to a combination of relations that organize, collect, assemble. As Jasbir Puar has argued, one of this concept's advantages is that "assemblages do not privilege bodies as human, nor residing within a human animal/nonhuman animal binary" (2012, 57). My use is also heavily indebted to Alexander Weheliye's (2014) concept of "racializing assemblages" in *Habeas Viscus*.

3. On the gendering of slavery's spaces, see Robert Reid-Pharr's *Conjugal Union*, in particular his analysis of the function of domesticity: "Domesticity should not be understood, then, as a static phenomenon. . . . Instead, domesticity is better understood as an irregular process of regulation, of law, in which the constant flight and return of desiring bodies is negotiated" (1999, 65). See also Christina Sharpe's *Monstrous Intimacies*: "The enslaved black woman in the house . . . , often in a better material position than the black woman in the field, is nonetheless positioned in the midst of the everyday intimate brutalities of white domestic domination, positioned within a psychic and material architectonic where there may be no escape from those brutalities but in the mind" (2010, 9).

4. Picking up on a use of the word in Gilroy's (1993) *The Black Atlantic*, Nyong'o writes, "Black subjects eavesdropped on an anxious discourse of white supremacy, black inferiority, and the dangers of racial contamination. Overhearing this discourse, they replayed and refracted it, precisely in the hopes of shaming whites about it as well as using it as evidence to rouse other blacks out of their acquiescence to the present state of affairs" (2009, 89).

5. Jodi Byrd argues that "indigenous critical theory . . . might provide an agnostic way of reading and interpreting colonial logics that underpin cultural, intellectual, and political discourses. But it asks that settler, native, and arrivant each acknowledge their own positions within empire and then reconceptualize space and history to make visible what imperialism and its resultant settler colonialisms and diasporas have sought to obscure" (2011, xxx). For an extended treatment of settler

colonialism as a material set of conditions of possibility for life in the United States, see Tuck and Yang's (2012) "Decolonization Is Not a Metaphor."

6. In a way, all humanization is dispersed, since its duration is indeterminate and it may well be interminable.

7. In the language of Sylvia Wynter, we can say that this claim is authorized by the descriptive statement of Man2 as the overrepresentation of the human. Wynter (2003, 267) writes of "our present Darwinian 'dysselected by Evolution until proven otherwise' descriptive statement of the human on the biocentric model of a natural organism." In other words, the belief in race as a biological logic is part of the global operations of coloniality in late modernity.

8. Hortense Spillers underscores the ubiquity of this when she writes, "Because it was the rule, however—not the exception—that the African female, in both indigenous African cultures and in what becomes her 'home,' performed tasks of hard physical labor—so much so that the quintessential 'slave' is not a male, but a female—we wonder at the seeming docility of the subject, granting her a 'feminization' that enslavement kept at bay" (2003, 215). Spillers thus underscores how imperialism and the transatlantic slave trade reconfigured a historically more trenchant gendered division of labor, and how it served to produce a particular, state-sanctioned destruction of the possibility of motherhood, one that has been an alibi of the US nation-state since then for blaming black poverty (which is itself the product of state action) on black families.

9. Following Fred Moten's (2003) *In the Break*, we have to consider how thinking about slaves as commodities forces a radical reconceptualization of the commodity. I take this up later in "Slavery, the Human, and Dehumanization."

10. I learned about galls from Monique Allewaert, who gave a talk entitled "Turning the Light: From the Enlightenment to the Plantationocene" at the Legacies of the Enlightenment conference at Michigan State University, East Lansing, on October 5, 2018.

11. I'm thinking of what Andrew Pickering (1995, 24) calls "the dance of agency" here.

12. Morrison writes, "Slaves are not supposed to have pleasurable feelings on their own" (1987, 247). Even earlier, the novel signals the joy of bare feet on grass: "Here . . . in this place, we flesh; flesh that weeps, laughs; flesh that dances on bare feet in grass" (103). On flesh as a biopolitical problematic of racialization, see Alexander Weheliye's (2014) *Habeas Viscus*, Hortense Spillers's (2003) "Mama's Baby, Papa's Maybe," and Mayra Rivera's (2015) *Poetics of the Flesh*. The concept of priming is from Brian Massumi's *Ontopower*: "What distinguishes priming from the outmoded concept of subliminal influence is that priming does not imply a straightforward stimulus-response operating by linear causality, akin to a reflex. Priming conditions emergent awareness (creatively modulates its formation) rather than causing a response (reproducing a preexisting model). It implies complex thought-like

processes occurring as a nonconscious dimension of emergent perception, too rapidly for thought actually to have been performed" (2015, 66).

13. Watkins writes that affect "operates independently [of emotion], accumulating as *bodily* memory that, while both aiding cognition and inducing behavior, may evade consciousness altogether" (2010, 279).

14. For an excellent analysis of the role of nonhuman animals (focusing on the rooster Mister) in *Beloved*, see Zakiyyah Iman Jackson's (2016) "Losing Manhood: Animality and Plasticity in the (Neo)Slave Narrative."

15. On the concept of the event in Whitehead's philosophy, see Didier Debaise's (2017) *Nature as Event*, Erin Manning's (2013) *Always More Than One*, and Steven Shaviro's (2009) *Without Criteria*.

16. Erin Manning refers to what I'm calling a situation as "the ecology or associated milieu of the event," which "will have been inseparable from its affect" (2013, 27). Isolating events, then, is a work of subtraction after the fact of emergence: "This hyperrelationality has not yet found the means to subtract singularities from the virtual web of the associated milieu, a subtraction that will later allow the foregrounding of discrete events to be separated out from the complex relational bombardment of their backgrounds" (8).

17. In a related context, Zakiyyah Iman Jackson writes, of *Beloved*, that "the text opens up a space for us to ask questions that may not have solutions or provide solutions that may not be legitimated by hegemonic regimes of knowledge and liberal humanist ethics" (2016, 126).

18. See the issue of GLQ edited by Dana Luciano and Mel Y. Chen (2015, "Queer Inhumanisms"), some of the essays in a *Symploke* issue that I coedited with Mina Karavanta (Snaza and Karavanta 2015, "Posthumanisms"), and Zakiyyah Iman Jackson's (2013) "Animal: New Directions in the Theorization of Race and Posthumanism."

19. Among others, I am here following Stacy Alaimo's lead in *Bodily Natures*, where she argues that "casting racism as environmental exposes how sociopolitical forces generate landscapes that infiltrate human bodies. . . . Environmental justice social movements and modes of analysis target the unequal distribution of environmental benefits and environmental harms, tracing how race and class (and sometimes gender and sexuality) profoundly influence material, often place-based inequalities" (2010, 28–29).

3. Haunting, Love, and Attention

1. Denver, another of Sethe's daughters, asks the newly arrived ghost Beloved, "Why you call yourself Beloved?" and the response is, "In the dark my name is Beloved" (Morrison 1987, 88).

2. See Susan Huddleston Edgerton's (1996, 84) *Translating the Curriculum*: "Love—especially perhaps mother-love—complicated by the ravages of the almost total

social marginalization that is slavery, can be cataclysmic. Killing the child to save her from slavery might have been, as Morrison said, 'the right thing to do [but] she had no right to do it' (Otten 1989, 83)."

3. Indigenous scholars such as Jodi Byrd (2011), Eve Tuck and K. Wayne Yang (2012), and Glen Sean Coulthard (2014) foreground the violence settler states do in representing colonialism as past harm instead of ongoing, material process. Writing about the Canadian government's "reconciliation" projects, Coulthard writes that "in such conditions, reconciliation takes on a temporal character as the individual and collective process of overcoming the subsequent *legacy* of past abuse, not the abusive colonial structure itself" (2014, 108–9).

4. See Coulthard (2014). Seeing the present reality of settler colonial dispossession as the material condition of the US state also opens up ways of linking the US context to the Israeli occupation of Palestine (Davis 2016; Kotef 2015).

5. As Mina Karavanta argues, "The difficulty of sharing this history of violence against practices and discourses of forgetting requires a structure of response and hence responsibility to the ghosts of history living in the present" (2015, 168).

6. I here follow Lauren Berlant, who writes, in *Cruel Optimism*, "I am extremely interested in generalization: how the singular becomes delaminated from its location in someone's story or some local's irreducibly local history and circulated as evidence of something shared. This is part of my method, to track the becoming general of singular things, and to give those things materiality by tracking their resonances across many scenes, including the ones made by nonverbal but still linguistic activities, like gestures" (2011, 12).

4. *Humanizing Assemblages I: What Is Man?*

1. Making a virtually identical claim, Nancy Armstrong writes that "the history of the novel and the history of the modern subject are, quite literally, one and the same" (2005, 3).

2. Harold Bloom (1998), for instance, gives William Shakespeare credit for "inventing the human." Closer to Hunt's case, Christopher Castiglia (2008) offers an argument for the eighteenth-century production of the contemporary concept of the human in the context of the antebellum United States, but sees interiority as the production of print literacy more generally.

3. Judith Butler writes that "the state is not a simple unity and its parts and operations are not always coordinated with one another. The state is not reducible to law, and power is not reducible to state power. It would be wrong to understand the state as operating with a single set of interests or to gauge its effects as if they are unilaterally successful" (2004, 116).

4. In *States of Fantasy*, Jacqueline Rose writes that "the modern state enacts its authority as ghostly, fantasmatic, authority. But it would be wrong to deduce from

this . . . that the state is any less real for that" (1996, 9). Or, again, Judith Butler's claim that while being recognized and legitimated by the state is a necessarily ambivalent phenomenon for many, "to be legitimated by the state is to enter into the terms of legitimation offered there, and to find that one's public and recognizable sense of personhood is fundamentally dependent on the lexicon of that legitimation" (2004, 105).

5. In conceptualizing this as investment, I am obviously referring to psychoanalytic models of attachment. This last sentence also underscores how the in-vest-ment can signify acts of wearing clothing, where the affects generated at the fabric/skin border accumulate in gendered, racialized, classed, sexualized, national, and subcultural styles. Finally, given the chapter's concern with the state as its borders are articulated via assemblages, I am thinking about questions concerning a Palestinian state—and the metonymically linked question of a one- or two-state solution—in relation to the international boycott, divestment, and sanctions movement, which includes divestment as a key demand.

6. I expand on this point in chapter 7.

7. Zakiyyah Iman Jackson writes that "the question of race's reality has and continues to bear directly on hierarchies of knowledge pertaining to the nature of reality itself" (2015, 216).

8. Man, as the hegemonic form of the human today, picks up on and puts to political use an older ambiguity in the very concept in the sense that the human has been understood to be both a particular kind of being or creature, and the result of a particular developmental project (Snaza 2013a, 2014). Even in Plato's *Republic*, this doubling is at work. First, the human is differentiated as a kind of entity from other entities, classically the animal and the divine. Second, an educational-political apparatus is invented that would maximize what is most human in those creatures in order to humanize them, making them into fully human persons. Within modernity, two crucial changes appear in the structure of this narrative fiction. First, the pressure to distinguish the human from the divine lessens but is augmented by a need to dialectically distinguish the human from the machine and from the animal (in Cartesian philosophy, for instance). In Sylvia Wynter's terminology, this is the shift from Man1 to Man2. Second, under the auspices of seeing humanity itself as a kind of project, one that involves what a range of thinkers would come to call enlightenment, the individual subject also became a project. Immanuel Kant, then, can claim that "Man only becomes man through education" (1960, 3).

Foregrounding Man as a telos of development is axiomatic in imperialist ideology, for the idea was, officially, to civilize and humanize the "savage" or "primitive" or "underdeveloped" natives. Of course, this civilizing and humanizing mission was configured to fail, always leading to the production of what Homi Bhabha (1994, 92) calls "not quite/not white" humans. The operationalized failure of the humanizing apparatus—which included an entire educational structure to which

I will return—meant that colonialism, no matter how much intervention occurred, would always find justification for more intervention (Coulthard 2014, 100). Put differently, the colonial humanizing machine that claimed to seek the teleological production of fully human persons in fact generated the not-quite-human as Man's constitutive outside (something we saw in Schoolteacher's lesson in *Beloved*), and this produced remainder was then taken as reason to insist upon the necessity of further humanization. This same logic appears in mutated form underwriting state investments in control of preindividual affects and capacities in order to manipulate the economy and security of the nation-state. Control is always more subtle and more data driven.

9. She argues that "for the hominid-into-human, psychogeny replaced phylogeny as the determinant of its cognitive mechanisms or ratio-morphic apparatuses" (Wynter 1984, 24).

10. Patricia Clough argues that "memory might be better understood not as unconscious memory so much as memory without consciousness and therefore, incorporated memory, body memory, or cellular memory. As a surfacing of a difficulty in remembering or in being certain about the truth of memory, the body becomes a memorial, a ghosted bodily matter" (2007, 6–7).

11. She maps a two-stage production of Man as "processes made possible only on the basis of the dynamics of a colonizer/colonized relation that the West was to discursively constitute and empirically institutionalize on the islands of the Caribbean and, later, on the mainlands of the Americas" (Wynter 2003, 264). In the first stage, which "was from the Renaissance to the eighteenth century" (264), the human was reconfigured as a secular concept linked to early modern scientific reason and a Western state imperative to explore the new world (beginning, to use the title of one of her essays, in 1492). She calls this "Man1." In the second, "from then until today," the human was rewritten around the trauma that we can call Darwinian, as a natural phenomenon, a move that, on Wynter's reading, naturalizes the social and political forces of colonialism and racism. This is "Man2."

12. See Judith Butler (1990, 1993), *Gender Trouble* and *Bodies That Matter*. It's worth noting that Sylvia Wynter explicitly refers to Butler's work on gender performativity in her account of the human as praxis. She writes, "I am suggesting that the enactments of such gender roles are always a function of the enacting of a specific *genre* of being hybridly human. Butler's illuminating redefinition of gender as a praxis rather than a noun, therefore, set off alarm bells ringing everywhere! Why not, then, the performative enactment of *all our roles . . . ?*" (Wynter and McKittrick 2015, 33).

13. See Michelle Murphy's (2017) arguments in *The Economization of Life* that the biopolitics of population get tied to macroeconomic models of value in such a way that racialization is recast specifically as a question of probabilities for economic growth as measured by the GDP. I take up this argument in more detail in chapter 8.

14. On branding, see Simone Browne's (2015) *Dark Matters*.

15. This phrase is the title of a chapter in Elizabeth Grosz's (1994) *Volatile Bodies*.

16. This is important to underscore precisely because we need to resist the urge to see the individual body as a passive site of inscription for agents of power, while also avoiding giving an individual a false sense of freedom to do or become anything.

17. This conception of power is indebted to Foucault (1977, 1978), Deleuze (1988), Deleuze and Guattari (2002), and Puar (2007, 2012).

18. See Michael Omi and Howard Winant's (1986) account of "racial formation," which similarly sees the subject and the state in relations of mutual investment.

19. See Hagar Kotef's (2015) *Movement and the Ordering of Freedom*.

20. And, as Dean Spade (2015) has noted, a great deal of state power functions primarily in the less-than-spectacular mode of what he calls "administrative violence": a realm where bureaucrats use data to administer everyday life.

21. What Erin Manning (2013) calls an "affective tonality" is a near synonym for the literacy situation.

22. See Gilles Deleuze's (1992) "Postscript on the Societies of Control."

23. I take the notion of delinquency from Puar: "Control masks itself, or masks its effects, within the endless drive to recoup the resistant subject. We must instead advocate that resistance give way to delinquency" (2007, 162). On failure as something to affirm, see Halberstam (2011). On the virtual, see Deleuze and Guattari (2002), Manning (2013), and Shaviro (2009).

24. Castiglia offers a complementary account of the complex emergence of interiority via disciplines of character in the antebellum United States: "Self-possessed character was measured not by empirical effects on other people, but on its likeness to definitions made familiar to citizens through circulation in newspapers, pamphlets, and manuals" (2008, 26). Character, then, is a fiction produced through "interiorization of the social," and it "did not produce disciplined subject positions in the image of state ideology. . . but [rather] generated a site for negotiating the contradictions and conflicts of the state's myriad ideologies . . . in ways that belied the coherence of national or market interests" (4). Paradoxically, the goal of character reform "was not self- or collective management but *failed management*," which created the conditions of possibility for the historical emergence of new forms of state surveillance (10). Simone Browne's (2015) *Dark Matters* tracks some of these forms of state surveillance as they were articulated in relation to slave mobility. For both, these surveillance technologies endure and are reconfigured into what I have been calling the control society and its modulations of information and "machinically assembled bodies" (Clough 2004, 11).

25. For Whitehead, any aggregate of matter is a society. Before turning to living societies, the part of Debaise's text I quote first takes up "the case of societies such as crystals or rocks" (2017, 73).

5. Slavery, the Human, and Dehumanization

1. Garrison's rhetoric consistently associates darkness with all that is evil and base, while he associates lightness and white with all that is good. Despite his abolitionist politics, the metaphorics of racist thought saturate his preface. As we shall see, recognizing that a slave could be a human is not exactly the same as recognizing the slaves as human beings, and race emerges as the single most salient factor in thinking this difference.

2. I borrow the word "prime" from Brian Massumi's (2015) *Ontopower*.

3. With regard to truthful description, it is worth remembering here that Douglass in fact wrote three autobiographies, which differ sometimes substantially about the truth of his life.

4. As I argue in an essay called "Class Time: Spivak's Teacherly Turn" (Snaza 2015a) realism can be understood not as a particular kind of text so much as a mode of reading texts.

5. As Saidiya Hartman explains in *Scenes of Subjection*, the slave code was an ambiguous recognition of slave humanity; given the legal circumscription of slaves—who were, constitutionally, only three-fifths human—when slaves were recognized as human in the United States, it was only to find them at fault: "In this case, the assignation of subject status and the recognition of humanity expose the enslaved to further violence in the case of criminal agency or require the event of excessive violence, cruelty beyond the limits of the socially tolerable, in order to acknowledge and protect the slave's person" (1997, 55).

6. Toni Morrison's (1992) *Playing in the Dark* and David Roediger's (1991) *The Wages of Whiteness*, among many other texts, elucidate how the white gaze upon black unfreedom produces whiteness itself.

7. On this, see Luciano and Chen's (2015) "Has the Queer Ever Been Human?" and other essays in the issue of *GLQ* it introduces, as well as Alexander Weheliye's (2014) *Habeas Viscus*.

8. The so-called object-oriented ontology stream of posthumanist thought has, beginning with Graham Harman's (2002) *Tool-Being*, underscored how humans tend to recognize the ontological and agential existence of objects only when they break down or otherwise disrupt human fantasies of their "ready-to-handness."

9. In taking the infliction of wounds on Douglass's body as a kind of inscription (one that might be read alongside the tree that appears on Sethe's back in *Beloved*), I am following Simone Browne's analysis of "branding during transatlantic slavery as a marking, making, and marketing of blackness as a commodity. Branding was a measure of slavery, an act of making the body legible as property that was put to work in the production of the slave as an object that could be bought, sold, and traded" (2015, 26).

10. Zakiyyah Iman Jackson writes, in "Losing Manhood," "I invoke Douglass's

equivocations here to suggest we read the inchoate and incomplete nature of his intervention, its fugitivity, as a provocation and an effort to refuse modes of relating that were established under slavery" (2016, 106).

11. See Che Gossett's (2015) "Blackness, Animality, and the Unsovereign" for a similar analysis of Douglass's *Narrative* in relation to animal studies, biopolitics, and black abolitionist thought.

12. See Donna Haraway's (2008) *When Species Meet* and Nicole Shukin's (2009) *Animal Capital*.

13. Mina Karavanta writes, "If the post in posthumanism promises anything new, it does so by attending to this human together in complexity and unevenness without the vantage point of a particular human and her history as the measure" (2015, 169).

6. Literacy, Slavery, and the Education of Desire

1. The allocation of duties to persons playing particular roles is a crucial feature of Kant's highly influential account of the Enlightenment, in particular conception of how the ethics of thinking are connected to the apparatus of nation-state power. See Immanuel Kant's (1970) "What Is Enlightenment?"

2. This logic, ironically, structures the preface to Douglass's narrative by an abolitionist (see chapter 5).

3. A progymnasmata is a book containing examples meant to instruct students in writing through copying.

4. See Valerie Smith's (2009, 178–79) "Born into Slavery."

5. The phrase comes from J. Elspeth Stuckey's (1991) book of the same name.

6. This is why Betty Ring can write that "the autobiography itself bears witness to a resistance to slavery and assertion of 'manhood,' being *in se* a dismissal of the argument that the slave is unable to master written language. For this reason autobiography is a performative text. It describes the progressive return of the slave from bondage to freedom but comes also to stand as one of the elements that constitute and emphasize that liberation. Nor does the writing merely exist as a chronicle of events, since the narrator also constructs and interprets the past through the text. Even as it sets out to describe, it enacts" (1994, 120).

7. Although I take this up in more detail later, it's worth noting here that in formulating it thus, I am drawing on Brian Massumi's (2014) claim in *What Animals Teach Us about Politics*, that animal play is the condition of possibility for all language. That is, writing is an aspect of what he calls "animal politics."

7. What Is Literacy?

1. I argue that even the extension of literature to the entirety of human culture is too narrow.

2. The texts of Roland Barthes proved as good an *Ansatzpunkt* for considering the shift in cultural studies as there is.

3. See Jussi Parikka's (2014) *The Anthrobscene*.

4. See Hayles's (1999) *How We Became Posthuman*, Cary Wolfe's (2009b) *What Is Posthumanism?*, and Lydia Liu's (2010) *The Freudian Robot* for extended discussions of the Macy Conferences.

5. It's worth noting that this anthropocentric understanding of the political is severely restricted. I propose, instead, that the political is coextensive with touching or contact and thus includes not only humans but all other entities, living and nonvital.

6. Haraway cites Chomsky, Hauser, and Fitch, saying, "We argue that the available data suggest a much stronger continuity between animals and humans with respect to speech than previously believed. . . . For now, this null hypothesis of no truly novel traits in the speech domain [of humans] appears to stand" (2008, 235).

7. Stephanie Springgay (2018) picks up on Deleuze and Guattari's (2004, 475) claim that felt is the "anti-fabric" to link felting, affect, and feminist politics and pedagogy. She writes: "Felting as a posthuman proposition demands that we stop thinking broadly about the field, category, concept, practice, discipline—or whatever you want to call it—of education. Instead we need to consider intimate transmaterial touching relations that do not intensify settler colonial mastery over human and nonhuman life" (n.p.).

8. This should have been true at least since the publication of Derrida's (1978) *Of Grammatology*, which deconstructs the speech/writing binary in order to offer a paleonymic concept of writing in general, one that is, rather explicitly, operative far outside of the human and which is a condition of the human's possibility.

9. See Erin Manning's (2006) *Politics of Touch*.

8. Humanizing Assemblages II: Discipline and Control

1. For more on this, see my essay "Bewildering Education" (Snaza 2013a).

2. "De-partmentalization" means both to break up or divide and to institutionalize, following the French verb *partir* (to depart, to divide, to split up, to share). For a more extended treatment of the departmentalization of language and its relations to universities, see my essay "Departments of Language" (Snaza 2015b).

3. Patricia Clough writes, "The bodies of a control society are a composition of dynamic matter invested into being, an investment of capital and technoscientific

experimentation. . . . Control is a biopolitics that works at the molecular level of bodies, at the informational substrate of matter" (2007, 19).

4. In using "mastery" as a general term for imperialist power cutting across discipline and control, I am indebted to Julietta Singh's (2017b) *Unthinking Mastery*.

5. See also Murphy's claim that "race did not have to be named in order to enact racist practices" (2017, 12).

6. There is, of course, a vast materiality to the social scientific project of data gathering. It involves NGOs, universities, medical institutions, government agencies, syringes, test tubes, enormous amounts of paper, petroleum, and so on. Murphy's book tracks the particular ways that this system was field tested in Bangladesh precisely because of asymmetries in the political and economic relations among states in the twentieth century at a moment of official (and still partial and unfinished) decolonization.

7. I do not say "professors" or "scholars." In the field of education, for instance, the widely distributed journal of the dominant professional organization—*Educational Researcher*, published by the American Educational Research Association—routinely publishes educational research authored by researchers working for think tanks or nonprofit education reform organizations. I haven't explored this, but I would be surprised if this were not the case in many fields that have substantial links to the work of state governments or corporations.

8. Clough writes, "Machinically assembled bodies are compositions of elements, assembled even across techno-ontological thresholds, in order to do something, to transform, expand, or contract themselves and other bodies, to move bodies or to speed bodies up or to keep bodies going at given speeds. Machinically assembled bodies have no organizing center; instead, they arise out of a plane of dynamism in a continuum of forces" (2004, 11).

9. Attention, Massumi argues, is "the perceptual automatism that consists in tagging a change in the perceptual field as new and potentially important and building awareness on that change, for the very good reason that it may signal a necessity of a response or an opportunity for action" (2015, 65). Clough writes that "preindividual bodily capacities are made the site of capital investment for the realization of profit—not only in terms of biotechnology, biomedicalization, and genetics, but also in terms of technologically disposed education/training in self-actualization and self-control at the preindividual, individual, communal, national, and international levels" (2007, 21).

10. See also Erin Manning's claim that "to posit identity politics as the starting point of the process is to background in advance the activity of the milieu's rhythmic in-forming and, even more importantly, to undermine the potential of coming, if not to a different answer, at least to a different way of asking the question" (2013, 209).

11. Jasbir Puar argues that "the factioning, fractioning, and fractalizing of iden-

tity is a prime activity of societies of control, whereby subjects (the ethnic, the homonormative) orient themselves as subjects through their disassociation or disidentification from others disenfranchised in similar ways in favor of consolidation with axes of privilege" (2007, 28).

12. See Edward Said's (2004) *Humanism and Democratic Criticism*. This is what Cary Wolfe is trying to signal when he maps scholarship along two axes: humanist versus posthumanist object and humanist versus posthumanist methods. It is entirely possible even to study objects that fall outside of traditional humanist conceptions but to do so in traditionally humanist ways. Much of what takes place in the academy today under the sign of animal studies seems to fall into this category, as the animal simply becomes one more topic to study within existing disciplinary frames. For an excellent account of how this works in one particular case, see Julietta Singh's (2013) "The Tail End of Disciplinarity," which addresses disciplinary responses to J. M. Coetzee's *Lives of Animals*.

13. See Barad's (2007) *Meeting the Universe Halfway*.

14. Viswanathan chronicles the rise of English literature as subject in schools in the colonial context of British India before it was institutionalized in England. That is, the colonial drive to discipline the native subjects of India was directly implicated in the construction of English literature as a body of work that can be studied— a curriculum—and in particular practices of reading that literature which can be instantiated in pedagogies. As she puts it, "The discipline of English came into its own in an age of colonialism . . . and no serious account of its growth and development can afford to ignore the imperial mission of educating and civilizing colonial subjects in the literature and thought of England, a mission that in the long run served to strengthen Western hegemony in enormously complex ways" (1989, 2). Viswanathan also tracks how, once imported back to England, this newly developed curriculum had to be put to work in different ways. This reminds us that discipline is a matter of what one studies and how.

15. In Donna Haraway's (2016) terms, we could say that disciplines are less autopoietic than sympoietic.

16. See Julietta Singh's (2017b) *Unthinking Mastery: Dehumanism and Decolonial Entanglements*.

9. Bewilderment

1. Obviously, then, this light functions according to a long-standing Western metaphorics linking knowledge and morality that appears in such ur-texts as Plato's *Republic* and the book of Genesis. Given the passage's focus on pulsation, though, it would also make sense to read this light as a way of figuring a material force, one that reveals the indeterminacy of matter. I'm thinking of Karen Barad's (2007) account of quantum physics that tracks how, depending on the measuring

apparatus, light is either a wave or a particle (this is not, for her, a question of representation). These experiments anchor her generative account of "posthumanist performativity" and the "entanglement" of matter and meaning.

2. Freud's *Interpretation of Dreams* was published in 1900, the year after *The Awakening*.

3. For an extended discussion of "self-vivisection" and its function in Nietzsche's conception of the human, see my essay "The Human Animal *nach* Nietzsche: Rereading *Zarathustra*'s Interspecies Community" (Snaza 2013b).

4. Already in Plato's *Republic* we can see this logic at work, when Socrates, thinking about the best mode of education, asks, "Does not the one subject the beast in us to our human, or perhaps I should say our divine, element, while the other enslaves our humaner nature to the beast?" (1987, 355).

5. Erin Manning insists that "the body . . . is what comes-to-be under specific and singular conditions. It is the amalgamation of a series of tendencies and proclivities, the cohesive point at which a multiplicity of potentialities resolves as this or that event of experience" (2013, 16).

6. I repeat this claim here from my essay "Bewildering Education" (Snaza 2013a, 49).

7. My quotation marks around "we" indicate that any collectivity that could be gathered pronominally is a problem. My thinking here follows Spivak's (2003) arguments about collectivities taking shape in particular spaces (which I take up in chapter 14), as well as Vaccaro's (2015) queries about the first person plural, and Singh's (2017b) "Coda," which extends Vaccaro's questions to think about the politics of coloniality and ecology. The issue here is that any "we" can mask violent erasures and asymmetries but is also crucial for utopian politics.

8. My use of the word "horizon" here is indebted to Luciano and Chen's (2015) introduction to an issue of GLQ, where they write, of the variety of streams of contemporary theory that seek to question the human, "These widely disparate domains all share a conviction that the 'human' (at least as traditionally conceived) has unjustly dominated and unduly limited the horizon of critical thought" (189). It obviously summons a history of hermeneutics and phenomenology as well, and following Sara Ahmed's (2006) *Queer Phenomenology*, that conception too can be helpful for thinking about politics in terms of spatiality and orientation.

9. On the relation between signal and noise as the result of an attunement to a particular system while adjacent to another, see Michel Serres's *The Parasite* (2007, especially 66–73).

10. This formulation is indebted to Jack Halberstam's (2011) *The Queer Art of Failure*.

11. With regard to utopia, or worse, "out there" in a space that Man might conquer. See Edward Said's *Culture and Imperialism*, where referring specifically to citizens in the United States, but within a political and rhetorical context that extends

its first-person plural toward a largely imagined entity called the "West," he asks, "Is there not an unquestioned assumption on our part that our destiny is to rule and lead the world, a destiny that we have assigned ourselves as part of our errand into the wilderness?" (1993, 55). See Julietta Singh's (2018) "Errands for the Wild" for a way of thinking about these errands as containing the possibility of errant, bewildering, decolonial redirection.

12. This leads to the famously open end of the novella, which sees Edna swimming naked out to sea past the point where she would have strength to swim back. While this could be read as a figuration of open-ended movement, Mademoiselle Reisz's statement casts a kind of pall over the end of the book, making it seem like a literally dead end.

13. This is why collective study is so crucial, as I explain in chapter 14.

10. Toward a Literary Ethology

1. This conception of literacy builds upon, but is different from, the notion of biosemiotics. I would agree with the general claim that "life is fundamentally grounded in semiotic processes" (Hoffmeyer 2008, 3), whereby "living nature is understood as essentially driven by, or actually consisting of, semiosis, that is to say, processes of sign relations and their signification—or function—in the biological processes of life" (4, emphasis in original). This conception is absolutely necessary in order to imagine an ethology of literacy practices. And yet I would push this a step further to insist that the semiosis at stake here always and inescapably includes within its operations—at the level of the literacy situation—nonliving entities and their semiosis as well. Life, as I would understand it, isn't simply about the living but about the contacts and collisions among living and nonliving entities. In extending biosemiotics in this way I am thinking of, among others, Ruth Miller, who notes that "the contagion that is thinking, feeling, sensing, perceiving, or remembering is also wrapped up in the communication of attractive qualities from mineral to mineral" (2017, 77).

2. While I have learned from postcolonial critiques of anthropology that see it as structurally racist (Ismail 2005), I am also aware that some anthropologists in the present are moving away from narrowly anthropocentric concerns and are thus, to my mind, reconfiguring the discipline and its methodological and political presuppositions. See Timothy Choy's (2011) Ecologies of Comparison, Anna Tsing's (2015) The Mushroom at the End of the World, Eduardo Kohn's (2013) How Forests Think, and Stefan Helmreich's (2009) Alien Ocean. The anthropology practiced by those associated with the new literacy studies is not such a reconfigured anthropology though, and its anthropocentrism is unthinking and unquestioned.

3. Didier Debaise notes that Whitehead "talks of 'sensation,' a general sense, a mood, or a vague awareness of a situation, that is, the affective tonalities, the act or action by which something is properly felt" (2017, 43).

4. As Donna Haraway argued in *Primate Visions*, primatology—which is sometimes ethological and sometimes based on laboratory observations—functions both as "simian Orientalism" and as a fiction that naturalizes patriarchal visions of the family and gendered power. Her account of how this works is instructive: "primatology is about an Order, a taxonomic and *therefore* political order that works by the negotiation of boundaries achieved through ordering differences. These boundaries mark off important social territories, like the norm for a proper family, and are established by social practice, like curriculum development, mental health policy, conservation politics, film making, and book publishing" (Haraway 1989, 10). This primatology, as part of the general episteme Foucault associates with the production of Man, is obsessed with taxonomy: with an insistence upon difference that orders it by producing and policing borders. Hence, as simian Orientalism, "the scene of origins [for primatology] is not the cradle of civilization, but the cradle of culture, of human being distinct from animal existence" (10). Primatology polices a range of borders—in material, affective, and institutional ways—that are ultimately oriented toward producing and maintaining the fiction of a rupture between humans and other animals.

5. This does not mean that I don't see differences between humans and other animals, but as Cary Wolfe argues, we must learn to see the human as "itself a specific form of animality, one that is unique and specific as other forms but no more different, perhaps, than an orangutan is from a starfish" (2009a, 572).

6. Hagar Kotef argues that "space becomes political via the moments it allows and prevents, and the relations that are formed or prevented via these im/mobilities. . . . Movement, in and of these various bodies, is the *material substance* of both freedom and violence" (2015, 114).

7. To appear together, a neologism I borrow from Jean-Luc Nancy's (1991) *The Inoperative Community*.

8. See Bergson's (1998) *Creative Evolution*.

9. Despret also locates the conditions for language in something like play: in "gestural communication," which is primed by throwing in chimpanzees. Such throwing "not only implicates the neural circuits responsible for intentional communicative behavior but also requires the ability to synchronize spatial and temporal information in precise ways. The gesture thus mobilizes the neural circuits that could prove to be essential to language acquisition" (2016, 25–26).

10. See Teresa Brennan's (2004) discussion at the beginning of *The Transmission of Affect* of how the "atmosphere" of a room affects a body.

11. Obviously, I am referring to Virginia Woolf's famous book, which is virtually omnipresent in my account.

12. Thus literacy comes to be a quantum in what Michelle Murphy (2017) calls "the economization of life" in that a nation's literacy rate is calculated into the Human Development Index. That is, the more of a population that has literacy under-

stood according to state measures, the more that nation's humans are developed. Literacy, in this sense, is more a preindividual capacity modulated by control rather than an aspect of disciplinary practice.

13. This is as good a description as any of what Andrew Pickering (1995) calls "the dance of agency" in *The Mangle of Practice.*

14. I will return to this, but this formulation returns me to Douglass's fugitive literacy education in chalk, which can be washed or wiped away.

15. By "barely perceptible," I mean that these consequences constitute what Timothy Morton (2013) calls a "hyperobject": an object that is too big to be seen, and which isn't an object in the usual epistemological sense because we live inside it.

16. See Dipesh Chakbrabarty's (2009) "The Climate of History" and Timothy Morton's (2013) *Hyperobjects.*

17. This is found, for example, in Rosi Braidotti's (2013) otherwise astute *The Posthuman.* I explain the problems with her vision of a future university anchored in global virtual space in a more detail in a note to chapter 16.

18. I play here on Dr. Seuss's *The Lorax.*

11. What Happens When I Read?

1. I have made a similar but different case about extending Said in my "Toward a Genealogy of Educational Humanism" (Snaza 2014).

2. See Wynter's (1995) "1492."

3. Erin Manning writes that "to touch is to become attuned to the ecologies of sensation always already activating the world as we embody it, as it embodies us" (2013, 131).

4. In calling this fragile, I am summoning William Connolly's (2013) *The Fragility of Things.*

5. The monster's account takes up much of chapters 4, 5, and 6 in volume 2. Indeed, the monster offers something remarkably like the ethology of literacy practice I sketched in chapter 10. I return to this in chapter 14.

6. Karen Barad's queer posthumanist reading of Stryker locates this scene of (dis)identification as a source of reconfiguring attunement to "the naturalizing discourses about the nature of nature" (2015, 392), opening up a line of inquiry into how Man is kept in place by discourses about the nature/culture distinction which are politically and scientifically questionable if not simply wrong.

7. For Miller and many other nineteenth- and twentieth-century Western comparatists, European or Western culture and literature offered a much more expanded frame than narrowly national ones.

8. I attend to this in more detail in "Class Time: Spivak's 'Teacherly Turn'" (Snaza 2015a).

9. This is the lesson of the field of science studies, in particular its feminist,

postcolonial, and queer versions. See Harding's (2008) *Sciences from Below*, Hekman's (2010) *The Material of Knowledge*, Barad's (2007) *Meeting the Universe Halfway*, Roof's (2007) *The Poetics of DNA*, Latour's (1993) *We Have Never Been Modern*, and Willey's (2016) *Undoing Monogamy*.

10. Wilson looks to the psychoanalysis of Melanie Klein and Sándor Ferenczi and to clinical data from antidepressant trials to build her case, foregrounding what Ferenczi calls "the biological unconscious."

11. I am drawing here, primarily, from Protevi's (2009) *Political Affect* and Massumi's (2002) *Parables for the Virtual* and (2015) *Ontopower*.

12. It's worth recalling here from chapter 1 how Sethe's feet in contact with the grass prime her attention and perception.

13. On generating lists, see Ian Bogost's (2012) *Alien Phenomenology* for a celebration of the "litany."

14. On boredom, see Martin Heidegger's (1995) *Fundamental Concept of Metaphysics*. On disgust and arousal, see Laura Kipnis's (1999) *Bound and Gagged*. On discomfort, see Megan Boler's (1999) *Feeling Power*, Sara Ahmed's (2015) *The Cultural Politics of Emotion*, and Julietta Singh's (2017b) *Unthinking Mastery*.

15. We could think here about Jonathan Kozol's (1991) *Savage Inequalities*, which repeatedly notes how US citizens in poor and mostly black and brown communities are much more likely than affluent whites to live near toxic manufacturing facilities, or lack access to functional sewage, water, and trash utilities. Or we can look at Mel Y. Chen's (2012) *Animacies*, which tracks how toxic metals in manufacturing stick to Asian bodies and racialized ideas about Asianness.

16. See Flynn and Schweikart's (1986) *Gender and Reading*. Standpoint epistemologies in feminist and antiracist theory have contributed enormously to this project as well. See Alcoff and Potter's (1993) *Feminist Epistemologies*.

17. I return to the political necessity of thinking literacy outside of the politics of identity in both chapters 14 and 15.

18. See Hayles's (2012) *How We Think* for analysis of how studies are tracking differences between neural plasticity in print literacy and in digital literacies. For a more general overview of the idea of brain plasticity, see Pitts-Taylor's (2016) *The Brain's Body*.

12. The Smell of Literature

1. See Hsuan Hsu's (2016) essay, "Olfactory Art, Transcorporeality, and the Museum Environment."

2. On the importance of vision for Man's imperialist pedagogies, see William Spanos's (1993) *The End of Education*.

3. And even, perhaps, in certain forms of plant life. I refer to this argument below in a footnote on Anna Tsing's (2015) *The Mushroom at the End of the World*.

4. Buttigieg writes that a "facet of Stephen's aesthetic theory which traditional Modernist critics find irresistible is the insistence on the artist's detachment, difference, and distance" (1987, 15). Accordingly, "these readers have been caught in a vicious circle of interpretation: their expectations have so governed their approach to A Portrait that their reading of the novel cannot help confirming their expectations" (18). I'm also motivated by Schaefer's more explicitly materialist argument that "Catholic readings of Ulysses view it backwards: Joyce is not exhuming the transcendent, but burying it in the mundane" (129).

5. For more extensive accounts of Joyce's relation to colonialism, see Semicolonial Joyce, edited by Derek Attridge and Marjorie Howes (2000), and Howes's (2004) contribution to The Cambridge Companion to James Joyce, "Joyce, Colonialism, and Nationalism."

6. I am thinking here about Judith Butler's account of how discourses materialize as bodies, although much of my focus in this chapter is going to be about how matter itself participates in that materialization. See Bodies That Matter (Butler 1993).

7. Indeed, Wolf's book title's reference to Proust almost automatically reminds those of us disciplined in the study of literature of À la recherche du temps perdu's most famous scene where the taste (never separable from smell) of a madeleine cookie calls forth the memories that take up the bulk of the novel's more than three thousand pages.

8. One of Tsing's first examples of smelling mushrooms involves elk: "The smell [of the mushrooms], they said, draws elk from one patch straight to another" (2015, 45).

9. Tsing suggests that if you think of smell as a "particular form of chemical sensitivity . . . trees too are touched by the smell of matsutake, allowing it into their roots" (2015, 45–46). Smell is, then, resolutely vital and corporeal, but may not even be restrictable to animals.

10. The double meaning here is crucial: to give off the smells that a fully human is supposed to, and to use one's sense of smell as a human being ought.

13. Pleasures of the Text

1. One could offer readings of pornography's force in terms of representation, and Laura Kipnis's Bound and Gagged goes quite far in this regard. She writes that "pornography can provide a home for those narratives exiled from sanctioned speech and mainstream political discourse, making pornography, in essence, an oppositional political form" (1999, 123). As the title of her chapter on Hustler Magazine—"Disgust and Desire"—makes clear, though, this is not just about representation, but about affects. In an account of how classed, raced, and gendered affects are policed by the state during modernity as part of what Norbert Elias calls "the

civilizing process," Kipnis considers how visual and verbal texts actually agitate the reader, setting her or his body moving.

2. See Melissa Adler's (2017) *Cruising the Library*, a study of Library of Congress (LOC) practices of segregating obscene, pornographic, and dangerous materials in secret collections (the so-called "Delta Collection"), and the uses of LOC subject headings to discipline sexuality. The United States LOC "must be understood as a state institution, and its classifications as state apparatuses" (100). Hunt's (1996) *The Invention of Pornography* takes up similar collections in France and England.

3. Hunt writes, "Production of both novels and pornography seem to be related, and countries that did not produce novels did not produce much pornography either" (1996, 23–24). Moreover, "pornography was not a given; it was defined over time and by the conflicts between writers, artists, and engravers on the one side and spies, policemen, clergymen, and state officials on the other. Its political and cultural meanings cannot be separated from its emergence as a category of thinking, representation, and regulation" (11). Bakhtin, in "Discourse in the Novel," writes that novelistic prose "is in fact an organized microcosm that reflects the macrocosm not only of national heteroglossia, but of European heteroglossia as well" (1981, 295). Watt is more explicit in the link not just to the nation but to the state. For Watt, "the novel's mode of imitating reality may therefore be equally well summarised in terms of the procedures of another group of specialists in epistemology, the jury in a court of law. Their expectations, and those of the novel reader coincide in many ways: both want to know 'all the particulars' of a given case" and so on (1957, 31). That is, Watt sees the novel as a kind of extension of a general trend in Western modernity, one consonant with the emergence of what Foucault (1977), in *Discipline and Punish*, calls the "carceral" system, which supplants the feudal regime of punishments. What is at stake is precisely a shift in object from crimes to cases: singularities whose identities and histories are discursively verified. Donovan, while almost reversing the standpoint from which she approaches things, sees the novel as similarly entangled with the nation-state's shift toward a carceral system. She writes that "another probable source of the novel's crucial irony is in a kind of folk-culture resistance to the growing colonization of everyday life by nation-state bureaucracies and by the increasing dominance of scientific and pseudo-scientific regulation and/or (in Michel Foucault's terminology) 'discipline' of the everyday life-world" (Donovan 1999, 5). This resistance, however, might end up being like the "speaker's benefit" Foucault (1978) describes in *The History of Sexuality, Volume 1*, where what seems like resistance is simply a scripted thrill affectively produced by the operations of power on and through the self. That is, Donovan claims that "because of its unique blend of realism and critical irony, the novel can foster ethical understanding of individual characters' plights and the forces responsible better than perhaps any other medium" (1999, 5). I'm not sure I would want to disagree,

but it's not clear how this is not precisely the sort of power at work in constituting the case as an object of discourse in the first instance.

4. This linking of nation-states and literacies was, as Robert Young (2016) has argued, also the condition of possibility for imagining that there are such things as discrete languages.

5. An important exception here is D. A. Miller's (1989) *The Novel and the Police*, which picks up on "the possibility of a radical *entanglement* between the nature of the novel and the practice of the police," since both "systematically participate in a general economy of policing power" (2). Gauri Viswanathan (1989), in *Masks of Conquest*, begins to conceptualize English literature as a subject as a mode of colonial discipline, and Edward Said's (1993) *Culture and Imperialism* more or less proposes that Western literature (again, writ larger than simply the novel) functioned as a crucial vector in Western imperial conquest.

6. There are precedents, such as Bataille's strange pornographic and philosophical novels.

7. See Paulo Freire's (2000) *Pedagogy of the Oppressed*, bell hooks's (1994) *Teaching to Transgress*, and Jane Tompkins's (1994) "Pedagogy of the Distressed."

8. This reminds me of Roland Barthes's discussion of keeping a diary: "if I reread my journal pages several months, several years after having written them, though my doubt hasn't dissipated, I experience a certain pleasure in rediscovering, thanks to these lines, the events they relate, and even more, the inflections (of light, of atmosphere, of mood) they bring back. In short, at this point no literary interest (save for problems of formulation, i.e., of phrasing), but a kind of narcissistic attachment (faintly narcissistic—let's not exaggerate) to my doings (whose recall is inevitably ambiguous, since to remember is also to acknowledge and to lose once again what will not recur" (1982, 480).

9. I return to this in chapter 14, as I think attuning to such differences is crucial to understand the affective politics of education, especially in classrooms.

10. See Julietta Singh's (2017b, 157–58) "Cultivating Discomfort" in *Unthinking Mastery*, where she recalls composing poems while replanting clear-cut Canadian forests.

14. Those Changeful Sites

1. In chapter 11, I argue that claims such as this one about the importance of literary reading have to be understood as taking place at the material and corporeal site of the body as a processual conglomeration of systems in relation to the myriad agencies, mostly more-than-human, that swirl in the literacy situation.

2. See Benjamin's (2003) "On the Concept of History."

3. Ferguson writes that "this new biopower would take as its representative the

subject constituted through difference, the one who had to learn what it meant to have a particularized history, the one who would have to access how probabilities for life have everything to do with those particularities; this is the subject who has to confront publicly or privately how those particularities and differences have historically shaped the quality and meanings of life, and whether to maneuver these historical legacies for conservative or disruptive ends" (2012, 34).

4. While *Frankenstein* affords some particular opportunities to dwell on the literacy situation, a vast range of texts—literary and otherwise—can open up similar questions and conversations. My aim here, as in many of my other writings (Snaza 2013a, 2015b, 2018) is not to offer classroom methods but to call for teachers and students to experiment with ways of attuning to the more-than-human situation of education.

5. Because I teach at a private liberal arts university, this list may come across as somewhat idyllic. At the very least, I would expect there to be a far larger range of circumstances generated by students at large state schools or community colleges.

6. This formulation is informed by Sara Ahmed's (2015) *The Cultural Politics of Emotion* and Teresa Brennan's (2004) *The Transmission of Affect*.

7. Contemporary practices of acknowledging indigenous territory in the Americas (and Australia) are best understood in terms of such affects. But if such acknowledgments do not also include a foregrounding of the ongoing politics of settler colonialism, they are not only empty gestures but become part of a statist politics that would pretend such violence is in the past. See Coulthard (2014), Tuck and Yang (2012), and paperson (2017).

8. One of the most publicized cases involved the University of Chicago banning safe spaces on campus (see Jaschik 2016).

9. The complexity is partly due to how the classroom is rhizomatically connected to a range of other debates about the limits or parameters of speech. These include the often volatile and anonymous spaces of internet forums (which have sparked controversies like Gamergate) and public events promoting white supremacist or ultranationalist politics (such as the white pride march in Charlottesville, Viriginia, in 2016, or the appearances on university campuses by Milo Yiannopoulos and Charles Murray). On Gamergate, see Hathaway (2014). On Charlottesville, see Gobar (2017). On Milo Yiannopoulos and clashes at UC Berkeley with Antifa protestors, see Richardson (2017). And on controversies surrounding Murray, especially the event at Middlebury College, see Beinart (2017).

10. For a fairly comprehensive collection of local demands made by students in Black Lives Matter, see http://www.blackliberationcollective.org/ourdemands/.

11. This is inseparable, in the United States, from the ubiquity of mass shootings in schools, which happen, statistically, once a week. They are so common that most classrooms at all levels now have signs on the walls detailing procedures for active school shootings (next to information about responding to earthquakes, tor-

nadoes, and hurricanes). While these shootings are also often about race (it is white men who most often commit mass shootings), the politics of safety in these cases are rather different than those about the violence of engaging in textual analysis or group discussions.

12. Jen Gilbert notes, "If education is a relation of hospitality, then we will affect and be affected by our encounters with others. This relation exceeds affirmation and risks ambivalence" (2014, 93).

13. While by "manufacturing of illiteracy" I mean the everyday ways in which statist schools actively produce the very illiteracies they ostensibly aim to reduce through instruction, Ruth Miller offers an extreme example of how this operates: "In 1928, Turkey's parliament legislated a nationwide shift from Arabic to Latin alphabetic characters . . . thereby rendering its reading and writing population illiterate in a single legal-political stroke" (2017, 10). On shifting curricula, sociologists of higher education make a similar point: even dramatically expanding access to postsecondary education hasn't significantly reduced class, race, or gender inequalities in wealth and overall conditions of living. See Jenny Stuber's (2012) *Inside the College Gates*, and Ann Mullen's (2011) *Degrees of Inequality*.

14. The notion of epistemicide is from João M. Paraskeva's (2011) *Conflicts in Curriculum Theory*, and my gloss is also informed by Sandy Grande's (2004) *Red Pedagogy* and Coulthard's (2014) *Red Skin, White Masks*.

15. In relation to the conception of hospitality cited above through Singh (2017a) and Gilbert (2014), we have to say that the university's hospitality is a sham hospitality structured by a refusal of the "infinite openness" of what Singh calls "future hospitalities."

16. Occupied in a very literal sense in settler colonies like those in the Americas, Australia, and Palestine. For an analysis of university education that foregrounds its relations to technologies and assemblages of settler coloniality, see paperson's (2017) *A Third University Is Possible*.

17. See chapter 2.

18. See Donna Haraway's (2008) *When Species Meet* (especially the chapter "Training in the Contact Zone"), Eduardo Kohn's (2013) *How Forests Think*, and Brian Massumi's (2014) *What Animals Teach Us about Politics*.

19. As Karen Barad argues, "If 'humans' refers to phenomena, not independent entities with inherent properties but rather beings in their differential becoming, particular material (re)configurings of the world with shifting boundaries and properties that stabilize and destabilize along with specific material changes in what it means to be human, then the notion of discursivity cannot be founded on an inherent distinction between humans and nonhumans" (2007, 136).

20. See Jordy Rosenberg's (2014) "The Molecularization of Sexuality."

21. See Deleuze and Guattari's *Anti-Oedipus*: "*There is only desire and the social, and nothing else*" (1983, 29, emphasis in original).

22. We might ask, with Vicki Kirby, "What do we forfeit if we concede that Nature reads and writes, calculates and copulates with itself in the most perverse, creative, and also destructive ways? What if it is political through and through, and this very discussion, here, in this book, is a manifestation of natural intent?" (2011, 95).

15. *Literacies against the State*

1. See Michelle Murphy's (2017, 23–30) *The Economization of Life*.

2. This aligns with Harney and Moten's (2013) rejection of critique and with Brian Massumi's (2014) insistence on play as the engine of animal politics.

3. Jasbir Puar writes that "identity is foundational to the control of population through state racism and the division of bodies" (2007, 158–59). See also Michael Omi and Howard Winant's (1986) *Racial Formation in the United States*, which sees racial identity as always constituted in relations between political demands and state bureaucracies.

4. Writing about the crisis in the very form and endurance of the nation-state, Arjun Appadurai speculates that in its wake we will see chaos, but then, perhaps, a new kind of order: "It may well be that the emergent postnational order proves not to be a system of homogeneous units (as with the current system of nation-states) but a system based on relations between heterogeneous units (some social movements, some interest groups, some professional bodies, some nongovernmental organizations, some armed constabularies, some judicial bodies)" (1996, 23).

5. For a historical account of the emergence of big data as a *modus* of biopolitics, see Orit Halpern's (2014) *Beautiful Data: A History of Vision and Reason since 1945*. Her book opens with an analysis of Songdo in South Korea, where "developers . . . envision an interface-filled life, where the currency of the realm is human attention at its very nervous, maybe even molecular, level" (3).

6. As Jayna Brown has argued, "We need not temper our utopian urges," but "it may be in fact that the forms of life excluded from the protective categories of able-bodied, white, and male human will be most open to seeing and imagining new life forms and 'utterly new modes of existence'" (2015, 328). This utopian writing of new modes of sociality is spurred on by an affective literacy of the violence of humanization: "We feel the politics by which the human is legitimated, how the lines around the human are policed, and the inhuman ways that racialized, disabled, and queer bodies are treated" (337).

7. Erin Manning writes that "to posit identity politics as the starting point of the process is to background in advance the activity of the milieu's rhythmic informing and, even more importantly, to undermine the potential of coming, if not to a different answer, at least to a different way of framing the question" (2013, 209).

8. This politics of touch involves what William Connolly calls self-organization.

Every literacy event brings together a host of bodies that "possess varying degrees of self-organizing power" (2013, 25).

9. Connolly writes, "To be human . . . is to be organized by a host of nonhuman processes and to be entangled with others" (2013, 49). Or, as Manning puts it, "We are massive colonies of microorganisms. Human bodies are open, growing systems. Our bodies are continually changing" (2006, 97).

10. We could also say, with Samantha Frost, that the human is a biocultural creature existing only because of the agency of various kinds of energy—oxygen, proteins, protons, neurons, electrons, hydrogen, and so on—that continually make, unmake, and remake who we are in dizzyingly complex and fast processes. While Frost's account has a family resemblance to many other feminist theories of the body as open process, one of the signal benefits of her account is the way she articulates differences among systems in terms of temporality. She writes, "It is the long histories of response-and-adjustment-to-habitat that enable an organism to live in and meet the provocations of its extant habitat. The histories of habitat-induced responses through which an organism composes and decomposes itself mean that an organism is not wholly contemporaneous with its environment. Indeed, it is through conceiving of organisms as noncontemporaneous with their habitats that we can grasp conceptually both their porosity and their distinctness. It is through organisms' noncontemporaneity with their habitats that we can conceptualize what it means to say that they are biocultural creatures" (2016, 123).

11. Tavia Nyong'o calls this "the pedagogical temporality of the nation-state" (2009, 163); Jack Halberstam calls it "a middle-class logic of reproductive temporality" (2005, 4); and Elizabeth Freeman (2010) calls it "chrononormativity."

12. Nancy writes, "It is *man*, taken absolutely, considered as the immanent being par excellence, that constitutes the stumbling block to a thinking of community" (1991, 3).

13. I am thinking here, among other things, of Judith Butler's (1997) patient consideration of the harms of hate speech that ultimately rejects redressing such violence by asking the US settler state to adjudicate the wrongs. By taking up the court's protection of racist acts of burning crosses (52–65), she tracks how the court "assert[s] its state-sanctioned linguistic power to determine what will and will not count as 'speech' and, in the process, enact[s] a potentially injurious form of juridical speech" (53). Put more directly than she does: the settler state is the last apparatus we should trust with deciding what does and does not count as (hate) speech.

14. Debaise (2017) is glossing Alfred North Whitehead. Also drawing on Whitehead, Steven Shaviro has written that "the subject cannot be given in advance; it must always emerge anew, in an unforeseeable way, as it is precipitated out of a metastable transcendental field. What's basic, for Simondon and Deleuze, is not the individual, but the always ongoing, and never complete or definitive, process of individuation" (2009, 81).

1. In *Living Oil*, petromodernity refers to "modern life based in the cheap energy systems made possible by oil" (LeMenager 2014, 67).

2. See Mark Kurlansky's (2016) *Paper*. The second Appendix to LeMenager's *Living Oil* is an excellent account of "the amount of energy used to publish the book" (2014, 202), tracking the energy needed to power a computer to write it, the printing of the book, transportation of the book to warehouses and retailers, energy needed to consume (read) the book, and the book's afterlife after disposal (recycling or transportation to a landfill).

3. While I generally affirm the cartography Rosi Braidotti (2013) lays out in *The Posthuman* and would even say that most of my work fits within the tradition of what she calls "critical posthumanism" (especially the feminist/queer/Deleuzian version she also practices), I find her account of the future of the university to be troubling. I fully agree with her suggestion that the humanities should study not Man but rather "co-presence, that is to say the simultaneity of being in the world together [that] defines the ethics of interaction with both human and non-human others" (Braidotti 2013, 169), and I likewise see the breakdown of disciplinary borders as crucial. Where I part ways is her vision of "new campuses [that] will be virtual and hence global by definition" (178–79). Arguing that such campuses will be housed in global cities that require and depend upon "intelligent spaces of high-technological interactivity and can thus be defined as . . . 'smart' city space[s] with dense technological infrastructure," she offers that "more Internet-backed interactivity will allow citizens to participate in all forms of planning, managing and assessing their urban environment. The key words are: open source, open governance, open data and open science, granting free access by the public to all scientific and administrative data" (179–80). I would schematically suggest three problems here. First, given what I say above about the ecological costs of internet connectivity and the dense materialities that subtend its virtuality, this vision strikes me as ecologically shortsighted. Second, I would reject any vision of global unification (which I think all too easily gets captured by Man) in favor of a multiplicity of scattered, differing, and even mutually antagonistic experiments in living. I would see the future of the university in ever more experimental forms of relationality that are entangled with local inhabitants (human and non-) without collating those into a unified global land/mediascape. While I don't think it can be said that affects don't circulate online, I also think corporeal proximity enables different—and politically important—affects. Third, I think Braidotti here privileges too quickly the modes of data collection and analysis that materially condition control societies. As Orit Halpern notes, "The web today is above all about the collection of personal data" (2014, 5), and this data is linked into the statist and corporate humanizing assemblages (see also Clough 2007). Indeed, as Michelle Murphy has argued, this

data-fication of life has dramatically shifted global power relations: "Even if nothing is improved, the larger surround was still miraculated as a firmament with as yet untapped potentials. In this way, experimentality could function as a form of subsumption, that is, of surrounding life with the forms of phantasies of economization, as well as the instruments and infrastructures of expectation" (2017, 81). While I think there is political potential in the microrelations among systems that are the affective scene of politics, I would caution against pitching our political futures and the future of the university on the very surround of informationalization of life that informs Man's contemporary biopolitical capture of human and more-than-human energies.

4. See Snaza's (2018) "The Earth Is Not 'Ours' to Save."

5. See Alaimo's (2008) "Trans-corporeal Feminisms and the Ethical Space of Nature" and (2016) *Exposed*.

6. On mastery, see Julietta Singh's (2017b) *Unthinking Mastery*.

7. William Spanos's *The End of Education* "suggest[s] the degree to which . . . the humanist *paideia* . . . is implicated in the imperial political project" (1993, xviii).

8. In la paperson's *A Third University Is Possible*, they argue that "Regardless of its colonial structure, because school is an assemblage of machines and not a monolithic institution, its machinery is always being subverted toward decolonizing purposes" (2017, xiii).

9. Sandy Grande has argued that any decolonizing education praxis has to involve precisely this moving away from humanism and its anthropocentrisms. She thus offers a pointed critique of Marxist and critical modes of pedagogy since for these "the end game remains human liberation: a profoundly anthropocentric notion, rooted in a humanist tradition that preserves the superiority of human beings over the rest of nature" (Grande 2004, 27).

10. Singh writes, "Once we begin to take seriously the animality of the human, we must rethink the reach and methods—as well as subjects and objects—of the humanities. . . . To cultivate the future humanimalities, we might first ask how our already existing skills as scholars can move us beyond the masterful human enclosures of disciplinarity" (2017b, 140–41).

11. See Angela Y. Davis's (2016) *Freedom Is a Constant Struggle*, which links the events in Ferguson, Missouri, in the US to the occupation of Palestine. See also Sylvanna M. Falcón's (2015) "The Globalization of Ferguson." Macarena Gómez-Barris has also linked the activism around the Dakota Access Pipeline to indigenous struggles across the Americas that seek decolonization through a politics of land keenly attentive to ecology and the politics of affect. She made the connection in "The Extractive Zone: Comparative Indigeneities in the Americas," a talk at the University of Richmond (February 23, 2017), drawing on her 2017 book *The Extractive Zone*.

12. For more on #IdleNoMore, see Coulthard (2014). For an analysis of struggles

against the Dakota Access Pipeline that link it to study and alternative ways to enact the university, see paperson (2017).

13. See especially "Bartleby; or, the Formula" by Gilles Deleuze (1997) and "Bartleby, or On Contingency" by Giorgio Agamben (1999). Deleuze foregrounds how Bartleby's repeated "I would prefer not to" is agrammatical English, stalling the statist capture of litercy.

14. In addition to being analogous to the way emotions are back-formations that describe affective modulations after the fact (Massumi 2002), I sense in this passage two ideas about language that Friedrich Nietzsche insisted upon. First, the passivity of the sentences signals that "a thought comes when 'it' will and not when 'I' will" (Nietzsche 1955, 18). This is, I would say, precisely because thought is conditioned by the literacy situation where the human subject is always being affected by a range of agencies that animate its thinking. Second, in "On Truth and Lies in a Nonmoral Sense," Nietzsche (1979) proposes that human language—which is verbal and conceptual—is always a translation of a translation since all animal thinking already involves a translation from nerve stimuli (the body's being affected) to thinking in images. For an extended discussion of Nietzsche's thinking about the human's animality and language, see my essay (Snaza 2013b) "The Human Animal *nach* Nietzsche" and Vanessa Lemm's (2009) *Nietzsche's Animal Philosophy*.

15. Elsie calls Mala "a helpless bird" (Mootoo 1996, 108).

References

Adler, Melissa. 2017. *Cruising the Library: Perversities in the Organization of Knowledge.* New York: Fordham University Press.

Agamben, Giorgio. 1998. *Homo Sacer: Sovereign Power and Bare Life.* Translated by Daniel Heller-Roazen. Stanford, CA: Stanford University Press.

Agamben, Giorgio. 1999. "Bartleby, or On Contingency." In *Potentialities*, edited and translated by Daniel Heller-Roazen, 243–71. Stanford, CA: Stanford University Press.

Agamben, Giorgio. 2003. *The Open: Man and Animal.* Translated by Kevin Attell. Stanford, CA: Stanford University Press.

Ahmed, Sara. 2006. *Queer Phenomenology: Orientations, Objects, Others.* Durham, NC: Duke University Press.

Ahmed, Sara. 2008. "Imaginary Prohibitions: Some Preliminary Remarks on the Founding Gestures of the 'New Materialism.'" *European Journal of Women's Studies* 15 (1): 23–39.

Ahmed, Sara. 2014. "White Men." Feministkilljoys, November 4. https://feminist killjoys.com/2014/11/04/white-men/.

Ahmed, Sara. 2015. *The Cultural Politics of Emotion.* 2nd ed. New York: Routledge.

Alaimo, Stacy. 2008. "Trans-corporeal Feminisms and the Ethical Space of Nature." In *Material Feminisms*, edited by Stacy Alaimo and Susan Hekman, 237–64. Bloomington: Indiana University Press.

Alaimo, Stacy. 2010. *Bodily Natures: Science, Environment, and the Material Self.* Bloomington: Indiana University Press.

Alaimo, Stacy. 2016. *Exposed: Environmental Politics and Pleasures in Posthuman Times.* Minneapolis: University of Minnesota Press.

Alcoff, Linda, and Elizabeth Potter, eds. 1993. *Feminist Epistemologies.* New York: Routledge.

Anderson, Benedict. 1983. *Imagined Communities.* London: Verso.

Appadurai, Arjun. 1996. *Modernity at Large: Cultural Dimensions of Globalization.* Minneapolis: University of Minnesota Press.

Arendt, Hannah. 1968. *The Origins of Totalitarianism.* San Diego: Harvest.

Armstrong, Nancy. 2005. *How Novels Think: The Limits of Individualism from 1719–1900.* New York: Columbia University Press.

Attar, Karen. 2015. "Books in the Library." In *The Cambridge Companion to the History of the Book,* edited by Leslie Howsam, 17–35. Cambridge: Cambridge University Press.

Attridge, Derek. 2004. "Reading Joyce." In *The Cambridge Companion to James Joyce,* edited by Derek Attridge, 1–27. Cambridge: Cambridge University Press.

Attridge, Derek, and Marjorie Howes, eds. 2000. *Semicolonial Joyce.* Cambridge: Cambridge University Press.

Bakhtin, M. M. 1981. *The Dialogic Imagination: Four Essays.* Austin: University of Texas Press.

Barad, Karen. 2007. *Meeting the Universe Halfway: Quantum Physics and the Entanglement of Matter and Meaning.* Durham, NC: Duke University Press.

Barad, Karen. 2015. "Transmaterialities: Trans*/Matter/Realities and Queer Political Imaginings." *GLQ* 21 (2–3): 387–422.

Barthes, Roland. 1975. *The Pleasure of the Text.* Translated by Richard Miller. New York: Hill and Wang.

Barthes, Roland. 1977. "From Work to Text." In *Image Music Text.* Translated by Stephen Heath, 155–64. New York: Hill and Wang.

Barthes, Roland. 1981. *Camera Lucida: Reflections on Photography.* Translated by Richard Howard. New York: Noonday.

Barthes, Roland. 1982. "Deliberations." In *A Barthes Reader,* edited by Susan Sontag, 479–95. New York: Hill and Wang.

Barton, David, Mary Hamilton, and Roz Ivanic, eds. 2000. *Situated Literacies: Reading and Writing in Context.* New York: Routledge.

Beinart, Peter. 2017. "A Violent Attack on Free Speech at Middlebury." *The Atlantic,* March 6. https://www.theatlantic.com/politics/archive/2017/03/middlebury-free-speech-violence/518667/.

Benjamin, Walter. 1996a. "On Language as Such and on the Languages of Man." Translated by Edmond Jephcott. In *Selected Writings, Volume 1, 1913–1926,* 62–74. Cambridge, MA: Harvard University Press.

Benjamin, Walter. 1996b. "One-Way Street." Translated by Edmund Jephcott. In *Selected Writings, Volume 1, 1913–1926,* 444–88. Cambridge, MA: Harvard University Press.

Benjamin, Walter. 1999. "Unpacking My Library." Translated by Harry Zohn. In *Selected Writings, Volume 2, Part 2, 1931–1934,* 486–93. Cambridge, MA: Harvard University Press.

Benjamin, Walter. 2003. "On the Concept of History." Translated by Harry Zohn. In *Selected Writings, Volume 4, 1938–1940,* 389–400. Cambridge, MA: Harvard University Press.

Bennett, Jane. 2010. *Vibrant Matter: A Political Ecology of Things*. Durham, NC: Duke University Press.

Bergson, Henri. 1998. *Creative Evolution*. Translated by Arthur Mitchell. Mineola, NY: Dover.

Berlant, Lauren. 2011. *Cruel Optimism*. Durham, NC: Duke University Press.

Bernheimer, Charles, ed. 1995. *Comparative Literature in the Age of Multiculturalism*. Baltimore, MD: Johns Hopkins University Press.

Bérubé, Michael. 2013. "My View: What Will You Do with an English Degree? Plenty." *Schools of Thought*, CNN, January 4. http://schoolsofthought.blogs.cnn .com/2013/01/04/my-view-what-will-you-do-with-an-english-degree-plenty/.

Bhabha, Homi. 1994. *The Location of Culture*. New York: Routledge.

Bloom, Harold. 1998. *Shakespeare: The Invention of the Human*. New York: Riverhead.

Bogost, Ian. 2012. *Alien Phenomenology, or What It's Like to Be a Thing*. Minneapolis: University of Minnesota Press.

Boler, Megan. 1999. *Feeling Power: Emotions and Education*. New York: Routledge.

Braidotti, Rosi. 2013. *The Posthuman*. Cambridge: Polity.

Brennan, Teresa. 2004. *The Transmission of Affect*. Ithaca, NY: Cornell University Press.

Breu, Christopher. 2014. *Insistence of the Material: Literature in the Age of Biopolitics*. Minneapolis: University of Minnesota Press.

Brown, Jayna. 2015. "Being Cellular: Race, the Inhuman, and the Plasticity of Life." *GLQ* 21 (2–3): 321–41.

Browne, Simone. 2015. *Dark Matters: On the Surveillance of Blackness*. Durham, NC: Duke University Press.

Butler, Judith. 1990. *Gender Trouble: Feminism and the Subversion of Identity*. New York: Routledge.

Butler, Judith. 1993. *Bodies That Matter: On the Discursive Limits of "Sex."* New York: Routledge.

Butler, Judith. 1997. *Excitable Speech: A Politics of the Performative*. New York: Routledge.

Butler, Judith. 2004. *Undoing Gender*. New York: Routledge.

Buttigieg, Joseph. 1987. *A Portrait of the Artist in Different Perspective*. Athens: Ohio University Press.

Byrd, Jodi. 2011. *The Transit of Empire: Indigenous Critiques of Colonialism*. Minneapolis: University of Minnesota Press.

Casanova, Pascale. 2004. *The World Republic of Letters*. Translated by M. B. Debevoise. Cambridge, MA: Harvard University Press.

Casarino, Cesare. 2002. *Modernity at Sea: Melville, Marx, Conrad in Crisis*. Minneapolis: University of Minnesota Press.

Castiglia, Christopher. 2008. *Interior States: Institutional Consciousness and the Inner Life of Democracy in the Antebellum United States*. Durham, NC: Duke University Press.

Cesaire, Aimé. 2001. *Discourse on Colonialism*. Translated by Joan Pinkham. New York: Monthly Review Press.

Chakrabarty, Dipesh. 2009. "The Climate of History." *Critical Inquiry* 35 (2): 197–222.

Chen, Mel Y. 2012. *Animacies: Biopolitics, Racial Mattering, and Queer Affect*. Durham, NC: Duke University Press.

Chopin, Kate. 1993. *The Awakening*. 2nd ed. New York: W. W. Norton.

Choy, Tim. 2011. *Ecologies of Comparison: An Ethnography of Endangerment in Hong Kong*. Durham, NC: Duke University Press.

Clough, Patricia. 2004. "Future Matters: Technoscience, Global Politics, and Cultural Criticism." *Social Text* 22 (3): 1–23.

Clough, Patricia, ed. 2007. *The Affective Turn: Theorizing the Social*. Durham, NC: Duke University Press.

Connolly, William E. 2002. *Neuropolitics: Thinking, Culture, Speed*. Minneapolis: University of Minnesota Press.

Connolly, William E. 2013. *The Fragility of Things: Self-Organizing Processes, Neoliberal Fantasies, and Democratic Activism*. Durham, NC: Duke University Press.

Coulthard, Glen Sean. 2014. *Red Skin, White Masks: Rejecting the Colonial Politics of Recognition*. Minneapolis: University of Minnesota Press.

Damrosch, David. 2003. *What Is World Literature?* Princeton, NJ: Princeton University Press.

Davis, Angela Y. 2016. *Freedom Is a Constant Struggle: Ferguson, Palestine, and the Foundations of a Movement*. Chicago: Haymarket.

Debaise, Didier. 2017. *Nature as Event: The Lure of the Possible*. Translated by Michael Halewood. Durham, NC: Duke University Press.

Deleuze, Gilles. 1988. *Foucault*. Translated by Sean Hand. Minneapolis: University of Minnesota Press.

Deleuze, Gilles. 1992. "Postscript on the Societies of Control." *October* 59 (winter): 3–7.

Deleuze, Gilles. 1997. "Bartleby; or, the Formula." In *Essays Critical and Clinical*, translated by Daniel W. Smith and Michael A. Greco, 68–90. Minneapolis: University of Minnesota Press.

Deleuze, Gilles. 2000. *Proust and Signs*. Translated by Richard Howard. Minneapolis: University of Minnesota Press.

Deleuze, Gilles, and Félix Guattari. 1983. *Anti-Oedipus*. Translated by Robert Hurley, Mark Seem, and Helen R. Lane. Minneapolis: University of Minnesota Press.

Deleuze, Gilles, and Félix Guattari. 2002. *A Thousand Plateaus*. Translated by Brian Massumi. Minneapolis: University of Minnesota Press.

Derrida, Jacques. 1978. *Of Grammatology*. Translated by Gayatri Chakravorty Spivak. Baltimore, MD: Johns Hopkins University Press.

Despret, Vinciane. 2016. *What Would Animals Say If We Asked the Right Questions?* Translated by Brett Buchanan. Minneapolis: University of Minnesota Press.

Donovan, Josephine. 1999. *Women and the Rise of the Novel, 1405–1726*. New York: St. Martin's.

Douglass, Frederick. 1997. *Narrative of the Life of Frederick Douglass, an American Slave, Written by Himself*. New York: W. W. Norton.

Eagleton, Terry. 1987. Foreword. In *Social Figures: George Eliot, Social History, and Literary Representation*, by Daniel Cottom, viii–xvii. Minneapolis: University of Minnesota Press.

Edgerton, Susan Huddleston. 1996. *Translating the Curriculum: Multiculturalism into Cultural Studies*. New York: Routledge.

Falcón, Sylvanna. 2015. "The Globalization of Ferguson: Pedagogical Matters about Racial Violence." *Feminist Studies* 41 (1): 218–21.

Fanon, Frantz. 1967. *Black Skin, White Masks*. Translated by Charles Lam Markmann. New York: Grove.

Federici, Silvia. 2004. *Caliban and the Witch: Women, the Body, and Primitive Accumulation*. New York: Autonomedia.

Ferguson, Roderick. 2012. *The Reorder of Things: The University and Its Pedagogies of Minority Difference*. Minneapolis: University of Minnesota Press.

Finkelstein, David, and Alistair McCleery, eds. 2005. *An Introduction to Book History*. New York: Routledge.

Flynn, Elizabeth A., and Patrocinio Schweikart, eds. 1986. *Gender and Reading: Essays on Readers, Text, and Contexts*. Baltimore, MD: Johns Hopkins University Press.

Foucault, Michel. 1977. *Discipline and Punish: The Birth of the Prison*. Translated by Alan Sheridan. New York: Vintage.

Foucault, Michel. 1978. *The History of Sexuality, Volume 1: An Introduction*. Translated by Robert Hurley. New York: Vintage.

Foucault, Michel. 1994. *The Order of Things: An Archaeology of the Human Sciences*. New York: Vintage.

Freccero, Carla. 2006. *Queer/Early/Modern*. Durham, NC: Duke University Press.

Freeman, Elizabeth. 2010. *Time Binds: Queer Temporalities, Queer Histories*. Durham, NC: Duke University Press.

Freire, Paulo. 2000. *Pedagogy of the Oppressed*. Translated by Myra Bergman Ramos. New York: Continuum.

Freud, Sigmund. 2005. *Civilization and Its Discontents*. Translated by James Strachey. New York: W. W. Norton.

Frost, Samantha. 2016. *Biocultural Creatures: Toward a New Theory of the Human*. Durham, NC: Duke University Press.

Fuss, Diana. 1995. *Identification Papers*. New York: Routledge.

Garrison, William Lloyd. 1997. Preface to *Narrative of the Life of Frederick Douglass, an American Slave, Written by Himself*, by Frederick Douglass, v–xiv. New York: W. W. Norton.

Gates, Henry Louis, Jr. 1991. "Binary Oppositions in Chapter One of *Narrative of the Life of Frederick Douglass an American Slave Written by Himself*." In *Critical Essays on Frederick Douglass*, edited by William L. Andrews, 79–93. Boston: G. K. Hall.

Gilbert, Jen. 2014. *Sexuality in School: The Limits of Education*. Minneapolis: University of Minnesota Press.

Gilroy, Paul. 1993. *The Black Atlantic: Modernity and Double Consciousness*. Cambridge, MA: Harvard University Press.

Gobar, Wes. 2017. "This is Us: Charlottesville Represented Something Distinctly American." *Washington Post*, September 12. https://www.washingtonpost.com /news/grade-point/wp/2017/09/12/this-is-us-charlottesville-represented-some thing-distinctly-american-white-supremacy.

Gómez-Barris, Macarena. 2017. *The Extractive Zone: Social Ecologies and Decolonial Perspectives*. Durham, NC: Duke University Press.

Gordon, Avery F. 1997. *Ghostly Matters: Haunting and the Sociological Imagination*. Minneapolis: University of Minnesota Press.

Gossett, Che. 2015. "Blackness, Animality, and the Unsovereign." *VersoBlog*, September 8. http://www.versobooks.com/blogs/2228-che-gossett-blackness-animality -and-the-unsovereign.

Grande, Sandy. 2004. *Red Pedagogy: Native American Social and Political Thought*. Lanham, MD: Rowman and Littlefield.

Grosz, Elizabeth. 1994. *Volatile Bodies: Toward a Corporeal Feminism*. Bloomington: Indiana University Press.

Grosz, Elizabeth. 2004. *The Nick of Time: Politics, Evolution, and the Untimely*. Durham, NC: Duke University Press.

Grosz, Elizabeth. 2010. "Feminism, Materialism, and Freedom." In *New Materialisms*, edited by Diana Coole and Samantha Frost, 139–57. Durham, NC: Duke University Press.

Grosz, Elizabeth. 2011. *Becoming Undone: Darwinian Reflections on Life, Politics, and Art*. Durham, NC: Duke University Press.

Guillory, John. 1993. *Cultural Capital: The Problem of Literary Canon Formation*. Chicago: University of Chicago Press.

Halberstam, Jack. 2014. "You Are Triggering Me: The Neo-liberal Rhetoric of Harm, Danger, and Trauma." *Bully Bloggers*, July 5. https://bullybloggers.wordpress .com/2014/07/05/you-are-triggering-me-the-neo-liberal-rhetoric-of-harm -danger-and-trauma/.

Halberstam, Judith [Jack]. 1995. *Skin Shows: Gothic Horror and the Technology of Monsters*. Durham, NC: Duke University Press.

Halberstam, Judith [Jack]. 2005. *In a Queer Time and Place: Transgender Bodies, Subcultural Lives*. New York: New York University Press.

Halberstam, Judith [Jack]. 2011. *The Queer Art of Failure*. Durham, NC: Duke University Press.

Halberstam, Judith [Jack]. 2013. "The Wild Beyond." Introduction to *The Undercommons*, by Stefano Harney and Fred Moten, 5–12. New York: Minor Compositions.

Halpern, Orit. 2014. *Beautiful Data: A History of Vision and Reason since 1945*. Durham, NC: Duke University Press.

Haraway, Donna. 1989. *Primate Visions: Gender, Race, and Nature in the World of Modern Science*. New York: Routledge.

Haraway, Donna. 1991. *Simians, Cyborgs, and Women: The Reinvention of Nature*. New York: Routledge.

Haraway, Donna. 2008. *When Species Meet*. Minneapolis: University of Minnesota Press.

Haraway, Donna. 2016. *Staying with the Trouble: Making Kin in the Chthulucene*. Durham, NC: Duke University Press.

Harding, Sandra. 2008. *Sciences from Below: Feminisms, Postcolonialities, and Modernities*. Durham, NC: Duke University Press.

Harman, Graham. 2002. *Tool-Being: Heidegger and the Metaphysics of Objects*. Chicago: Open Court.

Harney, Stefano, and Fred Moten. 2013. *The Undercommons: Fugitive Planning and Black Study*. New York: Minor Compositions.

Hartman, Saidiya. 1997. *Scenes of Subjection: Terror, Slavery, and Self-Making in Nineteenth-Century America*. Oxford: Oxford University Press.

Hathaway, Jay. 2014. "What Is Gamergate, and Why? An Explainer for Non-geeks." *Gawker*, October 10. http://gawker.com/what-is-gamergate-and-why-an-explainer-for-non-geeks-1642909080.

Hayles, N. Katherine. 1999. *How We Became Posthuman: Virtual Bodies in Cybernetics, Literature, and Informatics*. Chicago: University of Chicago Press.

Hayles, N. Katherine. 2012. *How We Think: Digital Media and Contemporary Technogenesis*. Chicago: University of Chicago Press.

Heidegger, Martin. 1995. *The Fundamental Concepts of Metaphysics: World, Finitude, Solitude*. Translated by William McNeil and Nicholas Walker. Bloomington: Indiana University Press.

Hekman, Susan. 2010. *The Material of Knowledge: Feminist Disclosures*. Bloomington: Indiana University Press.

Helmreich, Stefan. 2009. *Alien Ocean: Anthropological Voyages in Microbial Seas*. Berkeley: University of California Press.

Highmore, Ben. 2010. "Bitter after Taste: Affect, Food, and Social Aesthetics." In *The Affect Theory Reader*, edited by Melissa Gregg and Gregory J. Seigworth, 118–37. Durham, NC: Duke University Press.

Hoffmeyer, Jesper. 2008. *Biosemiotics: An Examination into the Signs of Life and the Life of Signs*. Translated by Jesper Hoffmeyer and Donald Favareau. Scranton, PA: University of Scranton Press.

hooks, bell. 1989. *Talking Back: Thinking Feminist * Thinking Black*. Boston: South End.

hooks, bell. 1994. *Teaching to Transgress: Education as the Practice of Freedom*. New York: Routledge.

Howes, Marjorie. 2004. "Joyce, Colonialism, Nationalism." In *The Cambridge Companion to James Joyce*, edited by Derek Attridge, 254–71. Cambridge: Cambridge University Press.

Howsam, Leslie, ed. 2015. *The Cambridge Companion to Book History*. Cambridge: Cambridge University Press.

Hsu, Hsuan. 2016. "Olfactory Art, Transcorporeality, and the Museum Environment." *Resilience* 4 (1): 1–24.

Hunt, Lynn, ed. 1996. *The Invention of Pornography: Obscenity and the Origins of Modernity, 1500–1800*. New York: Zone.

Hunt, Lynn. 2007. *Inventing Human Rights: A History*. New York: W. W. Norton.

Ismail, Qadri. 2005. *Abiding by Sri Lanka: On Peace, Place, and Postcoloniality*. Minneapolis: University of Minnesota Press.

Jackson, Zakiyyah Iman. 2013. "Animal: New Directions in the Theorization of Race and Posthumanism." *Feminist Studies* 39 (3): 669–85.

Jackson, Zakiyyah Iman. 2015. "Outer Worlds: The Persistence of Race in Movement 'Beyond the Human.'" *GLQ* 21 (2–3): 215–18.

Jackson, Zakiyyah Iman. 2016. "Losing Manhood: Animality and Plasticity in the (Neo)Slave Narrative." *Qui Parle* 25 (2): 95–136.

Jagose, Annamarie. 2013. *Orgasmology*. Durham, NC: Duke University Press.

Jaschik, Scott. 2016. "Chicago Professors Fire Back." *Inside Higher Ed*, September 14. https://www.insidehighered.com/news/2016/09/14/u-chicago-professors-issue -letter-safe-spaces-and-trigger-warnings.

Joy, Eileen. 2015. "Improbable Manners of Being." *GLQ* 21 (2–3): 221–24.

Joyce, James. 1994. *A Portrait of the Artist as a Young Man*. New York: Dover.

Kant, Immanuel. 1960. Education. Translated by Annette Churton. Ann Arbor: University of Michigan Press.

Kant, Immanuel. 1970. "An Answer to the Question: 'What is Enlightenment?'" Translated by H. B. Nisbet. In *Kant's Political Writings*, edited by Hans Reiss, 54–60. Cambridge: Cambridge University Press.

Karavanta, Mina. 2015. "Human Together." *Symploke* 23 (1–2): 153–72.

King, Katie. 2011. *Networked Reenactments: Stories Transdisciplinary Knowledges Tell*. Durham, NC: Duke University Press.

Kipnis, Laura. 1999. *Bound and Gagged: Pornography and the Politics of Fantasy in America*. Durham, NC: Duke University Press.

Kirby, Vicki. 2011. *Quantum Anthropologies: Life at Large*. Durham, NC: Duke University Press.

Kohn, Eduardo. 2013. *How Forests Think: Toward an Anthropology beyond the Human*. Berkeley: University of California Press.

Kotef, Hagar. 2015. *Movement and the Ordering of Freedom: On Liberal Governance of Mobility*. Durham, NC: Duke University Press.

Kozol, Jonathan. 1991. *Savage Inequalities*. New York: Broadway.

Kurlansky, Mark. 2016. *Paper.* New York: W. W. Norton.

Latour, Bruno. 1993. *We Have Never Been Modern.* Translated by Catherine Porter. Cambridge, MA: Harvard University Press.

Latour, Bruno. 2004. *Politics of Nature.* Translated by Catherine Porter. Cambridge, MA: Harvard University Press.

Laura, Crystal. 2014. *Being Bad: My Baby Brother and the School-to-Prison Pipeline.* New York: Teachers College Press.

LeMenager, Stephanie. 2014. *Living Oil: Petroleum Culture in the American Century.* Oxford: Oxford University Press.

Lemm, Vanessa. 2009. *Nietzsche's Animal Philosophy: Culture, Politics, and the Animality of the Human Being.* New York: Fordham University Press.

Liu, Lydia. 2010. *The Freudian Robot: Digital Media and the Future of the Unconscious.* Chicago: University of Chicago Press.

Lorde, Audre. 2007. "The Uses of the Erotic: The Erotic as Power." In *Sister Outsider,* 53–59. New York: Crossing Feminist Press.

Lowe, Lisa. 2015. *The Intimacies of Four Continents.* Durham, NC: Duke University Press.

Luciano, Dana, and Mel Y. Chen. 2015. "Introduction: Has the Queer Ever Been Human?" *GLQ* 12 (2–3): 183–207.

Lukacs, Georg. 1974. *Theory of the Novel.* Translated by Anna Bostock. Cambridge, MA: MIT Press.

Manning, Erin. 2006. *Politics of Touch: Sense, Movement, Sovereignty.* Minneapolis: University of Minnesota Press.

Manning, Erin. 2013. *Always More Than One: Individuation's Dance.* Durham, NC: Duke University Press.

Massumi, Brian. 2002. *Parables for the Virtual: Movement, Affect, Sensation.* Durham, NC: Duke University Press.

Massumi, Brian. 2014. *What Animals Teach Us about Politics.* Durham, NC: Duke University Press.

Massumi, Brian. 2015. *Ontopower: War, Powers, and the State of Perception.* Durham, NC: Duke University Press.

McHugh, Susan. 2011. *Animal Stories: Narrating across Species Lines.* Minneapolis: University of Minnesota Press.

Miller, D. A. 1989. *The Novel and the Police.* Berkeley: University of California Press.

Miller, J. Hillis. 1990. *Versions of Pygmalion.* Cambridge, MA: Harvard University Press.

Miller, Ruth A. 2017. *The Biopolitics of Embryos and Alphabets: A Reproductive History of the Nonhuman.* Oxford: Oxford University Press.

Mootoo, Shani. 1996. *Cereus Blooms at Night.* New York: Grove.

Moretti, Franco. 1982. "The Dialectic of Fear." *New Left Review* 136: 67–85.

Moretti, Franco. 2005. *Graphs Maps Trees: Abstract Models for Literary History.* London: Verso.

Morrison, Toni. 1987. *Beloved*. New York: Vintage.

Morrison, Toni. 1992. *Playing in the Dark*. New York: Vintage.

Morton, Timothy. 2013. *Hyperobjects: Philosophy and Ecology after the End of the World.* Minneapolis: University of Minnesota Press.

Moten, Fred. 2003. *In the Break: The Aesthetics of the Black Radical Tradition.* Minneapolis: University of Minnesota Press.

Mullen, Ann. 2011. *Degrees of Inequality: Culture, Class, and Gender in American Higher Education.* Baltimore, MD: Johns Hopkins University Press.

Muñoz, José Esteban. 2015. "The Sense of Brownness." *GLQ* 21 (2–3): 209–10.

Murphy, Michelle. 2017. *The Economization of Life*. Durham, NC: Duke University Press.

Nancy, Jean-Luc. 1991. *The Inoperative Community*. Translated by Peter Connon, Lisa Garbus, Michael Holland, and Simona Sawhney. Minneapolis: University of Minnesota Press.

Nietzsche, Friedrich. 1955. *Beyond Good and Evil*. Translated by Marianne Cowan. New York: Gateway.

Nietzsche, Friedrich. 1967. *On the Genealogy of Morals/Ecce Homo*. Translated by Walter Kaufmann. New York: Vintage.

Nietzsche, Friedrich. 1979. "On Truth and Lies in a Nonmoral Sense." In *Philosophy and Truth: Selections from Nietzsche's Notebooks of the Early 1970s*, edited and translated by Daniel Breazeale, 79–97. Atlantic Highlands, NJ: Humanities.

Norman, Richard. 2012. *On Humanism*. New York: Routledge.

Norris, Margot. 1985. *Beasts of the Modern Imagination: Darwin, Nietzsche, Kafka, Ernst, and Lawrence.* Baltimore, MD: Johns Hopkins University Press.

Nyong'o, Tavia. 2009. *The Amalgamation Waltz: Race, Performance, and the Ruses of Memory.* Minneapolis: University of Minnesota Press.

Nyong'o, Tavia. 2015. "Little Monsters: Race, Sovereignty, and Queer Inhumanism in *Beasts of the Southern Wild*." *GLQ* 21 (2–3): 249–72.

O'Donnell, James J. 1998. *Avatars of the Word: From Papyrus to Cyberspace*. Cambridge, MA: Harvard University Press.

Omi, Michael, and Howard Winant. 1986. *Racial Formation in the United States from the 1960s to the 1980s*. New York: Routledge.

paperson, la. 2017. *A Third University Is Possible*. Minneapolis: University of Minnesota Press.

Paraskeva, João M. 2011. *Conflicts in Curriculum Theory: Challenging Hegemonic Epistemologies.* New York: Palgrave Macmillan.

Parikka, Jussi. 2014. *The Anthrobscene*. Minneapolis: University of Minnesota Press.

Pettman, Dominic. 2011. *Human Error: Species-Being and Media Machines*. Minneapolis: University of Minnesota Press.

Pickering, Andrew. 1995. *The Mangle of Practice: Time, Agency, and Science*. Chicago: University of Chicago Press.

Pitts-Taylor, Victoria. 2016. *The Brain's Body: Neuroscience and Corporeal Politics*. Durham, NC: Duke University Press.

Plato. 1987. *Republic*. Translated by Desmond Lee. New York: Penguin.

Preciado, Paul. 2013. *Testo Junkie: Sex, Drugs, and Biopolitics in the Pharmacopornographic Era*. Translated by Bruce Benderson. New York: Feminist Press.

Prigogine, Ilya, and Isabelle Stengers. 1979. *Order out of Chaos: Man's New Dialogue with Nature*. Toronto: Bantam.

Protevi, John. 2009. *Political Affect: Connecting the Social to the Somatic*. Minneapolis: University of Minnesota Press.

Puar, Jasbir. 2007. *Terrorist Assemblages: Homonationalism in Queer Times*. Durham, NC: Duke University Press.

Puar, Jasbir. 2012. "'I Would Rather Be a Cyborg Than a Goddess': Becoming-Intersectional in Assemblage Theory." *philoSOPHIA* 2 (1): 49–66.

Readings, Bill. 1997. *The University in Ruins*. Cambridge, MA: Harvard University Press.

Reid-Pharr, Robert F. 1999. *Conjugal Union: The Body, the House, and the Black American*. Oxford: Oxford University Press.

Richardson, Valerie. 2017. "11 Arrested as Milo Cuts Short Berkeley Speech Costing $800K over Antifa Concerns." *Washington Times*, September 24. https://www.washingtontimes.com/news/2017/sep/24/milo-yiannopoulos-berkeley-speech-cut-short-over-a/.

Ring, Betty. 1994. "'Painting by Numbers': Figuring Frederick Douglass." In *The Discourse of Slavery: Aphra Behn to Toni Morrison*, edited by Carl Plasa and Betty J. Ring, 118–43. New York: Routledge.

Rivera, Mayra. 2015. *Poetics of the Flesh*. Durham, NC: Duke University Press.

Roediger, David R. 2002. *The Wages of Whiteness: Race and the Making of the American Working Class*. Rev. ed. London: Verso.

Roof, Judith. 2007. *The Poetics of DNA*. Minneapolis: University of Minnesota Press.

Rose, Jacqueline. 1996. *States of Fantasy*. Oxford: Clarendon.

Rosenberg, Jordana [Jordy]. 2014. "The Molecularization of Sexuality: On Some Primitivisms of the Present." *Theory and Event* 17 (2).

Rothberg, Michael. 2000. *Traumatic Realism: The Demands of Holocaust Representation*. Minneapolis: University of Minnesota Press.

Rubin, Gayle. 2011. "The Traffic in Women." In *Deviations: A Gayle Rubin Reader*, 33–65. Durham, NC: Duke University Press.

Sade, Marquis de. 1966. "Reflections on the Novel." In *The 120 Days of Sodom and Other Writings*, compiled and translated by Austryn Wainhouse and Richard Seaver, 97–116. New York: Grove.

Said, Edward W. 1979. *Orientalism*. New York: Vintage.

Said, Edward W. 1993. *Culture and Imperialism*. New York: Vintage.

Said, Edward W. 2004. *Humanism and Democratic Criticism*. New York: Palgrave.

Sandoval, Chela. 2000. *Methodology of the Oppressed*. Minneapolis: University of Minnesota Press.

Saramago, José. 2006. *Seeing*. Translated by Margaret Jull Costa. Orlando: Harvest.

Schaefer, Donovan O. 2016. "Heavenbeast: A New Materialist Approach to *Ulysses*." *Angelaki* 21 (2): 119–37.

Schuller, Kyla. 2018. *The Biopolitics of Feeling: Race, Sex, and Science in the Nineteenth Century*. Durham, NC: Duke University Press.

Sedgwick, Eve Kosofsky. 2003. *Touching Feeling: Affect, Pedagogy, Performativity*. Durham, NC: Duke University Press.

Seigworth, Gregory J., and Melissa Gregg. 2010. "An Inventory of Shimmers." In *Affect Theory Reader*, edited by Melissa Gregg and Gregory J. Seigworth, 1–25. Durham, NC: Duke University Press.

Sellars, Roy. 1997. "Theory on the Toilet: A Manifesto for Dreckology." *Angelaki* 2 (1): 179–96.

Serres, Michel. 2007. *The Parasite*. Translated by Lawrence R. Schehr. Minneapolis: University of Minnesota Press.

Sharpe, Christina. 2010. *Monstrous Intimacies: Making Post-slavery Subjects*. Durham, NC: Duke University Press.

Sharpe, Christina. 2016. *In the Wake: On Blackness and Being*. Durham, NC: Duke University Press.

Shaviro, Steven. 2009. *Without Criteria: Kant, Whitehead, Deleuze, and Aesthetics*. Cambridge, MA: MIT Press.

Shaviro, Steven. 2014. *The Universe of Things: On Speculative Realism*. Minneapolis: University of Minnesota Press.

Shelley, Mary. 2012. *Frankenstein*. 2nd Norton Critical ed., edited by J. Paul Hunter. New York: W. W. Norton.

Shukin, Nicole. 2009. *Animal Capital: Rendering Life in Biopolitical Times*. Minneapolis: University of Minnesota Press.

Singh, Julietta. 2013. "The Tail End of Disciplinarity." *Journal of Postcolonial Writing* 49 (4): 470–82.

Singh, Julietta. 2017a. "Future Hospitalities." *Cultural Critique* 95: 197–215.

Singh, Julietta. 2017b. *Unthinking Mastery: Dehumanism and Decolonial Entanglements*. Durham, NC: Duke University Press.

Singh, Julietta. 2018. "Errands for the Wild." *SAQ* 117 (3): 565–78.

Smith, Valerie. 2009. "Born into Slavery: Echoes and Legacies." In *Cambridge Companion to Frederick Douglass*, edited by Maurice S. Lee, 173–82. Cambridge: Cambridge University Press.

Snaza, Nathan. 2013a. "Bewildering Education." *Journal of Curriculum and Pedagogy* 10 (1): 38–54.

Snaza, Nathan. 2013b. "The Human Animal *nach* Nietzsche: Re-reading *Zarathustra*'s Interspecies Community." *Angelaki* 18 (4): 81–100.

Snaza, Nathan. 2014. "Toward a Genealogy of Educational Humanism." In *Post-humanism and Educational Research*, edited by Nathan Snaza and John A. Weaver, 17–29. New York: Routledge.

Snaza, Nathan. 2015a. "Class Time: Spivak's Teacherly Turn." *Critical Literacy: Theories and Practices* 9 (1): 49–61.

Snaza, Nathan. 2015b. "Departments of Language." *Symploke* 23 (1–2): 91–110.

Snaza, Nathan. 2018. "The Earth Is Not 'Ours' to Save." In *Interrogating the Anthropocene: Ecology, Aesthetics, Pedagogy, and the Future in Question*, edited by jan jagodzinski, 339–57. New York: Palgrave.

Snaza, Nathan, and Mina Karavanta, eds. 2015. "Posthumanism." Special issue, *Symploke* 23 (1–2).

Spade, Dean. 2015. *Normal Life: Administrative Violence, Critical Trans Politics, and the Limits of Law*. 2nd ed. Durham, NC: Duke University Press.

Spanos, William V. 1993. *The End of Education: Toward Posthumanism*. Minneapolis: University of Minnesota Press.

Spanos, William V. 2015. "Posthumanism in the Age of Globalization." *Symploke* 23 (1–2): 15–40.

Spillers, Hortense. 2003. *Black, White, and in Color: Essays on American Literature and Culture*. Chicago: University of Chicago Press.

Spivak, Gayatri Chakravorty. 1997. "Teaching for the Times." In *Dangerous Liaisons: Gender, Nation, and Postcolonial Perspectives*, edited by Anne McClintock, Aamir Mufti, and Ella Shohat, 468–90. Minneapolis: University of Minnesota Press.

Spivak, Gayatri Chakravorty. 2003. *Death of a Discipline*. New York: Columbia University Press.

Springggay, Stephanie. 2018. "'How To Write as Felt': Touching Transmaterialities and More-than-Human Intimacies." *Studies in Philosophy of Education*. https://doi org/10.1007/s11217-018-9624-5.

Stoker, Bram. 2003. *Dracula*. New York: Penguin.

Stoler, Ann Laura. 1995. *Race and the Education of Desire: Foucault's History of Sexuality and the Colonial Order of Things*. Durham, NC: Duke University Press.

Street, Brian. 1984. *Literacy in Theory and Practice*. Cambridge: Cambridge University Press.

Stuber, Jenny. 2012. *Inside the College Gates: How Class and Culture Matter in Higher Education*. New York: Lexington.

Stuckey, J. Elspeth. 1991. *The Violence of Literacy*. Portsmouth: Boynton/Cook.

Tarc, Aparna Mishra. 2015. *Literacy of the Other: Renarrating Humanity*. Albany: State University of New York Press.

Tompkins, Jane. 1994. "Pedagogy of the Distressed." In *Changing Classroom Practices: Resources for Literary and Cultural Studies*, edited by David B. Downing, 169–78. Urbana, IL: NCTE.

Tsing, Anna Lowenhaupt. 2015. *The Mushroom at the End of the World: On the Possibility of Life in Capitalist Ruins*. Princeton, NJ: Princeton University Press.

Tuana, Nancy. 2008. "Viscous Porosity." In *Material Feminisms*, edited by Stacy Alaimo and Susan Hekman, 188–213. Bloomington: Indiana University Press.

Tuck, Eve, and K. Wayne Yang. 2012. "Decolonization Is Not a Metaphor." *Decolonization: Indigeneity, Education and Society* 1 (1): 1–40.

Tuck, Eve, and Marcia McKenzie. 2015. *Place in Research: Theory, Methodology, and Methods*. New York: Routledge.

Vaccaro, Jeanne. 2015. "Feelings and Fractals: Wooly Ecologies of Transgender Matter." *GLQ* 12 (2–3): 273–93.

Viswanathan, Gauri. 1989. *Masks of Conquest: Literary Study and British Rule in India*. New Dehli: Oxford University Press.

Wanzo, Rebecca. 2015. "The Deadly Fight over Feelings." *Feminist Studies* 41 (1): 226–31.

Watkins, Megan. 2010. "Desiring Recognition, Accumulating Affect." In *The Affect Theory Reader*, edited by Melissa Gregg and Gregory J. Seigworth, 269–85. Durham, NC: Duke University Press.

Watt, Ian. 1957. *The Rise of the Novel*. Berkeley: University of California Press.

Weber, Samuel. 1987. *Institution and Interpretation*. Minneapolis: University of Minnesota Press.

Weheliye, Alexander G. 2014. *Habeas Viscus: Racializing Assemblages, Biopolitics, and Black Feminist Theories of the Human*. Durham, NC: Duke University Press.

Wellek, René, and Austin Warren. 1942. *Theory of Literature*. New York: Harvest.

Willey, Angela. 2016. *Undoing Monogamy: The Politics of Science and the Possibilities of Biology*. Durham, NC: Duke University Press.

Wilson, Elizabeth O. 2015. *Gut Feminism*. Durham, NC: Duke University Press.

Wolf, Maryanne. 2007. *Proust and the Squid: The Story and Science of the Reading Brain*. New York: Harper Perennial, 2007.

Wolfe, Cary. 2009a. "Human, All Too Human: 'Animal Studies' and the Humanities." *PMLA* 142 (2): 564–75.

Wolfe, Cary. 2009b. *What Is Posthumanism?* Minneapolis: University of Minnesota Press.

Wolfe, Cary. 2013. *Before the Law: Humans and Other Animals in a Biopolitical Frame*. Chicago: University of Chicago Press.

Wynter, Sylvia. 1984. "The Ceremony Must Be Found: After Humanism." *boundary 2* 12 (3)–13 (1): 19–70.

Wynter, Sylvia. 1995. "1492: A New World View." In *Race, Discourse, and the Origin of the Americas: A New World View*, edited by Vera Lawrence Hyatt and Rex Nettleford, 5–57. Washington, DC: Smithsonian Institution Press.

Wynter, Sylvia. 2001. "Towards the Sociogenic Principle: Fanon, Identity, the Puzzle of Conscious Experience, and What It Is Like to Be 'Black.'" In *National Identities* and *Sociopolitical Changes in Latin America*, edited by Mercedes F. Durán-Cogan and Antonio Gómez-Mariana, 30–66. New York: Routledge.

Wynter, Sylvia. 2003. "Unsettling the Coloniality of Being/Power/Truth/Freedom: Towards the Human, after Man, Its Overrepresentation—an Argument." *CR: New Centennial Review* 3 (3): 257–337.

Wynter, Sylvia. 2007. "Human Being as Noun? Or Being Human as Praxis? Towards the Autopoetic Turn/Overturn: A Manifesto." Scribd. http://www.scribd.com/doc/237809437/Sylvia-Wynter-The-Autopoetic-Turn#scribd.

Wynter, Sylvia, and Katherine McKittrick. 2015. "Unparalleled Catastrophe for Our Species? Or, to Give Humanness a Different Future: A Conversation." In *Sylvia Wynter: On Being Human as Praxis*, edited by Katherine McKittrick, 9–89. Durham, NC: Duke University Press.

Yamashita, Karen Tei. 1997. *Tropic of Orange*. Minneapolis, MN: Coffee House Press.

Young, Hershini Bhana. 2006. *Haunting Capital: Memory, Text, and the Black Diasporic Body*. Hanover, NH: Dartmouth University Press.

Young, Robert J. C. 2016. "That Which Is Casually Called a Language." *PMLA* 131 (5): 1207–21.

abolition: of Man, 41, 46–47, 143–44; of slavery, 38–41, 50–52
affect, 38, 89, 137; in bewildering events, 77–78, 81, 149; as communication, 44; as corporeal system, 12; as emotion/feeling, 23; learning as accumulation of, 16, 138–40, 144, 168n13; as link between reading and politics, 39–40; in literacy situation, 17–18, 64, 69, 76, 93, 93–94, 99, 110–12, 115; political ecology of, 24, 45–46; as preindividual site of control, 32, 72, 170–71n8; in relation to reading, 105–7, 110–12; relation between two senses as preindividual capacity and emotion, 17; as part of safe spaces, 139–40
affective attunement, 6, 140
Adler, Melissa, 131, 184n2
Agamben, Giorgio, 145
agency, nonhuman: in Douglass's Narrative, 44; in literacy, 16–18, 63–64, 72–72, 87–88, 124, 144; in literature, 25; in the novel, 29; in reading, 130; in relation to the human, 36–37; in relation to human agency, 154–55
Ahmed, Sara, 17, 23, 48, 72, 93–94, 111, 113, 130, 132

Alaimo, Stacy, 124, 168n19
Anderson, Benedict, 126
animacy, 6–7, 61, 64, 88, 90, 92, 107, 144
animal, 4–5, 59, 60, 89–91, 94–97; in binary opposition to the human, 42–47, 49–52, 115–16
anima-literature, 5, 6, 154–59, 163
Anthropocene, 97, 153–55
anthropology, 88, 179n2
Appadurai, Arjun, 188n4
apparatus of capture, 9, 28, 53, 68, 70, 76, 77, 91, 98, 128, 146–47
Arendt, Hannah, 145–146
Armstrong, Nancy, 169n1
assemblages, 166n2; and bodily capacities, 128; and colonization, 52, 75; and constitutive outsides, 104; coupling of humanization and dehumanization, 9, 31–37, 68; and formation of desire, 134–35; and humanization, 8–9, 97–98; and literacy, 45, 58, 115; and Man as a diagram, 2, 68, 81; and the novel, 28–29; of racialization, 43; as site of posthumanist thinking, 58; relation to the political, 144, 147–48, 152

attention: of ethology, 137; to haunting, 20–21; and investment in state formations, 29; to literacy's affects, 111–13; as love, 22–24, 163; mastery of, 76; to materiality, 107; to nonhuman agency, 63–64; 82–83; politics of, 72, 132; in reading, 134; as shaped by the university, 9

Attridge, Derek, 123

Bakhtin, Mikhail, 184n3
Barad, Karen, 25, 60, 75, 90, 177n1, 181n6, 187n19
Barthes, Roland, 25, 58, 125, 175n2, 185n8
Beloved (Morrison), 8, 11–17, 19–22, 36–37, 144, 168n17
Benjamin, Walter, 65, 131–32, 134
Bennett, Jane, 64
Bergson, Henri, 90
Berlant, Lauren, 17, 32, 83–84, 88, 169n6
Bernheimer, Charles, 57–58
Bérubé, Michael, 1
bewilderment: and aesthetics, 112; as affective disorientation, 9–10; as affective event, 77, 140; in The Awakening, 79–80; in classrooms, 136; in Dracula, 77–79; as effect of anima-literature, 163; as effect of literacy situation, 99; in Narrative of the Life of Frederick Douglass, 51; in relation to Man, 36, 81–85, 143
Bhabha, Homi, 170n8
biocultural creatures, 5, 31–32, 61, 75, 102, 189n9
biopolitics: and affect, 68; of control, 72, 80, 175n3; and data, 188n5; and governmentality, 35; and humanization, 2; and human rights, 146; in Narrative of the Life of Frederick

Douglass, 174n11; population as object of, 70; and racialization, 167n12; in Testo Junkie, 126–28; as theoretical current, 3; of the university, 185n3
biosemiotics, 179n1
birds, 84, 89, 95, 162–63, 192n15
Black Atlantic, 20–21, 150
Black Lives Matter, 139, 158, 186n10
Boler, Megan, 72, 138–39, 150
book history, 59–64, 74, 88
Braidotti, Rosi, 181n17, 190n3
Brennan, Teresa, 110–11, 121, 180n10
Breu, Christopher, 97, 107
Brown, Jayna, 188n6
Browne, Simone, 33, 52, 172n24, 173n9
Butler, Judith: on bodies and materialization, 183n6; on constitutive outsides of the human, 13, 32–33; on disidentification, 103–4; on gender performativity, 37, 171n12; and gender trouble, 165n8; on hate speech, 189n13; on personhood in relation to the state, 169nn3–4; on remaking the human, 8, 36–37
Buttigieg, Joseph, 183n4
Byrd, Jodi, 166n5

capitalism, 1, 2, 29, 35, 46, 68, 92, 120, 126, 161
carceral system, 69–70
Casanova, Pascale, 5, 91–93
Casarino, Cesare, 22, 26, 140, 163
Césaire, Aimé, 59
Castiglia, Christopher, 169n2, 172n24
Chakrabarty, Dipesh, 154, 181n16
Chen, Mel Y., 6, 7–8, 148, 182n15
Chopin, Kate, 9, 77, 79–80, 83–84, 86, 179n12
class, 113, 131–32, 139, 168n19
Clough, Patricia, 32, 72, 80, 171n10, 172n24, 175n3, 176nn8–9

colonialism: in *Beloved*"s concept of natureculture, 36–37; and disciplinarity, 75–76; and emergence of English Literature, 177n14; as force shaping classrooms, 134; and human rights, 102; and literacy, 97–98; neocoloniality, 97; as ongoing violence of modernity, 20–21, 145; in *A Portrait of the Artist as a Young Man*, 117–18, 183n5; and primatology, 180n4; as rendered illegible by humanism, 13; and restrictions of the human, 59–60; settler colonialism, 13, 20, 83, 139, 140, 143–44, 150, 159, 166n6, 169nn3–4, 186n7, 187n16; in Wynter's account of Man, 29–36, 170n8. *See also* decolonization; humanism; state apparatus

commodity, 43–44, 45–46, 93, 167n9
commodity fetishism, 16, 133
comparative literature, 57–58, 134
Connolly, William, 109, 181n4, 188n8, 189n9
consciousness, 59
constitutive outsides, 13, 66
contact zone, 60, 64, 87–88, 106–7, 112, 132
control, as form of power, 9, 32, 34, 68–72, 77, 80, 115, 146
Coulthard, Glen Sean, 37, 54, 88, 129, 140, 150–51, 154, 169nn3–4
critical animal studies, 3, 165n7
critique, limits of, 3, 100, 143, 188n2
cultural studies, 57–58

Damrosch, David, 57, 156–57
Darnton, Robert, 60
Davis, Angela Y., 191n11
Debaise, Didier, 35, 151, 172n25, 179n3, 189n14
decolonization, 37, 41, 65, 144, 155–56, 158–59, 161, 166n4, 176n6, 191n9

dehumanism, 4, 7, 35, 37, 166n13
dehumanization: in abolitionist thought, 46–47; and affect, 86; as aspect of literature, 26–27, 126; as constitutive feature of modern politics, 9; as exhaust, 37, 76, 136; as inseparable from humanization, 13–14, 17, 33–37, 145; and literacy, 51–53, 114; in relation to human/animal binary in slavery, 40–44, 49–50; and slavery, 84
Deleuze, Gilles, 2, 25, 68, 71, 80, 145, 192n13
Deleuze, Gilles, and Félix Guattari, 17, 83, 89–90, 136, 146–47, 166n2, 187n21
de Réaumur, René-Antoine Ferchault, 63
Derrida, Jacques, 32, 102, 175n8
Despret, Vinciane, 90, 96–98, 180n9
diagram, concept of, 2, 31–32, 68, 81
digital media, 58–59, 153, 190n3
discipline, 68, 82–83, 92; as form of power, 3, 5, 9, 34, 66, 72, 77, 80, 115; as intellectual field, 5–6, 9, 67, 70–71, 73–76, 78, 86, 156–57, 177n12, 177n15
disidentification, 103–4, 129
distant reading, 5, 23, 92
dogs, 16–17, 116
Donovan, Josephine, 184n3
Douglass, Frederick, 9, 38–47, 48–54, 55–56, 84–85, 131, 132, 135, 159, 163, 173n2, 173n10
Du Bois, W. E. B., 43, 52

Eagleton, Terry, 2
eavesdropping, 7, 12–13, 17, 55, 166n4
ecological devastation, 35, 97–98, 145, 153–55

Edgerton, Susan Huddleston, 168n2
empathy, 28, 38, 42, 60, 101
energy, 1–3, 5–6, 70, 72, 75–76, 150
erotics, 21, 24–26, 125, 129–33
ethology, 5, 87–90, 130, 136–37
event, 17, 21, 69, 72, 77, 81, 86,
    168nn15–16. *See also* literacy event
excellence, in universities, 3, 71
exhaust, 37, 76, 136

failure, 5–6, 9, 34, 76, 83, 154–55,
    172n23
Fanon, Frantz, 30, 32, 88, 112, 161
Ferguson, Roderick, 71, 136, 185n3
fiction, 34–35
flies, 12, 16–17
Foucault, Michel, 66, 67, 69, 71, 127,
    184n3
Frankenstein (Shelley), 104–5, 136–38
Freccero, Carla, 21
Freire, Paulo, 11
Freud, Sigmund, 30, 80, 94, 102, 115–16
Frost, Samantha, 5, 31, 75, 86, 189n10
Fuss, Diana, 102–4

Garrison, William Lloyd, 38–41, 46,
    47, 173n1
Gates, Henry Louis, Jr., 42
gender, 4, 12–13, 30, 32–33, 59, 62, 68,
    71, 113, 127, 136, 139, 145, 166n3
gender performativity, 32, 171n12
Gilbert, Jen, 139–40, 187n12
Gilroy, Paul, 12, 136, 166n4
Gómez-Barris, Macarena, 191n11
Gordon, Avery, 20–21
Gossett, Che, 46–47, 174n11
Grande, Sandy, 191n9
grass, 12, 16
Gregg, Melissa, 64
Grosz, Elizabeth, 65, 107, 149–50
Guillory, John, 141

Halberstam, Jack, 6, 70, 73, 82–83, 105,
    139, 151, 156, 178n10
Hall, Stuart, 32
Haraway, Donna, 25, 30, 46, 59–61,
    109, 135, 165n7, 165n8, 175n6,
    177n15, 180n4
Halpern, Orit, 188n5, 190n3
Harding, Sandra, 166n12
Harman, Graham, 173n8
Harney, Stefano, 47, 83, 142–43, 157
Hartman, Saidiya, 42, 51, 53, 85, 173n5
Hayles, N. Katherine, 58–59, 107, 109,
    182n18
haunting, 19–22, 140, 150–51
Hegel, G. W. F., 97
Highmore, Ben, 122
hooks, bell, 139
horses, 26
hospitality, 90, 140, 142, 187n12,
    187n16, 187n15
human, concept of: abolitionist recon-
    ceptualization of, 44–47; in human
    rights, 28; limits of in relation to
    race, 40–45; as produced by assem-
    blages, 31–37, 72–73; relation to the
    humanities, 2, 30–31. *See also* Man
Human Development Index, 73, 146,
    180n12
humanism: history of, 66–67; as intel-
    lectual project, 3, 7, 21–22, 53; as
    political commitment, 46, 63–64,
    98, 99–102; and restricted concept of
    agency, 44, 73–74. *See also* colonial-
    ism; state apparatus
humanities, 5, 21–22, 31, 67; crisis of,
    1–2, 8, 155–58, 191n10
humanization: as colonialist project,
    30–37, 75, 97–98; as dispersed pro-
    cess, 11–12, 167; as function of liter-
    ature, 104, 126; as goal of education,
    11–12, 30–31; as inescapably tied

to dehumanization, 13–14, 142; in literacies against the state, 147–48; and literacy, 38; and pleasure, 130; as production of Man in assemblages, 9–10, 68–69; as synonym for education, 50; and the university, 134–36

humanizing assemblages. *See* assemblages; humanization

human rights, 2, 9, 28, 50–51, 101, 145–46, 165n5

Hsu, Hsuan, 115

Hunt, Lynn, 8–9, 28, 30, 38–40, 101–3, 185n3

identification, 38, 40, 42, 53, 101, 102–5

identity, 59, 68, 72, 113, 135, 148

imperialism. *See* colonialism

information, 32, 69, 71–72, 148

ink, 15, 93–94

instinct, 90–91, 115, 119, 151

Jackson, Zakiyyah Iman, 168n17, 170n7, 173n10

Jagose, Annamarie, 128

Joy, Eileen, 148

Joyce, James, 10, 114, 116–20, 121–23, 124–25, 183nn4–5

Kant, Immanuel, 11, 66, 174n1

Karavanta, Asimina, 169n5, 174n13

King, Katie, 8, 21–24, 56

Kipnis, Laura, 183n1

Kirby, Vicki, 188n23

Kohn, Eduardo, 60, 64–65, 155

Kotef, Hagar, 180n6

Kozol, Jonathan, 182n15

Kurlansky, Mark, 61–63, 190n2

labor, more-than-human, 16, 46

land, 37, 150, 154, 159

Lee, Li-Young, 113–14

LeMenager, Stephanie, 153, 190nn1–2

library, 29, 61, 131, 184n2

literacy: and affect, 17, 76; against the state, 147–49, 158–61; as animate practice, 4, 93–98; in *Cereus Blooms at Night*, 161–63; as inscription of race and gender, 32–33; in *Narrative of the Life of Frederick Douglass*, 38, 45, 48–49, 50–54, 55–56, 64–65; outside of classrooms, 140–42; and pleasure, 153; relation to humanization, 9; relation to personhood, 19; relation to violence, 26–27; as restricted by slavery, 41, 48–54, 56, 94; in restricted sense, 28, 87; of smell, 115, 122, 148

literacy event, 7–10, 17, 24, 64, 72, 77–78, 84, 87–88, 93, 94–95, 99, 103–4, 111, 122, 125, 130–31, 134, 141, 144, 157

literacy rates. *See* Human Development Index

literacy situation, 4, 8, 9, 17, 33, 53, 61, 69, 76, 82, 88, 94, 99, 110, 112–14, 138, 144, 149, 151–52

literature: as animate practice, 4, 133, 155; in *Death of a Discipline*, 106–7; definition, attempts at, 56–58; expanded framing of, 21–22, 26–27, 86; humanist framing of, 30–31, 86, 91–93, 123, 133; love for, 6, 163; and nonhuman agency, 7; in Plato's *Republic*, 66; pleasures of, 125–26, 133. *See also* anima-literature; comparative literature; world literature

Lorde, Audre, 25, 129–30

Lowe, Lisa, 33

love, 6, 20, 22, 25–27, 90, 140, 163, 168n2

Luciano, Dana, 7–8, 148

Macy Conferences on cybernetics, 58–59

Man, 2–4; and bewilderment, 9–10; and biopolitics, 71–73, 95; and disciplinarity, 73–76, 88–89, 92–94, 98; Douglass's critique and reconfiguration of, 41, 44; as fiction, 34–36; fragility of, 64–65; history of, 29–24, 67–68, 170n8, 171nn11–12; identification with, 100–101; knowledge produced at distance from, 7–8, 37, 135–36; and orientation, 81–83, 85–86, 152; and the politics of recognition, 53–54; in A Portrait of the Artist as a Young Man, 116–19; as produced by humanizing assemblages, 8–9, 148; and restricted sense of the political, 59–60. See also humanization; Wynter, Sylvia

Manning, Erin: on affective tonality, 172n21, 176n10; on the body, 178n5; on desire as movement, 54, 135; on ethology, 87; on the leaky self, 103; on politics as movement, 149; on the relational milieu, 130, 168n16, 188n7; on touch, 181n3

Marx, Karl, 44, 133

Massumi, Brian, 160; on affect, 17, 68–69; on attention, 176n9; on experimental acting out, 52, 54; on instinct, 90–91; on ontopower, 110, 128, 151, 167n12; on play, 96, 115, 151, 174n7; on priming, 24, 45

McHugh, Susan, 89

McKenzie, Marcia, 37

Melville, Herman, 159

Mignolo, Walter, 31

Miller, D. A., 185n5

Miller, J. Hillis, 105–6

Miller, Ruth, 179n1, 187n13

modernity, 7, 21, 44, 47, 52, 59, 66, 126, 145

Mootoo, Shani, 161–63, 192n15

Moretti, Franco, 5, 23, 81

Morrison, Toni, 8, 11–17, 19–22, 36–37, 167n12, 168n17, 168n1, 168n2

Morton, Timothy, 181nn15–16

Moten, Fred, 44, 47, 54, 83, 142–43, 157, 167n9

Muñoz, José Esteban, 148

Murphy, Michelle, 70, 146, 171n13, 176nn5–6, 180n12, 190n3

Nancy, Jean-Luc, 150, 180n7, 189n12

Narrative of the Life of Frederick Douglass, 9, 38–47, 48–54, 55–56, 84–85, 131, 132, 135

nation-state. See state apparatus

new literacy studies, 17, 87, 179n2

new materialism, 3, 7, 17–18

Nietzsche, Friedrich, 80, 192n14

Norman, Richard, 67

Norris, Margot, 165n7

novel, 28–29, 38–39, 57, 101–3, 125–26, 169n1

Nyong'o, Tavia, 12, 46, 81–82, 98, 166n4

O'Donnell, James, 58

Omi, Michael, 188n3

ontopower, 69, 110, 128, 151

orangutan, 96–98, 163

orgasm, 128–29

orientation: Sara Ahmed's account of, 93–94; in Beloved, 12–14, 16; as disciplinary structure, 25, 88, 118; and education, 48, 130; in ephemeral territories, 133; literacy as problematic of, 52–54; as relation between Man and humanizing assemblages, 32–33, 35–36, 75–76, 81–83, 147

oxen, 45–46

paper, 15, 55, 59, 61, 62–63, 88, 93–94, 97, 133
paperson, la, 191n8
Parikka, Jussi, 97–98
pedagogy, 8, 17, 134–44, 158–59
perception, 12, 109–10, 163
periperformativity, 13, 17, 19
Pettman, Dominic, 34
Pickering, Andrew, 73, 167n11, 181n13
Plato, 11, 66, 170n8, 177n1, 178n4
play, 91–92, 96, 115, 151, 180n9
pleasures, 10, 16, 72, 122–23, 124–25, 128–33
political, limits of the, 5, 7, 34–35, 38–40, 46–47, 59–60, 72, 144, 175n5
politics, as more-than-human, 56, 76, 149–52, 155, 163
politics of touch, 149, 150, 188n8
pornography, 125–127, 129, 183n1, 184nn2–3
Portrait of the Artist as a Young Man, A (Joyce), 10, 116–20, 122–23, 124–25
posthumanism, 2, 3, 18, 58–59, 74–75, 82, 111
Preciado, Paul, 10, 126–28, 133
Prigogine, Ilya, 161
primitive accumulation, 21, 46, 150
Protevi, John, 69, 110, 112
Proust, Marcel, 107–8, 113, 183n7
Puar, Jasbir, 34, 71–72, 148, 166n2, 172n23, 176n11, 188n3

queer inhumanisms, 3, 7–8, 81–82, 168n18, 173n7
Quijano, Aníbal, 31

race, 4, 13, 31–33, 40–42, 48–54, 56, 62, 68, 71, 113, 136, 139, 168n19
Readings, Bill, 165n6
recognition, politics of, 51–54, 81, 140, 150

Reid-Pharr, Robert, 166n3
rememory, 20
Ring, Betty, 174n6
Rose, Jacqueline, 169n4

safety, 139–40
Said, Edward, 11, 74, 100–101, 178n11, 185n5
Sandoval, Chela, 8
Saramago, José, 159–61
Schaefer, Donovan, 116, 183n4
school, as state institution (especially P–12): access to, 141–41, 157–58; as apparatus of capture, 91; biopolitics of, 95; as disciplinary site, 66–73, 110; literacy education in, 31, 56, 155; as site of bewilderment, 136
school-to-prison pipeline, 70
Schuller, Kyla, 144, 165n10
scoping and scaling, 8, 21–23
Sedgwick, Eve, 13, 17, 99, 107
Seigworth, Greg, 64
Sellars, Roy, 116
Serres, Michel, 178n9
sexuality, 4, 68, 71, 127–28, 136, 139
Sharpe, Christina, 19–20, 166n3
Shaviro, Steven, 64, 72
Shelley, Mary, 104–5, 136–38
Shukin, Nicole, 46
Singh, Julietta: on becoming sensitive, 161; on dehumanism, 7, 35, 166n13; on discipline as mastery, 76; on errands, 179n11; on future hum-animalities, 156, 191n10; on writing poems that aren't written down, 185n10
slavery, 12–17, 19–21, 38–47, 48–54, 69, 84, 94, 102, 145, 150, 173n5
smell, 10, 24, 115–16, 118–22
Snaza, Nathan, 170n8, 175n2, 178n6, 186n4

sociogeny, 9, 30–37, 101–4, 112, 144
sociology of scientific knowledge, 73, 88
Souriau, Étienne, 90
Spade, Dean, 172n20
Spanos, William, 156, 165n2, 165n6, 182n2, 191n7
Spillers, Hortense, 167n8
Spivak, Gayatri, 10, 102, 106–7, 134–36, 157, 178n7
Springgay, Stephanie, 175n7
state apparatus, 9, 19, 28–29, 30–33, 35, 38, 41, 47, 54, 59, 64, 67, 72, 81, 84, 91–93, 95, 98, 122, 126, 128–29, 140–41, 145–48, 150, 158–61, 169nn3–4, 184nn3–5, 188n4
Stengers, Isabelle, 161
Stoker, Bram, 9, 77–79
Street, Brian, 87
Stryker, Susan, 105
syllabus projects, 158–59, 161
synecdoche, 31, 40, 59, 101

Tarc, Aparna Mishra, 51
territorialization, 83, 89, 91–93, 122, 136, 147–49, 156
Testo Junkie (Preciado), 10, 126–28, 133
tiger, 45
Tompkins, Jane, 135
trauma, 19–20
trees, 5, 15–17, 45, 63, 94, 144, 162, 183n9
Tsing, Anna, 120, 182n3, 183nn8–9
Tuana, Nancy, 5
Tuck, Eve, 37

university: biopolitics of, 70–71; discipline in, 9, 67; of excellence, 3;

relation to class, 121; relation to the humanities, 1; relation to minority activism, 136; relation to the undercommons, 142–42, 157; as settler colonial and racializing institution, 140. See also humanities; school

Vaccaro, Jeanne, 62
Viswanathan, Gauri, 75, 177n14, 185n5

Wanzo, Rebecca, 139
Warren, Austin, 56–57
wasps, 16, 63
Watkins, Megan, 16, 138, 168n13
Watt, Ian, 29, 60, 126, 184n3
Weheliye, Alexander, 31–32, 41, 166n2
Wellek, René, 56–57
Whitehead, Alfred North, 17, 35, 88, 168n15, 172n25, 179n3, 189n14
Whitman, Walt, 121
Wilson, Elizabeth, 109, 165n9, 182n10
Winant, Howard, 31, 188n3
Wolfe, Maryanne, 107–8, 113, 112, 165n4, 165n7, 177n12
Wolfe, Cary, 74–75, 180n5
world literature, 57, 156–57
Wynter, Sylvia: account of human/ Man distinction, 2, 4, 29–32, 44, 59, 68–69, 82, 100–104, 145, 167n7, 170n8, 181n11; collating struggles against Man, 85; on genres of the human as praxis, 35–36, 72–73, 171n12; sociogenic principle in, 4, 81, 112, 171n9; on written history, 148

Yamashita, Karen Tei, 25–26
Young, Hershini Bhana, 20–21